"Carol Harris' *Consult Yourself*, is a must seriously considering leaving the corpo starting their own consulting practice. S preparation, planning and actions that i succeed. Her approach, integrated with ᴎᴸᴘ, ᴡᵢₗₗ ₑₙₐᵦₗₑ ᵧₒᵤ ₜₒ harness your conscious and below conscious strengths. And she has lots of useful tips for even the most seasoned consultant."
– **Shelle Rose Charvet**, author of *Words that Change Minds*.

"Carol Harris has written a book that covers all you ever need to know about consultancy. The book is excellent – it describes brilliantly what a consultant has to demonstrate to become successful."
– **Roger Walker**, Consultant People Agenda Network.

"Consulting can mean all things to all people. Not after reading Carol Harris' book – she breaks the topic right down into its constituent parts so it is quite clear what is being talked about. Readers, whether part- or full-time consultants already – possibly with a big firm and considering going it alone – or those thinking about entering the field for the first time, can see at a glance what the options are, what is involved in each and the pitfalls. The book spells out how to get started and, essentially, how to do the job. The totally seamless integration of NLP thinking into the explanations of the necessary skills and techniques adds a valuable dimension and Harris never resorts to jargon or fad. Anecdotes keep the tone personal, practical, down-to-earth ... A sharp knife through the fudge and gobbledegook that's talked about consultancy today. Harris paints a crystal clear picture of what it means to be a consultant – from what rates to charge to responding to tenders to how to do the job. The consultant's consultant."
– **Susanne Lawrence**, Deputy Chairman, Personnel Publications Ltd.; Chief Executive, Indigo Publishing Ltd.

"I wish Carol Harris's book had been on the market when I first set up my business many years ago. Her new book is comprehensive, dealing with many of the more difficult issues of setting up and running a business."
– **Philip Atkinson**, Director Transformations UK Ltd.

"Carol Harris has written a book for all consultants, whether the would-be sole practitioner or the seasoned, big practice consultant wanting to re-calibrate what he/she is doing … Down-to-earth, practical advice, distilled from a now maturing profession, is combined with information on trends within a profession undergoing enormous change. Readers will find the book written in an accessible style and, if they want more information on a particular topic, the pointers to other authors and professional, support organisations are there … Readers will be challenged by new and thought-provoking ways of thinking. Any consultant will have his/her understanding of their profession enhanced by this book, whether it is read from cover to cover or used as a source of ideas and approaches on a more casual basis."
– **Ian Barratt**, Chief Executive, Institute of Management Consultancy.

"I commend this book to all those who are not afraid to look within for guidance on the external consulting journey."
– **Barry Curnow**, Vice-Chairman, International Council of Management Consulting Institutes; Principal, Maresfield Curnow School of Management Consulting.

"*Consult Yourself* is a 'must have' book for anyone considering consultancy as a new career. Although targeted at independents, the book is a veritable asset to all aspiring consultants. … Subtly and wisely, Harris draws the reader into critical self-analysis, introspection and educated reasoning, for consultancy is not just about on-the-job skills. This she achieves by using proven tools of NLP (Neuro-Linguistic Programming) in an acceptable and impactful way. Well-written and logically developed this is a book for reading and then referencing time and again. If you are considering a career in consultancy, read this book and act on your learning."
– **Angus McLeod**, author of *Me, Myself, My Team* and *Performance Coaching*.

Consult Yourself

The NLP Guide to
Being a Management Consultant

Carol Harris

Illustrated by Roy Elmore

Crown House Publishing Limited
www.crownhouse.co.uk
www.chpus.com

First published by

Crown House Publishing Ltd
Crown Buildings, Bancyfelin, Carmarthen, Wales, SA33 5ND, UK
www.crownhouse.co.uk

and

Crown House Publishing Company LLC
6 Trowbridge Drive, Suite 5, Bethel, CT 06801, USA
www.CHPUS.com

British Library of Cataloguing-in-Publication Data
A catalogue entry for this book is available
from the British Library.

10 Digit ISBN 1904424821
13 Digit ISBN 978-190442482-6
LCCN 2004117849

Printed and bound in the UK by
Cromwell Press, Trowbridge, Wiltshire

Contents

Biography

Carol Harris is a Certified Management Consultant and a Fellow of the Institute of Management Consultancy, as well as a member of the Richmond Group, a leading UK consortium of independent consultants. She is also a Fellow of the Chartered Institute of Personnel and Development and a Member of the British Association of Communicators in Business. She has been active in the Institute of Management Consultancy, serving on the Women in Consultancy special interest group, helping with membership development, running IMC accredited courses and contributing to the Institute's publications.

Carol established her independent consultancy practice, Management Magic, in 1986. Management Magic's expertise is in human resource management, organisational development, change management, teambuilding, training, development and employee communications. The practice offers consultancy and training services to the public, private, charitable and voluntary sectors. Management Magic specialises in the application of NLP (Neuro-Linguistic Programming) to business, and Carol has been Chair of the Association for Neuro-Linguistic Programming in the UK for four years and Editor of the Association's international magazine *Rapport* for ten years. Management Magic offers NLP-based in-house training in various parts of the UK, and also runs open courses in London and Wales, where, in addition to enhancing their business skills, delegates can enjoy exploring the local countryside, eating home-cooked meals and meeting the resident rare-breed pigs and piglets.

Carol is the author of *The Elements of NLP*; *NLP – New Perspectives*; *Think Yourself Slim* and *Networking for Success* and has produced the *Success in Mind* series of audiotapes on various aspects of personal effectiveness. She is also the Editor and publisher of *Effective Consulting*, the international magazine for independent management consultants.

Acknowledgements

I would like to thank the following people and organisations for their help with this book:

The Institute of Management Consultancy in the UK for their general help and for permission to use extracts from their publications, including *Inside Careers,* published in conjunction with Cambridge Market Intelligence Ltd.

Management Consulting Information Service, which conducts salary surveys on behalf of the IMC, for providing me with some of the information on UK salaries.

The Kennedy Information Research Group in the USA for providing information on salary/fee rates and billing practices.

Kennedy Information LLC for permission to reproduce information on the top USA consultancy firms.

The AMCF for permission to quote from its publication *Operating Ratios for Management Consulting Firms: A resource for Benchmarking.*

Management Consultant Decisions International for permission to reproduce the foreword to their 2000 edition.

William M Mercer for permission to use information from their joint study with Cranfield School of Management, *European Trends in HR Outsourcing.*

Russam GMS for permission to reproduce information from their publication *Interim Management: The Russam GMS Market Research Report.*

Don Leslie, of Beament Leslie Thomas, for supplying some of the information on consultancy recruitment practices.

Paul Harris for helping with the research on industry information.

Philip Atkinson for sending me much useful information and chatting on the phone.

Nick Cotter and Calvert Markham for supplying one or two anecdotes.

And everyone else who has contributed to my own experience, enabling me to produce this book.

Finally, I would like to dedicate the book to my mother, Sylvia Leibson, who was regarded by all her friends and acquaintances as the best unofficial consultant they knew.

Foreword

This is a welcome and timely book. The title *Consult Yourself* is apt and points to the importance of learning to become a reflective consultant and a reflexive practitioner of consultancy: reflective in thinking about professional practice and reflexive in learning from experience and feeding that learning back into future client work.

Consultants must use their whole selves, body, mind and spirit in the service of the client and the consulting journey. This consulting truth was enunciated nearly two decades ago by Peter Block in Chapter Two of the first edition of his legendary *A Handbook of Flawless Consulting*, which was entitled 'Techniques Are Not Enough'.

We have been waiting ever since then for a practical handbook, a do-it-yourself guide or consultant's survival kit that tells consulting practitioners how to master themselves in the service of the client/consultant relationship, whether in private practice or corporate life. Here it is! Carol Harris is herself a Certified Management Consultant, an experienced Fellow of the Institute of Management Consultancy and a thoughtful consulting practitioner. She has now written the "workshop manual" for how to go beyond techniques to live the consulting life as a journey of inquiry, learning and self-development, as a joint venture with the client.

There is a sense in which we are all consultants now. The end of lifelong careers, the downsizing and restructuring of organisations, and turbulent change in markets, have led to the need for consulting skills as the survival edge in the post-employment labour markets of the digital economy where self-employed, freelance and consulting engagements are the daily bread of work.

There are life cycles in the consulting business. There are life cycles in client-consultant relationships. There are life cycles in consulting careers, whether employed, self-employed or leading the portfolio life of the third age. Consulting skills are life skills, survival skills. There are principles and proven practices that govern these life cycles of the consulting journey. And Carol Harris sketches them well, giving good, down-to-earth, practical guidance about what to do and how to do it. These guidelines are more than common sense – they blend good theory with best practice and provide a map with which to navigate across the territory of service provider-client relationships, teaching and learning for life.

Many aspiring internal consultants turn to NLP in order to accelerate the professionalism of their consulting services. Many external consultants turn to NLP in order better to understand the process aspects of their own psychology and that of others. To the extent that this magical book helps the practitioner to look within, to their own psychology, as the basis for understanding what works in their relationships with their colleagues and with clients, it is pointing to a fundamental truth and requirement of consulting endeavours. I commend it all those who are not afraid to look within for guidance on the external consulting journey.

Barry Curnow
Vice-Chairman, International Council of Management Consulting Institutes; Principal, Maresfield Curnow School of Management Consulting.
London, December 2000.

Preface

Over the years, many people have asked me how they could become independent consultants. Most of these people were experienced professionals in particular fields and now wished (or had no choice but) to change direction, although a few were starting out on their careers and had little work experience under their belts.

My immediate response to the 'new starters' was usually to tell them that one doesn't take up consultancy in the way one does other jobs – that is, feel attracted to it, do some training and launch into a career. I felt that consultancy was something to be done only when one had sufficient experience of a particular function, sector or process to be able to pass on one's own knowledge and skill to others. And, to a large extent, I still believe this.

However, management consultancy is now such a rapid growth area that it is commonplace for young graduates, or specialists with only a few years' work experience, to be taken on by the large consultancy practices, which then mould them to their own image. There sometimes seems to be a sharp contrast between this route to consultancy success and that of the seasoned professional who turns to consultancy after many years in line management, a functional specialism or business development.

There are many different routes to consultancy success, but they have in common the requirement for excellent skills in order to help others grow, develop, innovate, solve problems, manage, lead and achieve business results. Although the focus of this book is the independent consultant, the chapters that follow will take you through a range of consultancy issues and ideas. I hope they will give you food for thought, whatever your route into consultancy.

I have used various concepts in this book, many of them – as the title indicates – from NLP (Neuro-Linguistic Programming). Although I have kept the book as jargon-free as I can, I have indicated at the end of chapters the terminology for the NLP techniques used so that those who are unfamiliar can track them back and, if motivated to pursue them, learn more about their origins, applications and practice. The application of all the techniques mentioned is, of course, far broader than their usage here.

So use the book in whichever way suits you best; either read it from start to finish, or dip in at those points that attract your interest the most. And if you have any interesting consultancy anecdotes to recount, do get in touch – I like collecting tales of endeavour and result.

Author's note: Throughout this book I have used the term 'consultancy', as it is the word used in the UK to describe both the industry and the function. In the USA the term 'consulting' is used instead and readers may prefer to substitute this if it is more familiar to them.

Chapter 1
What Is Consultancy?

This chapter introduces a range of topics including the origins of consultancy, its purposes, the kind of people who can be consultants, the issues faced by consultants, what clients want from consultants (and vice versa), and consultancy elements and processes.

How Can Consultancy Be Defined?

There are two ways of considering the field of consultancy. There is the 'technical' definition – consultancy as a formal business activity. There is also the more commonplace definition – consultancy as an activity that takes place on a daily basis between people in all contexts.

The first definition encompasses many discrete processes, for example: ◆Management consultancy, ◆Medical consultancy, ◆Design consultancy, ◆Financial consultancy, and so forth.

The second definition covers activities such as an employee asking a colleague for ideas on how to tackle a task, a teenager asking an older friend for advice on relationships and a new house purchaser asking a neighbour for the addresses of local garden centres.

In this book I concentrate on the first definition of consultancy, that is, the formal processes in which people engage in business. I will be focusing especially on management consultancy, with brief glimpses at consultancy in other fields. The Management Consultancies Association (MCA) in the UK defines management consultancy as '…the supply of independent advice and assistance to clients about management issues'.

How Did Consultancy Originate and Develop?

Probably consultancy in its informal sense has existed for as long as people have been together in social groups. However, the origins of consultancy as a business practice are quite recent. The impact of the Industrial Revolution gave rise to 'industrial engineering', aimed at improving efficiency and productivity and, in the UK and the USA, some early consultancy activities were in evidence in the late 1880s; their origins being in management costing and accountancy. The 1920s were probably the starting point for modern consultancy as we know it and, in the decades that followed, many firms came into existence, with the 1950s being the real growth times for the consultancy industry, linked to postwar business expansion/reconstruction, technological advancement and growth in developing countries.

The early period of consultancy featured many consultancy products and processes, many of them trademarked 'off-the-shelf' solutions to problems. Some of these products, and their associated 'Here's the solution, now what's the problem?' approach have still survived, although nowadays consultancy tends to be much more client-focused and flexible, offering approaches and processes rather than guaranteed solutions.

Although there were some periods when consultancy services fell in popularity – the early 1970s in Britain being one of those times – consultancy survived and grew. Today it is one of the most popular work sectors for both employed and self-employed people.

The Management Consultancies Association survey of consultancy trends showed that, in the UK, between 1960 and 1998 there was a steady rise in the number of consultants employed by MCA firms, from around 1,500 in 1960 to almost 15,000 at the end of 1999. Bruce Petter, Executive Director of MCA, has said that management consultancy is one of the fastest-growing industries in the United Kingdom.

Revenues in the UK now exceed £6 billion, with exports well over £1 billion, and consultancy services offered include IT consultancy, IT systems development, strategy, financial services, project management, production management, human resources, marketing, economic/environmental and outsourcing.

Management Consultancy magazine reports annual growth rates of around 20% in consultancy, with a good proportion from fee income overseas. Growth appears higher in financial services and manufacturing and lower in central and local government, and much of the growth is in IT and project management. According to the MCA, over 90% of the FT–SE 250 companies employ MCA firms on a repeat basis.

According to the Federation of European Management Consultants, FEACO, there are now 200,000 management consultants operating in Europe. Some 75% of these are based in just five countries: Germany (62,500), UK (35,000), Italy (32,000), Spain (16,000) and France (15,400). The northern European market seems to be the 'most mature' and the UK and Germany represent the largest management consultancy markets (around 60%). And in a research project carried out by one training organisation in the UK, it was estimated that there are over 10,000 one-person consultancies offering people skills development, and over 300 companies in the same field.

In his foreword to 'Management Consultant Decisions International 2000', Gil Gidron, Chairman of the Federation of European Management Consultants, said:

> *Consultancy is undergoing an unprecedented period of growth and it has become one of the most dynamic and strategic industries as a result of the added value it generates and its contribution to the competitiveness of companies and institutions.*

> *The economic, business and social environment is changing rapidly. Factors such as the globalisation of markets, the increase in pan-European operations, the deregulation and liberalisation of some industries, the wave of consolidation and concentration, the new opportunities arising from technological development, monetary union and, above all, the e-economy, are all influencing the demand for consulting services.*

> *The management consultancy industry in Europe now represents 200,000 professionals and a market worth more than 25 billion*

euro is not only important in size, but also in what it represents for the economy, for consultants are wealth creators who capitalise on change.

The 1980s required delivery excellence in consultancy. The objective was to deliver quality on time and on budget. In the 1990s a different dimension was added. Clients not only required delivery excellence but were interested in value created through implemented business solutions. Now, at the beginning of the new millennium, clients want to add another dimension: speed. Modern change is characterised by speed and consultants will be competitive only if they manage to successfully deliver value at superior speed. Accelerated change will be the common denominator of the twenty-first century.

In this context, consulting firms have to change rapidly to maintain their competitiveness. In the future they will be required to develop new skills and capabilities in two areas; those of envisioning and realising new business models and those of adapting and transforming human performance in the economy.

All of these changes will require new profiles of consultants, diverse compensation models, different financial and organisational structures and new client 'relationships' that will allow consulting firms to be competitive.

I am optimistic about consultancy in the new environment. In a world of unlimited business opportunities generated by these new electronic channels, management consultancy should be a point of reference and a source of innovation for all organisations across the world in the twenty-first century. The new challenge for consultancy is to be at the forefront of changes, delivering value to clients at superior speed.

Why Is Consultancy Needed?

There is a range of reasons for the growth in consultancy services; some of these are as follows:

Specialisation and the pace of change

The world of work has tended to become compartmentalised, with people knowing 'more and more about less and less'. Because of this, no one person in an organisation can know everything, nor can they keep up to date with developments in all fields. This means that there is an increased demand for the services of specialists who may be too expensive to afford on a full-time basis, or whose expertise is needed too infrequently to justify their permanent employment.

Downsizing, outsourcing and virtual working

As companies streamline their activities, many departments are reduced in size. This leads to more use being made of resources outside the organisation. In some cases activities are carried out by contractors rather than permanent staff; in others, networks of contacts are used to boost internal resources. Consultants may also be used for a period while in-house skills are being developed in employees. Whichever of these reasons applies, there is a growing demand for help from people outside the organisation.

Differing perspectives, collaboration and challenge

It is very easy to become complacent, fail to see new opportunities and fall into a rut. Having access to people with new ideas and having one's approach scrutinised can lead to a healthier and more productive way of working. It may not be easy to accept the viewpoints of others, but keeping an open mind can lead to surprisingly useful results.

What Is a Consultant?

Just as there are two definitions of consultancy, so there can be two definitions of a consultant. The first is a person who has 'consultant' in, or implied in, their job title; the second is anyone who provides information, advice or assistance to another. Again, I will be taking the first definition in this book. Within this definition, there are a number of recognisable consultancy roles; I will mention a few of them here.

Internal/external

An internal consultant is one who provides a service to other members of the same employing organisation. Not long ago, this term would have been unusual, but it has become more common-place over the past couple of decades. There are various reasons for having internal consultants. For example, internal consultants are more likely than outsiders to understand the nature of the business, and to have well-established relationships with people within the organisation; also, in some very large firms, it is more cost-effective to provide consultancy internally than to buy it in at high daily rates. The tendency within businesses to designate dis-crete functions or departments as individual cost centres for finan-cial control purposes has meant that internal consultancy can become a transferable cost. This has a number of implications. One is that the cost effectiveness of the service is more likely to be assessed. Another is that, when purchasing departments weigh up the benefits of using one source rather than another, internal consultants are more likely to face competition from external consultants.

An external consultant is one who is brought in from 'outside' for a specific project or time period. This is probably how most people understand consultancy, and the growth of external consultants has been one of the business success stories of recent years. There will be further discussion of the internal/external consultancy dimension later in this chapter.

Specialist/generalist

Specialist consultants offer services in one or more areas. These may be functionally oriented (for example finance, IT, HR, mar-keting) or they may be sector or industry oriented (for example public sector, voluntary sector, pharmaceuticals, manufacturing).

Specialist consultants are likely to have worked previously in the particular areas they cover and will need to keep up to date with developments in their field. Specialism brings advantages of relevant knowledge and expertise; the downside can be a narrow focus that limits understanding of broader business issues.

Generalist consultants are able to take an overview of business activities. They may well have expertise across a range of functions and sectors and may therefore have a breadth of understanding that can be a great asset to clients. Generalisation may, however, make it more difficult for such consultants to define their particular assets (or 'unique selling points', to use marketing jargon) and they will be competing in the marketplace against many others with a similar range of services.

Process/analytical/strategic consultant

Process consultants work collaboratively with their clients to help them handle important issues. This kind of consultancy is not so much about offering solutions or providing guidance, but is more about facilitation and development – helping clients enhance their own capabilities and skills. (The old adage 'Give a person a fish and they have a meal; teach them how to fish and they have meals for life' is a good analogy for this kind of consultancy.) In the past ten or fifteen years, process consultancy has tended to be most popular.

Analytical consultants are more content driven, working on current operational activities, and are often brought in where there is a particular problem to be solved, for example a production breakdown that can be 'fixed'. In these cases the consultant acts as more of a specialist adviser/troubleshooter, providing expertise that is not available within the organisation. Although both process and analytical consultants have roles to fulfil, it is likely that the process consultant, in the long run, is better able to help the clients enhance their own capabilities rather than just giving them a 'solution' to a problem.

Strategic consultants work on high-level, long-term issues to help their clients develop and achieve their overall business aims.

Interim manager/project consultant/'outsourced' services

While the majority of consultants work on specific assignments on an independent basis, some act as interim managers or executives for client organisations.

An assignment-based consultant is brought in to conduct an assignment or project for the client. The consultant tends to be slightly at arm's length, advising and guiding. An interim manager or executive is more 'hands on', taking an operational role within the client organisation and helping implement action rather than simply recommending it. It could be argued that this latter role is not a true consultancy role, but many clients benefit as much from such injections of assistance as they would from the services of a purely external consultant. For those readers who are happiest with seeing a total project through from start to completion, interim work may be more satisfying and give more of a feeling of involvement and commitment.

As well as interim or project work, activities may simply be 'outsourced' so that an external person is brought in to carry out tasks; this is sometimes considered to be consultancy but may simply be purchasing subcontracted services rather than the provision of consultancy advice. Outsourced work can be a good source of additional income for consultants, although it does seem different in kind from much consultancy work.

There is an enormous growth in outsourcing, and in a recent survey 'Trends in HR outsourcing', Cranfield School of Management (in association with William M Mercer) surveyed almost 4,000 organisations employing over 200 employees throughout Europe (excluding Germany) and showed that organisations throughout Europe made great use of external providers. Training and development was generally the function with the highest use of external providers (an average of 77%), followed by recruitment and selection (59%); pay and benefits (30%) and outplacement/down-sizing (29%). Overall, the outsourcing process tended to be used on an 'opportunistic' basis rather than as a result of deliberate strategy. In a table showing the geographical spread of organisations outsourcing three or more services, the top three countries were Belgium, the Netherlands and France, with the UK next and then the other countries in the study.

The authors of the above study did comment that the word 'outsourcing' is ambiguous, so, in their survey, they simply used the term 'external providers' (also, in some languages the word 'outsourcing' is difficult to translate, which adds to any possible confusion).

Sole trader (solo)/partner/associate/employed consultant

There is a wide range of organisational types within the field of consultancy. Sole traders work on a self-employed basis, offering services to their chosen market. Some consultants work in partnership with others, perhaps one other person, or possibly several; the term 'partner' is also used for senior members of larger consulting firms, who generally have a stake in the business. Many consultants work in association with others, either personal contacts or through organisations set up to offer consultancy services through a network of affiliated people. Others work as employees of various-sized consultancy firms.

There are advantages to both consultant and client in each type of organisation and, if you are considering a career in consultancy, there are various issues to consider when deciding which route is most appropriate for you to take. In Chapter 3 I will be discussing how you can either set up on your own as a consultant, or get a job in a larger consultancy firm.

Local/national/international

Some consultants operate in a small geographic region, some within one country, while others work across a broader geographical range. Within the larger consultancy firms, consultants will often be sent overseas on assignments for periods of time; equally, many sole traders or smaller firms will have an international focus.

Working nationally can build up particular expertise in the needs and characteristics of a 'local' market, whereas operating internationally can give either a specific expertise in particular cultures or a broader understanding of comparative business issues.

What Kind of Person Can Be a Consultant?

If you take the 'informal' definition of consultancy, anyone can be a consultant. If, however, you take the 'formal' definition – someone who is a consultant professionally – then, although probably most people *could* be a consultant, in practice there are certain factors that make it likely that such a career will appeal to, and work better for, people with particular attributes.

Chapter 2 deals with how to assess your personal potential as a consultant and will give you some ideas about your own suitability for a career in consultancy.

What Issues Are Faced by Consultants?

There is a wide range of issues that come up in consultancy. Many of these have an ethical element and many consultants, especially new ones, find it hard to know how to handle them. I will be covering many of these issues (together with other topics) in the chapters that follow; the list here is just a selection to give you a taste of what will follow in the chapters ahead.

The issues are not in order of priority, but similar issues have been grouped together.

Business development issues

- Raising finance.
- Generating business.
- Overcoming peaks and troughs of work.
- Managing risk.

Self-management issues

- Combating loneliness.
- Avoiding stress.
- Managing time.
- Maintaining motivation and fitness.

Work issues

- Being client-focused.
- Providing quality.
- Producing results.
- Maintaining effectiveness.

Relationship issues

- Balancing work and home life.
- Using home as an office.
- Collaborating with other consultants.
- Developing a personal network.

Client management issues

- Developing rapport.
- Understanding the 'real' issues.
- Handling disagreement and conflict.
- Ensuring commitment.

Ethical issues

- Remaining impartial.
- Maintaining confidentiality.
- Separating professional from personal issues.
- Abiding by professional codes of conduct and ethics.

Cultural issues

- Fitting in with different client organisations.
- Handling individual and cultural diversity.
- Responding to differing systems of values.
- Being aware of your own cultural patterns.

Development issues

- Reviewing effectiveness.
- Keeping up to date.
- Finding personal mentors and coaches.
- Financing personal training.

In the skills chapters I will be taking you through various issues facing consultants and giving you practical ways of anticipating and dealing with them.

What Trends Are There in Consultancy?

- The MCA (Management Consultancies Association) says that overall issues facing the consultancy industry today include: ◆New organisations entering the field; ◆Regulatory legislation (including disaggregation issues – that is, the separating of auditing and consultancy services); ◆Mergers and the rise of e-business (in the current year, the MCA assessed that over 17% of their members' revenues were predominantly e-business related).

- Barry Curnow, Past President of the IMC in the UK and currently Vice-Chair of the international management consultancy organisation ICMCI, says that two trends that will become even more prominent in the future are: ◆Globalisation and ◆Virtual consultancy.

- The AMCF (Association of Management Consulting Firms) US report on consulting industry results (see Bibliography) says that: ◆Women have moved ahead in consulting firms, with almost a quarter of management consultants in responding firms being women (compared with a fifth in 1993); almost two-thirds of junior partners are women (compared with just under half in 1992) and just over a quarter of senior partners were women (compared with a fifth in 1993); ◆Minority groups make up around a third of the entry-level positions, although only 6% of senior partners; ◆The highest demands for services were in compensation and benefits and health care consulting, while production management and strategic planning growth decreased.

- FEACO (Federation of European Management Consulting Associations) says, in its latest survey of the European management consultancy market (December 1998), that: ◆The majority of member firms predicted that IT work had the best prospects, followed by corporate strategy and organisation development and financial and administrative systems; ◆The key markets were seen as financial services, retail and international business; ◆The key drivers for the industry were predicted to be intensification of competition through globalisation, privatisation and deregulation, rapid advancement in IT and e-commerce, mergers and acquisitions. (Members also reported on the outlook for service areas, by country, and this information is available in the full report, or in extract form in *Management Consultant Decisions International 2000*).

What Are the Elements of Consultancy?

Consultancy can often be recognised through its elements; here are a few that are common to many consultancy activities.

'Problem' issues or development needs

Before a consultancy relationship can be entered into, there needs to be some requirement that has to be met. Sometimes there is an actual problem, in other words something that is causing concern, preventing achievement or stopping progress – for example, lack of finance, interpersonal conflict or a technical process breakdown. In these cases, the way forward may not be apparent; people may simply know that something needs to be done. At other times there is an identified need for intervention or development – for example, rearranging shift patterns to cope with an increased product demand, or a requirement to train staff in new practices. In these cases, some analysis has been carried out so that people are aware of the issues involved and are beginning to grasp their impact. And sometimes there is a need that has not been expressly clarified, but which still presents as an issue to be addressed – for example, a sense that a change of direction may be needed, or an awareness of a shift in the success of an organisation.

Parties to the interaction

Generally there are two distinct parties involved in a consultancy interaction; a supplier and a client. Within this framework there may be more than one person involved on each 'side'; there may be a management team which is the client, and there may be several consultants involved if the activity is substantial. However, there can also be 'self-consultancy', where a person assesses and works on their own issues, or debates issues with himself or herself ("Part of me would like to do ... but part of me would prefer to do ..."; "On the one hand I could ... and on the other hand I could ...").

Transfer of knowledge/expertise/advice

For consultancy to be effective, there should be some transfer of resources from one party to another. The resources may include knowledge, skill or information and the transfer may be conscious or, on occasion, unconscious. What I mean by this is that in some cases the transfer may be made explicit, so the client knows exactly what he or she is gaining from the process, but in other cases the recipient may be unaware at the time of any gains, although these might subsequently become apparent, or may even benefit the client without that person really knowing why. Explicit transfer is likely to be perceived as more valuable, as it is apparent what kind of benefit has been gained by the receiver. If unconscious transfer processes are used deliberately, care must be taken as this can be a powerful process and should not be attempted by the untrained.

What Consultancy Processes Are There?

There are numerous processes involved in consultancy, with their associated models, frameworks and techniques. Some of the processes are patented or trademarked, but many have simply slipped into general usage and their origins are sometimes shrouded in the mists of time. It can be very helpful to follow existing approaches to consultancy, but I believe the most successful consultants are constantly devising their own approaches and solutions and continuously reinventing and redeveloping how they work. In this way they stay up to date, move ahead of the competition and become known for innovative and resourceful handling of client issues.

I will be dealing with consultancy processes and techniques in some depth in Chapter 7.

An Example of a Consultancy Framework

One simple framework for consultancy that I have found makes sense to many people was developed by the then Manpower Services Commission and used within the Civil Service in the UK as 'a consultancy approach to getting things done through others'. I can no longer trace the original documents or authors, so am unable to credit it further. This framework has five elements, but I have adapted one of them because I think the original version does not quite cover what goes on.

The framework as it was originally devised uses a mnemonic (EDICT) and has five stages, as follows:

> **E** ntry
> **D** iagnosis
> **I** nfluencing
> **C** ontracting
> **T** ransition

I have changed the third stage to 'Intervention' as I believe influencing goes on at all times, whether we are aware of it and use it consciously, or not. This is acknowledged by the authors of EDICT, but I do not believe it is truly reflected in the model.

So, taking the adapted version, this is how it can be described.

Entry

This is a stage where the consultant is making a first entrance into the consultant/client relationship and building a working relationship. Entry is characterised by activities such as initial contact, ice-breaking, finding common ground, developing rapport and trust, gaining credibility, reducing ambiguity, overcoming concerns and exchanging basic information. At this stage the emphasis is on defining roles and building a working relationship, rather than on carrying out formal consultancy 'work'. Entry is built each time contact takes place with a client and it deepens the working relationship; total credibility and trust may only be achieved over a period of months or years.

Diagnosis

This is the stage where analysis of the situation, its causes, the people involved and any other relevant issues takes place. Diagnosis can happen in discussion, through research, through thinking and so on. It involves elements such as listening, questioning and reflecting. The purpose of diagnosis is to gather sufficient quantity and quality of information on which to base a judgement, including the 'key levers to change'. Diagnosis includes content (what you need to find out) and process (how you set about doing it). It is important at this stage not to jump to conclusions and make premature suggestions for improvement; it is simply a fact-gathering and investigation stage.

Intervention

This stage is about developing appropriate strategies for getting client commitment, facilitating movement and making changes. The changes may come through proposals, recommendations, guidance, collaboration, implementation and so on and include the development of appropriate strategies for gaining client commitment. The consultant may take a more or less active part in intervention work, depending on the assignment; and problem-solving, benefit demonstration, commitment maintenance and influencing may take a high profile during this phase.

Contracting

This is about agreeing/confirming roles, responsibilities and relationships; it is also about enhancing trust and support. The authors of EDICT say it is "… a continuous process towards developing a clear plan of action". Although it is placed near the end of the EDICT process, contracting may run in parallel with intervention, or it may come before or after it, depending on what is being contracted. This dispersal of the contracting function is not made entirely clear in the model.

Transition

This is about "… managing the client relationship in a manner that ensures the achievement of objectives and … considers the longer term objectives". It also ensures moving from one situation to another. As an assignment ends, the consultant will need to move on to other work and the client will need to move into a more autonomous role in implementation. Transition may involve follow-up, maintenance, or support activity, depending on circumstances. Transition can be a difficult time if the client has become over-dependent on the consultant; it can also be a sensitive time if the consultant is (for whatever reason) reluctant to leave the client to his or her own devices. Transition may lead to re-entry, and the start of another assignment or a further stage of activity, in which case the whole cycle may begin again.

The EDICT cycle does not always run in a linear manner; stages may cycle, or be omitted or repeated, depending on circumstances. It also does not cover some important elements, such as the research you need to do before the entry stage. It is, however, a simple concept and one that sums up much of the activity that takes place within a consultancy relationship.

What Are the Differences Between Internal and External Consultants?

In the same way that external consultants differ in what they are like and in what they do, internal consultants also vary. There can be differences between the roles and activities of internal and external consultants, and there can also be some particular constraints on the internal consultant that tend not to be faced by the external consultant. I would like to consider some of these issues here.

What is an internal consultant?

The same definition may be used as with consultancy in general: i.e., a person may be an informal or a formal internal consultant. An informal internal consultant is simply someone who is consulted for advice by others within the organisation. A formal internal consultant is one who has 'consultant' as part of their role definition and has official responsibilities to help others achieve their goals.

In their roles as managers, coaches, mentors and facilitators, people may take on aspects of a consultancy role within an organisation, but the true internal consultant has very a specific role in helping the organisation adopt, or adapt to, change. Internal consultancy can be a challenging role, for a variety of reasons, which will be explored in the paragraphs that follow.

Where does an internal consultant fit in?

Internal consultancy can take various forms. In larger organisations there are internal consultancy departments, running into tens, and occasionally hundreds, of people. In smaller organisations, the internal consultant may reside in any one of a range of specialist functions – for example IT, HR, training – or may be found elsewhere in the hierarchy – for example reporting directly to the chief executive. In multi-site businesses the internal consultant may come from a different location, or business unit, and still be regarded as internal to the business as a whole.

Comparing the internal and external consultant

In respect of what they do, there are many similarities and also many differences between the internal and external consultant. Here are some of the issues involved:

- The external consultant often has more apparent credibility (nobody is a prophet in their own land!). It may be harder for the internal consultant to be taken seriously, as he or she is probably well known within the organisation and specialist skills are often more valued if they seem to come from 'experts' outside the organisation. Internal consultants may also be seen as allied with particular factions or approaches and may be regarded with suspicion because of this. Against this, however, the internal consultant already has many internal contacts, knows the systems, procedures, attitudes and values, and so has less groundwork to do than the external consultant may.

- The internal consultant may have reporting relationships with others within their organisation that may make them less 'free' to act than an independent consultant from outside would be. The internal consultant may also experience some conflict if their own manager is not the initiator of the particular assignment; the manager and the initiator may have differing interests or demands and, at times, it may be hard for the internal consultant to reconcile these. Of course, being inside an organisation and having established working relationships may also make it easier to get ideas adopted in some instances.

● There are other stakeholders in the internal consultant's immediate working environment, for example the sponsor or initiator of the project on which they are working, the recipient of the initiative and any others within the organisation who have an interest in the changes being brought about. Although all these people may still have an interest if an external consultant is brought in, the working relationships and personal investments may be substantially different.

● Sometimes there are people referred to as 'champions' within an organisation. These are people who either sponsor or, often, are simply extremely supportive of an assignment and do their best to promote it at any opportunity. There can be operational problems if the internal consultant and the project 'champion' go around giving different messages, or carrying out overlapping tasks, and this relationship needs to be managed skilfully.

What does an internal consultant need to consider?

Arising from the points above, there are several issues that need to be given attention if an internal consultant is to be successful. These include:

● Having clear role definitions and reporting responsibilities, so it is obvious who is responsible for what and whether the internal consultant is a service provider or a thought leader.

● Knowing who are the important people to deal with and having open access to any people who are important to the conduct of the assignment, even if this would normally be unusual for a person at the consultant's job level.

● Having open access to any information required for the conduct of the assignment.

- Having all the consultancy skills that apply in any consultancy role, including problem definition, information gathering, analysis, interpersonal and facilitation skills and the ability to present evidence and recommendations and, if appropriate, help ensure implementation.

- Acting as a liaison point with any external consultants so that there is dovetailing of interests and activities.

- Understanding internal political issues and having the sensitivity to take them into account in any work conducted.

- Avoiding being seen as aligned with either management or staff – an independent stance is important if the consultant is to be able to function effectively.

- Marketing internal consultancy services so that they are known about, understood and valued by others within the organisation.

What Do Clients Want from Consultants?

All consultants will tell you their own version of what is important to clients. However hard anyone tries to generalise on this topic, each client is different, each consultant is different and the dynamics between the two will vary according to many different factors. In writing this book, I decided to consult some of my own clients, some other consultants, some consultancy organisations and some users of different consultancy services about what they felt was most important in choosing a consultant and having a client/consultant relationship.

I deliberately left it open for each person to respond in their own way as I did not want to bias their thinking with my own preconceptions about the topic. In the event I obtained an interesting set of opinions. Have a look at the following responses and see how they correspond to your own expectations, or experience, of these issues. Most of the comments relate to management consultancy, but a few are from other fields, and I have given these first:

21

Medical consultancy

Doctors believe there are three essential elements in a consultant/client (patient) relationship; they are referred to as the three A's of:

- Availability.
- Amiability.
- Ability.

These three factors are perceived, in the medical profession, as having just that order of importance. In other words, a consultant's skills are often felt to be less important than their responsiveness to the patient. If they can be contacted easily and develop a good rapport with their patients, their reputation is good. If their ability is excellent, but they are poor at interpersonal relations and hard to get hold of, opinions of them may take a nosedive. Other factors mentioned in the medical context were empathy and listening, patience and transfer of information.

Design consultancy

A key factor here seems to be accessibility. In common with the medical consultants, designers are often expected to be on call 24 hours a day. Because clients often want design work done rapidly, especially in the field of graphic design, a fast turn-around time matters to them. Being available when the client wants you is frequently of prime importance.

IT consultancy

The main points in this kind of technical consultancy seem to be fourfold: a good understanding of the particular client's problems, experience of the issues raised and their possible solutions, good interpersonal skills in order to get on with clients and not antagonise them and good project management (and, where appropriate, implementation) skills in order to achieve results.

Financial consultancy

In this field, the main needs seem to be for good, speedy and accurate advice, at a price that can be afforded, and a person who will work in the client's best interests. There was also some perception that, whereas small independent consultants would work for their clients' interests, the larger consultancies could be more worried about their own reputation than about their clients and, if there were any 'grey areas', they could interpret them against their clients' interests.

General management consultancy

There was a very varied set of responses here. Although some common principles run through most of them, the actual top priorities did vary considerably from client to client. The following are some of the points made by individuals, grouped according to topic. As many of them are from my own clients they may, of course, reflect my own client base rather than consultancy purchasers in general, although I think this is unlikely:

Experience and Expertise

Particular specialist expertise

A good track record to give the client reassurance, and up-to-date experience – including sector experience – are required, although most consultants themselves do not believe that sector experience is so important as long as specialist and process skills are good. Experience may be in paid work or as a consultant; it does not always matter to the client as long as the experience is practical, relevant and up to date.

Having both good process skills and professional subject knowledge
Being able to manage processes and facilitate interactions between people is important. However good the consultant, if they can

only offer specialist expertise and not process skills, they are likely not to be favoured. Conversely, knowing their subject well is basic to effectiveness so that process skills are balanced with a depth of knowledge and information about the topic concerned.

Breadth of understanding beyond the client's own industry and their own experience

Practical experience across a range of contexts is sought after. Although specific sector experience is important, the ability to conceptualise more broadly, and to apply knowledge gained in different contexts, is also valued. This means a balanced approach where there is a focus on more than one element. A real understanding of both the client's business and of the business world in general is appreciated.

Being good at what they do

Actually delivering results matters. However good a consultant looks and sounds, and however wonderful they make the client feel, business results are what count in the long run.

Credibility

Establishing their credentials for doing the work.

Delivering what they profess to do

Keeping to agreements is important, as is providing everything that has been promised and not just part of the discussed package.

Offering practical solutions and delivery to the business

Past practical experience is seen as a good indication of expertise, and carrying out activities which have a relevance to client needs is important. Being able to give ideas over and above what the client would have thought of is a valued asset. Not just giving off-the-shelf solutions – 'I have the solution; you must have the problem' – 'Been there, done that and got the answer'.

Encouraging client ownership
Being able to leave the client believing they can get on with implementation is vital. It is also important for client staff to see their own view in what the consultant produces.

A balanced approach
Being objective and impartial is another important element. It is good to have personal opinions and ideas, but they need to be kept in perspective and the total context dealt with.

Bringing current best practice to the work area
Keeping up to date and knowing about developments in the particular field is important.

Having appropriate qualifications
One good qualification tends to be seen as better than none, but numerous ones may give the impression of 'qualification fatigue'. One comment, however, was that it was sometimes difficult for clients to know exactly what qualifications indicated: e.g., is a particular professional body hard to join or is it simply expensive?

Quality assurance
Keeping the people with the purse-strings happy matters. Having a good client list and good qualifications are important factors in this process.

Having basic marketing skills
Being able to demonstrate what makes you different from anyone else, being able to understand the client's problems and showing the benefits rather than just doing a sales pitch were points made.

Providing a skills transfer to staff
Enabling staff to take responsibility for, and carry out, appropriate activities is appreciated. In other words, allow your skills to be given to others, rather than kept as consultant mystique.

Relationship skills

Some kind of bond
Having a sense of connection. This may mean that the consultant will call just to talk on a personal level, without there necessarily being a work connection. Clients generally need to like the consultant if they are to work with him or her.

Trust
Knowing that the consultant will respect confidentiality, do what has been agreed and act appropriately.

Being a good team player
Being able to get on with client staff and work with any others associated with the assignment is an important element.

Good communications
Keeping in touch, explaining what is going on and managing the client's involvement in what they are doing were mentioned. Being concise and not garrulous, although comprehensive enough to cover all the elements required, was another point covered. Not blinding with science and technical or academic jargon.

Good relationship skills
Being able to relate to people at all levels within the organisation. Not being 'pushy'.

Listening
Having the ability to listen and empathise with the people doing the job, because many of the best ideas come from those doing the job, who may never have been listened to before. Being prepared to listen rather than just talk.

Being receptive
Not seeming to understand everything within the first ten minutes, but listening and discussing in order to get a real understanding.

Understanding the client's values and being able to speak a language that can fit these
Being able to take on the client's perspective and work with what is important to the client; sharing 'core values'.

Involving the client
Some external consultants may take over the client's own internal clients and stakeholders and leave out the client themselves. So involving the client is important.

Being able to show empathy
Not necessarily being like the client, but empathising. Being able to look as if they fit in.

Fit of character, personality and style
A similarity of temperament and approach between consultant and client; the right personality to deal with personalities in the client organisation so the consultant can sell him or herself and relate to people, especially of different types from the consultant.

Cultural fit
No inappropriate formality or orientation towards financial results at the expense of relationships. Some people can seem too polished and glossy, which may make less affluent clients, sub-consciously, think they are too expensive.

Establishing longer-term relationships
This sometimes involves moving away from the bigger firms to establish relationships with a selected few firms that can work well with the client.

Valuing relationships, understanding and talking at more than a superficial level
Knowing that there is a real depth of understanding and a real concern to assist the client to the greatest extent possible. Not just watching without letting you know what they are seeing.

Availability

Responsiveness
Being able to ask for help with problems at any time and knowing that the consultant will never say 'No'.

Has time available for the work needed
Knowing that the person you select can commit the time to the assignment.

Ethics

Being prepared to lose work because what the client is asking is wrong
Not always agreeing with the client. This can be perceived as a powerful thing to do and can gain respect rather than lose it.

Open and honest accounting
Letting the client know about any hidden extras in the billing; being clear about what the costs are from the start.

Impartiality
Not having any hidden agendas; being able to stay outside the politics of the organisation.

Honesty
Being able to have open and honest discussions that both parties can gain from. Admitting if there are things that the consultant does not know, rather than 'pretending to be God'.

Reliability

Having a reliable backup from the company should a particular consultant become unavailable
Knowing that the job will be done, whatever happens.

Reliability with commitment
Having a steady working pattern with a view to getting the job done rather than watching the clock.

Having confidence that the consultant will be around long enough to do the job
Knowing the practice is stable and that the person who is involved will continue to be so.

Personal Qualities

Flexibility and, in some contexts, being multi-skilled
Being able to tailor their products to the client, rather than the client having to fit in with them. Not having their own agenda. Being able to deal with what the client needs rather than what you have planned. Being able to 'change things on their feet'.

General willingness and an ability to listen
A proactive approach and a genuine interest in the client's concerns.

Political awareness of various stakeholders, not just the sponsor and the consumer
A broad understanding of the client's environment and interests.

Being more organised than the client
Having reliable systems and approaches to make things work.

Responsiveness to client needs
Being able to pick up the style wanted in tune with what the client is saying.

Having people who are willing to do some work up front
Visiting, talking, sitting in on meetings and doing research to show they are taking the job seriously.

Doing their homework
Reading the brief and understanding the organisation.

Being a chameleon
Responding appropriately to each person and situation encountered.

Commitment
Being fully in support of the client and the assignment.

Humour
Being able to bring a sense of humour to groups within which the person is working.

Independence
Being able to provide a new view of the organisation from the outside, rather than the clients constantly looking internally.

Purchasing Issues

Being able to understand the relationship between the organisa-tion and the consultant
Is the consultant a franchisee, salaried, on commission, sub-contracted, etc.?

Being able to see not just the sales team but what you are buying
Better practices use their consultants as the sales team, and clients may be suspicious of those who don't. WYSIWYG – What You See Is What You Get – is important.

Availability
Being free to do the work.

Clarity of costing
Knowing what the total charge is, whether VAT and expenses will be additional, etc.

And finally, a few specific additional comments:

- A long-established consultant said that what clients want is different from what they need and is different again from what consultants actually do.

- A client who used to be an independent consultant said that having been independent himself made him more aware of his commissioned consultants' positions.

- A client-turned-consultant said there was a difference between consultants who favoured methodology and those who favoured outcomes – those driven by methodology may be very familiar with new techniques, but those who are focused on the client's needs tend to be more effective.

- Some clients felt that a low price (as long as the provider pro-duced results) meant good value, while others felt that a high price indicated that the value would be good; and in fact many clients do choose high-charging firms simply because they believe their fee levels reflect their expertise.

- It can be 'lonely at the top', so some clients welcome a good consultant as much for the personal interaction and support they bring as for their particular expertise and ideas.

- It was also reported that some clients regard a consultant as an 'insurance policy'. This can be because they simply want external validation for their own ideas – or those of their board – or it can be so they have someone to blame if the ideas are not well received.

And an anecdote:

One consultancy purchaser said he was visited by a consultant who drove a very expensive XJ6 Jaguar car. The car gave him the sense that the consultant was either a charlatan, out to impress, or a very successful and effective person (had he been driving a battered old Ford, he said, his impressions would have been different!). He decided to go with the latter assessment of success and effectiveness and turned out to be right. An interesting thought, however, for both providers and purchasers – impres-sions do count.

What Do Consultants Want from Clients?

Having thought about what clients want from consultants, it is also worth considering what consultants want from their clients. As with any relationship, it is good when the interaction itself is pleasant, as well as the end result being achieved, so here are a few things that consultants like to find in their clients:

- Well-defined objectives or an openness to the consultant clarifying what the needs are.

- Good briefing and clarity about what is required.

- Reasonably prompt decisions about selection for assignments.

- An agreed contract.

- Appropriate people designated for client management, liaison and decision-making.

- Availability for discussion.

- Adequate information and briefing.

- Openness and honesty about requirements, issues and people.

- Realistic expectations.

- Adequate internal communication about the consultancy project and the consultant.

- Implementation of recommendations and feedback on results.

- Appreciation.

- Prompt payment.

Final Points

This chapter has illustrated some of the issues relevant to consultancy as a career. If you are now stimulated to consider pursuing this course of action, the next chapter will give you ways of identifying how you might react to the reality of a consultancy life.

Chapter 2
Consultancy and You

This chapter will help you consider whether consultancy is right for you. It will enable you to explore your own motivation and aptitudes, assess the benefits and risks of a consultancy career and help identify your own consultancy products and positioning in your market.

I am often called by people with questions about consultancy. The two most common questions are: "How can I tell whether consultancy is the right thing for me?" and "How can I get into consultancy?"

There was a period a decade or so ago, when many people who were made redundant decided that consultancy would be the best (and perhaps the only available) career move for them. Nowadays there seems to be a different attitude on the whole and people are recognising that consultancy is an option that needs careful consideration, as should any major change in direction in life. So how do you tell whether consultancy is a good career step for you, and how can you become a consultant if that is what you choose? Here are some aspects for you to consider.

Will Consultancy Be Right for You?

Here are a few scenarios, each followed by some questions. This is not a test and it is not scored. The questions are there for you to imagine each situation and assess your own reaction to it. So consider each possibility and think which of the options seems most like you.

Make sure, with each of the options, that you really project yourself into the situation and consider how it would actually *feel* in reality.

You are sitting at your desk. It is 11.45 p.m. You have spent since 8.00 a.m. calling potential new clients, doing urgent administration, catching up with current reading, revising a brochure, and you still have three sections of a new proposal to write and get in the post first thing tomorrow. Are you:

a) Still full of energy and capable of completing the task effectively?

b) Exhausted and incapable of rational thought?

c) Wishing you had a 9–5 job with a life outside work?

d) Anything else?

You look in your diary. The next five weeks are very busy but after that there are large empty spaces. You know you will hardly have any time to spare in the short term, but really don't know if you will be earning fees in much more than a month's time. How do you feel?

a) Anxious that no more work may come in?

b) Enthusiastic at the prospect of seeking new assignments?

c) Glad that you will have time to do those odd jobs around the house?

d) Anything else?

You visit a potential client. You have spent two days preparing for a presentation, following an invitation to tender. You get the impression that you are there to make up the numbers, the client apparently having the inclination to give the assignment to a previously used consultancy firm.

Do you:

a) Do your best to come across as so excellent that the client has no option but to choose you?

b) Assume there is no point in making an effort and do the minimum necessary to fill in the time?

c) Ask directly what you would need to do to convince them to select you?

d) Anything else?

You have been working on an important project for some weeks. You have no other day-to-day work associates with whom to compare notes or discuss ideas. Are you:

a) Happy to work alone?

b) Longing for some interaction with others in similar lines of work?

c) Able to call up a network of contacts with whom to exchange ideas and approaches?

d) Anything else?

You are extremely busy on a major assignment that takes up all your time. Do you:

a) Decide to do more marketing once the assignment is completed?

b) Make time to research and contact new prospects while working on the assignment?

c)   Trust that fate will bring you more work when you need it?

d)   Anything else?

You have been working on a major assignment and it is time for you to leave the client to implement your recommendations. Do you:

a)   Believe they are the best people to implement their own business development?

b)   Feel sorry that you will not personally be putting the plans into action?

c)   Want to keep in touch to see how they are getting on?

d)   Anything else?

Another consultant phones and asks how you generate new business. Are you:

a)   Flattered to be asked and happy to respond?

b)   Worried that if you give away your techniques you may lose out in the future?

c)   Concerned that you have no real strategy for business development?

d)   Anything else?

You receive a leaflet about an interesting training course, which may well be relevant to your business. Is your response:

a)   "I will find the money to pay for it as it is a good investment for my future business"?

b)   "It sounds really good but I can't afford to take that much time off"?

c)   "If I don't go on the course I could buy a new fax machine or mail a flyer to 200 new prospects"?

d)   Anything else?

You come across a job advertisement from a major consultancy firm. Do you:

a)   Feel confident you could get the position?

b)   Think you lack sufficient confidence to apply?

c)   Wonder if you would like the job if you were successful?

d)   Anything else?

You are a junior member of a team of consultants in an important meeting with a client. Are you:

a)   Content to listen and learn from the more senior members of your team?

b)   Anxious to contribute and looking out for every opportunity to do so?

c)   Concerned you may come across as inexperienced and uninformed?

d)   Anything else?

You have been working on a large project and your contribution is key to its success. When the final report is submitted, your name does not appear in it. Do you:

a)   Feel aggrieved that you have not been credited?

b)   Accept that the report is best submitted under the name of the consultant in charge of the project?

c) Look forward to a time when you will be the lead person?

d) Anything else?

You have written to 200 potential clients to tell them of your services, but only three have responded and then only with an indication that they will keep your details on file. Do you:

a) Feel pleased that three people, at least, have expressed some interest?

b) Worry that, if this is typical, your business will never be successful?

c) Decide to target your future sales and marketing literature more carefully?

d) Anything else?

You have a scheduled meeting with senior managers in a client organisation, due to take place in a week's time; they contact you to say it is difficult for one or two people to attend and ask if it can be rescheduled. Do you:

a) Happily re-organise your diary to fit in with their wishes?

b) Feel annoyed at the disruption?

c) Try to get them to keep to the original date?

d) Anything else?

You have been working for a client company and a member of staff complains to you about how the organisation is run. Do you:

a) Agree and commiserate about the problems?

b) Tell the person to take up their complaints internally?

c)   Listen and say you will raise the issues with the management team?

d)   Anything else?

I hope these scenarios have given you an idea of some typical consultancy situations and allowed you to think out how you might feel if faced with them. Although consultancy jobs vary considerably, there are some features that tend to be common to them. I would, however, distinguish between working as an independent consultant and working as a member of a large consultancy practice. So now, let's consider some of the things that people mention as pros and cons of a consultancy career.

Benefits and Risks of Consultancy

Although each person is individual and has his or her own concept of consultancy work, there are some features of the consultancy lifestyle that are commonly mentioned by practitioners. I have listed a few, split between independent and employed consultants.

Independent consultants

People working as sole practitioners often report the following features of their day-to-day activity:

Positive

- Freedom – ability to choose when, where and how you work.

- Variety – a range of projects with different features.

- Independence – not having to account to others for your activities.

- Home-based work – the convenience of working at your own premises.

Negative

- Loneliness – nobody to discuss work projects with.

- Peaks and troughs of work – not knowing if you will be earning anything next month.

- Pressure – never having an hour free as there are no set hours of work.

- Marketability – finding it difficult to re-enter the job market if consultancy does not work out.

Large practice consultancy work

People working for large consultancy firms often mention the following features of their work:

Positive

- Resources – readily provided training, equipment, information and support staff.

- Career advancement – progression opportunities internally or externally.

- Teamworking – having colleagues for support and interaction.

- Mentoring – having more experienced colleagues there for advice and guidance.

Negative

- Conformity – needing to convey the company image and values to others.

- Enforced relocation – being allocated projects in possibly undesirable regions.

- Competition – having to prove your worth against others.

- Client confidence – being treated as less competent than more senior colleagues.

Of course, some of the things I have listed as positives, some people might think of as negatives, and vice versa. And smaller consultancy firms, partnerships or associations can have a mix of the features mentioned. The important thing is to be aware of some of the issues faced by consultants and then to think out whether you would be enthused or demotivated by dealing with them yourself.

Two of the issues that are particularly relevant in consultancy are, firstly, the extent to which you can handle uncertainty and risk and secondly, the extent to which you are happy in a non-operational role. Have a look at the next two sets of questions and see how you respond to them.

A) Uncertainty and risk

Here are a few sets of alternatives; in each, tick the one you think applies most to you:

Would you be more likely to choose:

- A job offering £40,000 p.a.
  or
  a job offering basic pay of £15,000 plus the opportunity to increase your earnings to £60,000 p.a. through performance-related payments?

- Joining an old established firm that will give good basic experience
  or
  joining a firm just starting up that will offer fast-track development if it stays in business?

- A guaranteed six-month contract
  or
  a one-month contract with the possibility of it being extended to twelve months if you achieve agreed results?

- Putting all your invested money into setting up your practice to as high a standard as you can manage
  or
  keeping some money back for unexpected need, although this will limit the resources for your practice?

- A high proportion of interim management work to provide a regular income
  or
  one-off assignments that could produce an unpredictable income level?

- Keeping a second source of income until your practice proves viable
  or
  putting all your effort into establishing your practice, foregoing the security of established work?

B) *Level of operational activity*

Again, some sets of alternatives:

Do you prefer:

- 'Hands-on' activity
  or
  letting others do the spadework?

- Implementing your own recommendations
  or
  handing over implementation to others?

- Control
  or
  influence?

- Responsibility
  or
  an advisory role?

- Things to be done your way
  or
  things to be done appropriately for others?

- Managing
  or
  facilitating?

So you have now completed various sets of questions about aspects of consultancy. Taking all the questions into account, if you are thinking of embarking on a career as an independent consultant, did you consider the questions and think, "Yes, I would really be excited by working on my own, balancing work and home life, coping with uncertainty, being solely responsible for the satisfaction of my clients and having constantly to seek and respond to new work possibilities"? Or did you think, "No, I couldn't see myself existing from day to day, worrying about whether I could pay the bills next week, knowing I couldn't afford to take a day off sick because nobody would be there to cover for me and having no work colleagues to complain to or to cheer me up if I was having a bad day"? Of course these are extremes, but they can be a good description of the life of the sole practitioner.

And if you are thinking of embarking on a career in a large consultancy firm, did you think, "Yes, I would be motivated by having a visible promotion ladder, senior people to guide me, colleagues for support and scope for international travel"? Or did you think, "No, I would be frustrated by having to get the approval of senior colleagues, hampered by having to take what projects were allocated to me and miserable at being sent overseas at the drop of a hat"?

Factors Contributing to Success in Consultancy

Understanding your own motivation, attitudes and aptitudes is vital if you are to make a success of consultancy. Once you know what makes you enthusiastic and able to maintain commitment and energy, you are well placed to embark on your new career. It is also important to have the right combination of skills and knowledge for your chosen field. So the next part of this chapter will deal with identifying your own knowledge, skills, aptitudes, attitudes and motivation, as well as your strengths and weaknesses, likes and dislikes, successes and 'failures'. Let's take them in turn. In the sections that follow I use simple, commonsense definitions of each of the terms; you may well find more sophisticated ones in textbooks, but I believe the following will be helpful in allowing you to assess yourself effectively.

Knowledge

One definition of knowledge is 'The state that exists when you have assimilated, and understood, information you have collected'. Knowledge is a major underpinning element of performance. In consultancy, knowledge is probably the single most vital commodity and there is a strong current trend towards the development of what is termed 'knowledge management'. What clients buy, first and foremost, is knowledge. I am reminded of the old story of a plumber who was called in to deal with a faulty boiler. He simply tapped the boiler and it started working perfectly. He then sent in a bill for £100. The customer thought the bill was far too high and questioned it. The plumber sent in a more detailed bill, which read: "To tapping the boiler, £5; to knowing where to tap, £95".

This story is commonly used and is still worth retelling; it illustrates the importance of knowledge as the foundation for expertise. So what knowledge do you have that could be relevant to consultancy? Take a little time to consider the following questions and write down your answers so you can have access to them again later.

- What fields does your knowledge cover?

- What depth of knowledge do you have in your major fields of activity or interest?

- How up to date is your knowledge in these fields?

- Is your knowledge gained from personal experience, from speaking to others, from reading, listening to or viewing material, or from any other sources?

- How do you think your knowledge in these fields compares with other people's?

Aptitudes

An aptitude is a natural tendency to be good at something. Just because you have a particular aptitude, however, does not mean that you have actually developed a skill in that area. You may, for example, have an aptitude for learning languages, but only discover this when you go abroad and find you can pick up words and phrases easily – you may not have known this before you went.

Identifying your aptitudes is a good foundation for a move to consultancy as it helps you understand your areas of strength and the likely focus for your business products. So consider the following questions, which should help you be more aware of your own aptitudes.

- Are there certain things which seem to come very naturally to you; if so, what are they?

- Given the opportunity, which activities do you choose to spend time on?

- Which things have you found it very easy to learn and practise?

- Which subjects did you do best in at school or further education?

Skills

Skills are things people are able to do effectively. For example you may be skilled at teaching, writing, gardening, listening, analysing, managing stress, managing a team or riding a bicycle. You will notice that these skills differ from each other in various ways. Listening is a 'small' skill, whereas teaching is a 'large' skill. Riding a bicycle is an 'activity' skill, whereas analysing is a 'thinking' skill. Managing stress is a personal (emotional control) skill whereas team management is an interpersonal skill.

Skills are developed as we go through life. Whereas an aptitude seems to be inherent, skills can be more easily enhanced. So consider the following questions, some of which relate to your current skills and some to skills you may develop in the future.

- Which skills do you have at present?

- Which skills would you like to develop?

- Which skills do you practise most often?

- Which skills have you not utilised for some time?

- Do you believe you are more skilled at:

  - Physical activities.
  - Mental activities.

  - Technical activities.
  - Non-technical activities.

  - Personal activities.
  - Interpersonal activities.

  - A broad range of activities.
  - A narrow range of activities.

Attitudes

Attitudes are coloured by your thoughts, feelings and beliefs about things. When you have an attitude towards something it tends to govern your actions and reactions in relation to that thing. Your attitudes are important factors when considering consultancy work – attitudes to your own performance, to your clients, to your employers, to your colleagues, to your work assignments, to your long-term future and to much, much more. Take a little time to consider the following questions on attitudes.

- What is your attitude towards your current employment status?

- What is your attitude towards being employed or self-employed?

- What is your attitude towards uncertainty in employment?

- What is your attitude towards status?

- What is your attitude towards responsibility?

- What is your attitude towards providing a service to clients?

- What is your attitude towards people who make substantial demands on your time and effort?

- What is your attitude towards personal development?

- What is your attitude towards conflict?

- What is your attitude towards change?

Motivation

Motivation is a topic that has given rise to numerous theories and interpretations. While it is possible to generalise about motivational patterns, each person is unique and therefore has a unique set of criteria that impact on his or her motivation. Motivation is an important aspect of consultancy, especially if you are self-employed and single-handed, so consider the following questions and assess your responses to them.

- Are you generally self-motivated or do you need others around to motivate you?

- Do you find it easy to maintain your motivation levels?

- Are you demotivated if you are criticised or if you make a mistake?

- Are you more motivated by some stages of activity than by others (e.g. planning, initiating, implementing, etc.)?

- Are you more motivated by achievement, money, status, recognition, helping others, or anything else?

- Are you more motivated by getting results or by avoiding problems?

Strengths and weaknesses/likes and dislikes (preferences) /successes and 'failures'

Now you have worked through the preceding topics you should have a good idea about your own position on the questions asked. Now let's use these as a foundation to consider your strengths and weaknesses, likes and dislikes, successes and 'failures'. I use the word 'failures' in inverted commas because things that may have seemed like failure at the time are almost invariably, on reflection, opportunities for learning and development. Many people learn more from things they do badly than from things they do well, so considering relative 'failures' can be a good pointer to future success.

Although some of these points are similar to issues raised earlier in this chapter, please take a little while to think about the following issues.

- What do you think are your main strengths?
- What do you think are relative weaknesses?
- What kind of things do you like or enjoy?
- What kind of things do you dislike and avoid?
- What have you done really well in the past?
- What do you feel you have not done particularly well in the past?

Now you have taken this time to assess yourself in a variety of ways, you can use the information gathered to consider what products or services you would offer if you went into consultancy as a career. Let's think about that next.

Your consultancy product or expertise

It is perfectly possible to choose a field of consultancy without having any prior experience within it. It is generally better, however, to tailor your consultancy offerings to reflect your own personal abilities and expertise. So, taking your answers to the above questions, and considering some of the consultancy choices mentioned in the introduction, you can now think about what you would be best at. As a reminder, here are some of the options; can you tell which would suit you best?

- Internal or external consultancy.
- Specialist or generalist consulting.
- Process, analytical or strategic consultancy.
- Interim management, project consultancy or provider of 'outsourced' services.
- Sole trading, partnership, associateship or employed consultancy.
- Local, national or international consultancy.

And, following on from this list, perhaps you could qualify some of your answers. For example:

- If specialist:
  - What function – e.g. IT, HR, marketing?
  - What sector – e.g. public sector, financial services, voluntary organisations?
  - What 'level' – e.g. strategic, process, operational?

- If international:
  - Which countries would you prefer to work in?
  - And why?

And now, perhaps you could qualify your choices even further, by thinking about whether there is any particular specialist 'niche' you could fulfil within your broad areas of activity. Perhaps some of the following apply to you, or perhaps there are other aspects that you feel are more relevant.

Examples of niche products and services

- Advising on company mergers.
- Setting up wide-area computer networks.
- Training in particular software products.
- Producing client-based training videos.
- Introducing supermarket stock control systems.
- Devising performance management systems.
- Creating company operations handbooks.
- Advising on company mergers.
- Developing call centre operations.

And, finally, some thoughts about positioning. There are many ways in which you can position yourself in your particular market; here are a few and, again, you may well think of others.

Examples of positioning elements

- Top end of the market – high-quality, high-priced services.
- Serving low-budget clients – e.g. voluntary organisations.
- Innovation – new approaches and creative ideas.
- Flexibility – solutions tailored very specifically to individual clients.
- Industry, or sector, based – assistance to discrete parts of the client population.

The more you can refine your thinking and be specific about your products, services and positioning, the more likely it is that you will be able to find a unique focus for what you do, which will give you a good market advantage and enhance your reputation as an expert in your particular field. I will be returning to the subject of marketing in Chapter 5.

Getting professional advice

I hope this chapter has helped you identify whether consultancy is a good career choice for you and, if so, which aspects of it would most suit you. If you are still undecided, however, you might wish to consult a professional careers adviser and do some more formal aptitude and personality tests to help you decide.

There are many specialist careers advisers available, and it is worth finding some independent sources of advice on which will be most appropriate for you. There are also tests in existence to check on whether somebody has entrepreneurial skills and is well suited to an independent career, and this kind of test could be a useful resource for you.

Final Points

I said at the beginning of this chapter that people often ask me how they can tell whether consultancy is right for them. If you now believe that consultancy could be a good option for you, the following chapters will help you to become an effective consultant and give you a variety of techniques that will be useful in consultancy work.

Chapter 3
Becoming a Consultant

This chapter will give you some ideas on setting up as an independent consultant or on joining a consultancy practice.

Becoming an Independent Consultant (Solo)

Having made the decision to be a sole practitioner, how do you get started? My belief is that, although you can join a large firm and be trained in consultancy skills, as an independent, you need experience and credibility before you start.

The experience and credibility do not need to be in consultancy, but they will carry far more weight if they have been gained in areas relevant to those in which you intend to offer services. There is something to be said for having an open mind, uncluttered by experience, so you bring a fresh approach to issues, but, in my experience, most clients prefer someone who they feel can bring a practical, real-life, down-to-earth, informed approach to their business.

So let's assume you have relevant experience; what do you need to do to set up in business? Here are some of the elements you are likely to require:

- A product or service.
- A business plan.
- Adequate finance.
- An office base.
- Administrative resources.
- A marketing plan.
- A fee structure.
- Terms of business.
- Personal contacts.
- Membership of a professional body.
- Insurance cover.

- An information base.
- Advice and support.

This list may not be exhaustive, but it does give you an idea of the areas which need to be considered when setting up your business. Let's take them in turn and see what they comprise and how they may be tackled.

A product or service

Knowing what you are offering is essential, as it forms the basis for your marketing and sales and, ultimately, your success and that of your organisation. I hope the preceding chapter will have helped your thinking about products, services and positioning, and in Chapter 5 I will be talking more about how to promote your activities. The important thing is to be clear yourself about your products and services and how they can offer unique benefits to your potential clients.

Because there are so many consultants in business you really do need to stand out if you are to be successful, so your consultancy offerings must be distinctive and saleable, otherwise you will have problems keeping afloat.

One useful point to consider is non-time-based income. Examples are sales of your own products, such as books or computer software, which will carry on earning you income well after the time you have spent on producing them; commission on work passed to associates and licence agreements. Each of these will bring in income either without you having to do much direct work, or for a longer time period than that during which the work took place. This kind of income is a useful addition to other activities and, as well as being financially useful, can spread your activities so you are not reliant on one single source of income.

A business plan

A proper business plan is – theoretically – vital to any successful business. I only say 'theoretically' because when I set up my first business (not consultancy) many years ago, my bank, which was asked to help finance it, never asked me and my co-director to produce a business plan. Although the business was successful, it might well have done better if we had known at the start about some of the factors that could have been predicted through good business planning.

As an example, cash flow was a problem we, together with many small businesses, faced. Much of our work was for large organisations and they could take anything up to three months to pay our invoices. Business volume was not a problem; getting payment for services rendered was.

So, a business plan will enable you to think out all the elements of your business, including many of the items I mentioned at the start of the chapter. There are numerous books on business planning, and your local bank will be only too happy to give you booklets on the topic and help with your thoughts.

If you produce your business plan on your computer it will be easy to make changes, update it and assess progress as you go along; it will also look more professional when you present it to any potential backers. And also think carefully about how you write your plan; its layout and language will considerably influence its impact. You will find more detail about writing business plans in Chapter 5, and Chapter 14 covers business writing skills, which will also help in producing your plan.

Adequate finance

There are a number of factors to consider here, including what funds are needed for capital investment (office, car, computer and so on), business development (marketing, advertising and so on), product development (writing manuals, computer programs workbooks, training material and so on), business maintenance (travel, insurance, stationery, memberships, telephone and post and so on), your own survival (household, food, clothes and so on) and for your development needs.

There is a saying that goes, 'In the first year, you keep your business. In the second year, your business keeps itself. In the third year, your business keeps you'. Although you may be successful very early on, it can take a long time for a consultancy business to get off the ground, so you must make sure you have enough funds to keep you going through your development period.

Remember too that cash flow can be an issue. If you work for organisations that take a long time to pay, you may have sufficient overall income, but your cash flow may mean that you cannot pay your bills on time. This is one of the major reasons for small businesses going under so, when you take on assignments, remember that it may be better to earn a lower daily rate but be certain of payment, than to go for a higher rate that can take months to arrive – months during which you may be borrowing money in order to survive. A recommended approach to finance is to exaggerate the expenditure and underestimate the income, which is likely to give you a realistic estimate of cash flow.

An office base

Unless you have a lot of money to spare, or are offered free or very inexpensive space, it is most likely that you will have to base your business in your own home. There are several things to consider if you do this, including:

- Domestic arrangements.
- Tax implications.
- Noise.
- Interruptions.
- Overlap between work and personal life.
- Impression given to visitors.
- Ease of access.

There are many advantages to working from home. It avoids the time and expense of travelling to work; it enables you to have access to your working materials whenever you want; it allows you to customise your own environment and it allows you to move between work and non-work activities at short notice.

There can also be disadvantages to being home-based. It is easy to blur the distinctions between work and private life, so that you are never off duty; it can encroach on your family's activities and it can seem less professional to some business contacts.

One interesting way of working from home has been adopted by some independent practitioners I know. Both husband and wife work from home and, instead of taking up space in their house, they have put up some wooden cabins in their garden and work from there. The cabins are well made, light, airy and warm and have plenty of space for their needs. The advantages are numerous: they keep their house for domestic purposes, they find it easier to separate work and domestic activities, they have dedicated areas to see clients and they have a pleasant environment in which to work.

If you do not wish to use your own home as an office base in any way, there is another alternative to bought or rented office accommodation; this is to use a 'virtual office' service. With such services, you are given an address and contact numbers, but you do not have a physical space of your own. Services are provided by staff of the service provider and they deal with your telephone messages, faxes and so forth at a distance. Callers receive the impression that you have a fully staffed office and the service costs are considerably less than those involved in buying or renting accommodation and employing staff.

Administrative resources

This can be a difficult factor. A fledgling business can probably not afford staff, yet doing your own administration takes time away from marketing, fund-raising, planning and service provision. Some options are to share staff with other independent consultants, have a part-time secretary/administrator, use a 'virtual office' as referred to in the previous section or contract out some of your activities, such as bookkeeping or secretarial work.

One of the difficulties with consultancy support is that consultancy work often comes in peaks and troughs, so having permanent assistance for spasmodic activity can be difficult to justify and possibly demotivating for the support staff themselves.

A marketing plan

You should already have considered marketing in your business plan, but possibly not in sufficient detail for all of your operational use. Marketing and sales are vital activities for small consultancies and there is a wide range of activities that can help you generate business and sell your products.

I will be covering marketing in more depth in Chapter 5.

A fee structure

This is a difficult one for a number of reasons. Firstly, you may not be aware of market rates for consultancy services. Secondly, you may be tempted simply to get what you can for your work. Thirdly, you may not know where to position yourself within the market.

There is a range of different methods of charging for consultancy services, and you will need to decide which of these is most appropriate for you. To some extent this will be determined by the kind of work you are doing, the clients you work for and the countries you work in.

The major ways of fee charging are as follows:

Time-based
This means charging a rate for time spent. The most commonly found is a day rate, but it is possible to charge on smaller units of time, such as a half-day or hourly rate. In the UK, the day rate is the most common method of charging, although there can be variations in how a day is assessed, with some consultants counting any time spent during a particular calendar day as being within that day's fee rate, while others charge on the basis of a day consisting of a set number of hours (say seven or eight) and possibly charging more if time exceeds that number of hours. One way of calculating a day rate is to add up the hours and then charge each seven or eight hours as a day, regardless of when they were spent.

Time-based accounting is open to exploitation by consultants who are either not very efficient or who spin out their work so that the client is charged more than is necessary for an assignment. Also, it can be hard for a client to know exactly what cost will be involved in a total project, so an indication should be given of the total number of days that will be likely, while leaving room for flexibility should circumstances merit it.

Assignment-based

This means quoting a total fee for a whole assignment. This lets the client know at the start what the total cost of the project is; the difficulty comes if much more time than anticipated needs to be spent, or if the client asks for other things to be done within the project: it may be difficult to say they are outside the remit and therefore cannot be done, or that they will incur an extra cost.

If you charge in this way, you need to make sure your calculations regarding what needs to be done are very well estimated. An alternative way is to agree a total consultancy price, but tailor the work to be done to fit within the budget available. Again, there needs to be advance agreement between both parties for this to work well.

Value-based

This is a method that is still used by the minority, although it is being promoted more actively by some, especially in the USA, where Alan Weiss is one of its main supporters.

With value-based billing, your charges relate to the value (or perceived value) your client receives as a result of your intervention, and the extent to which your activity is seen as an investment by the client. This process means that the relationship with the client is all-important and has to be developed before a fee is discussed. The detailed breakdown of your activity and expenses remains your responsibility and does not have to be accounted for to the client. If the client wishes to reduce the fee, then you remove some of the value accordingly.

Weiss suggests that some points to consider with this kind of billing are: ◆What the outcome of the project is worth to the client, both quantitatively and qualitatively; ◆What your direct contribution to that outcome is; ◆What your relationship is with the client and what costs there are to you in conducting the assignment.

Billing Methods – USA

Billing Method	% of sample using this method 1996	% of sample using this method 1998
Hourly	22	24
Daily	19	16
Monthly	8	5
Project-based	38	39
Time and materials-based	8	7
Value-based	4	7

Source: 'Pricing Trends in Management Consulting', Kennedy Information Research Group, 1999.

Terms of business

Your terms of business are the basis for your side of the contract with your clients. Your fee and expenses structure, fee rates and period of credit will be part of your terms of business, and there will also be other elements. Some other things you can include are liability and insurance, provisions for sickness or accident, use of associates or sub-contractors, confidentiality, intellectual property/trademark rights, charges for additional work or for cancelled assignments, termination of contract and so forth. Having these items clearly documented can save disputes and misunderstandings. However, you will still have to reconcile your own terms of business with those of your clients so they are compatible.

You will need to consider the frequency of billing; monthly is very common, but you can also bill in instalments, for example a third at the start of a project, a further third halfway through and the final third at the end. It will help your cash flow if you can either bill at fairly frequent intervals, or gain agreement for an upfront payment at the start of an assignment.

Sometimes clients may want to pay you in advance, so they can put payments through during a particular budgeting period when they have funds available. While this can be excellent for your own cash flow, if you are subsequently unable to do the work, or the client's need changes, it can cause problems with reimbursement or negotiating changes to the original contract.

Personal contacts

One of the best ways to develop your business is through personal networking. Networking means building a circle of personal and professional contacts, whereby you can ask for, and give, information, advice and assistance on a mutual basis.

Networking at a basic level simply means considering each person you meet as a potentially useful business contact. Each person you know, or meet, will have other personal contacts of their own and so a network is developed which is much larger than your own direct contacts.

Remember that business contacts are not only gained through business situations. You may meet people at social events, clubs, holidays, educational establishments and so forth. In order to make use of these contacts you should have business cards to give people, and you should have a system for annotating and recording information you are given so that it is readily accessible when you need it.

As an example of consultancy networking, the Richmond Group, which is a consortium of independent consultants in the UK (see Resources List), has an e-mail link between its members. Many members regularly exchange ideas, opportunities and information and collaborate on assignments or put in joint proposals and tenders for work. There are other similar bodies elsewhere and I have listed one or two US consultancy groups in the Resources List too.

Membership of a professional body

It is helpful to belong to a professional consultancy organisation for a variety of reasons. Some of the benefits of belonging are:

- Professional recognition and status through the use of designatory letters after your name.

- The opportunity to network with fellow consultants.

- The availability of membership support services such as libraries, information services and legal helplines.

- Conferences and events.

- Publications.

Insurance

As an independent consultant, you will need to have insurance cover for various circumstances.

Cover that is useful to have includes:

- Professional indemnity insurance – important in case any claim is made against you. Although this is unlikely, you should protect yourself against possible claims, especially if you work in a sector where bad decisions could cost a lot of money, or where you might cause an accident or damage. Do shop around for this insurance, as rates can vary enormously. If you can join a group scheme from a professional body it may save you a good deal of money.

- Public liability – especially if you have business visitors to your home.

- Product liability – if you use products that have the potential to cause damage in any way.

An information base

Having adequate information is vital in building your consultancy business. You may choose to maintain your own database of information or you may support your own data through access to external databases.

Professional bodies, specialist libraries and information services and local business development centres are just some of the providers of information to consultants. It is well worth checking what is available in your own field so you do not have to re-invent the wheel when you are researching topics and creating marketing and development systems.

Advice and support

It is helpful to have sources of advice and support, both when you are starting your business and on an ongoing basis. Support can come from your friends and family, from work associates, from professional advisory services and also from selected counsellors, mentors and coaches.

Many people in consultancy find it useful to have a mentor; a person who can help them think through different issues and who has experience that is relevant to their own situation. Mentoring can be a two-way process, whereby both parties gain from the exchange of ideas.

As well as mentoring, coaching is now growing in popularity, and there are numerous organisations offering coaching services. I cover coaching and mentoring in more depth in Chapter 13.

You may think you do not need advice from anyone else, but in independent consultancy it can be valuable to have access to independent sources of help and support.

Training and development

However experienced you are, development activities are invaluable. Most professional organisations now have a requirement for what is termed CPD, or continuing professional development. There are a number of reasons for this requirement; one of the main reasons is the need to keep up to date in an ever-changing world, and I will be returning to this topic in Chapter 6.

Quite apart from the need to update your skills, if you are starting out as a newly fledged consultant, you will need to learn the skills required to survive and be effective. Many of these skills are covered in this book, but there are others, and it can be useful to learn in a social environment, where you can observe how other people respond to situations and discuss the various implications and options involved in different courses of action.

There are various ways of embarking on consultancy training, including the following:

- Taking a degree course in the subject. There are many specialist courses now, for example MBA and MSc programmes, in general or specialist consultancy.

- Taking a short course offered by an institution or an independent training body. There is a growing range of courses provided on consultancy as a whole, or on different aspects of it.

- Becoming associated with a consortium, agency or network. There are many networks of consultants that provide development opportunities for their associates. Some of the provisions include training days, conferences and support groups.

- Joining an Internet discussion group. This is a developing field and one that can be very useful to you. By exchanging ideas and opportunities with others in a similar field of activity, you can extend your own knowledge and skills.

Details of many of these training sources are given in the Resources List.

Collaboration

When working as an independent consultant, you may find you are happy on your own, or you may wish to be associated with others for a variety of reasons, for example:

- Liking the intellectual stimulus of other people's ideas.
- Needing the additional skills that associates can bring.
- Having substantial work projects that need additional help.
- Lending credibility to your business.
- Wanting to help develop less experienced consultants.

Here are a few thoughts about aspects of collaboration:

Will you actively seek it?
Some people deliberately set out to work in association with others, some wait for others to approach them, and others collaborate if such a situation arises but will not otherwise seek it out. It is worth considering your own opinions early on and taking steps to put in place the system that will work best for you.

Whom do you choose (or are you chosen by others)?
It is important to select people with whom you feel comfortable, share values, can meet easily and so forth. An example, from personal experience, of the importance of shared values was a time, many years ago, when I was involved in a joint business venture with two other people. Two of us shared a similar approach to activities, and felt that certain elements were important – we had similar values concerning the venture and ways of working. The third person, who was actually funding most of the start up, had a very different approach from us – in manner, focus and interaction. Eventually the differences between us became too great to continue with the venture, although the two of us who were closest in approach have worked together on other activities since then.

So, knowing that you will be able to work with the people you select, or at least thinking about the way in which the relationship might go in the future, is a vital step, both personally and financially.

What kind of collaborative relationships might you have?

Some examples of collaboration are the following:

- *Working with associates*

  In this case you will have one or more people with whom you work on a more or less ad-hoc basis, when suitable assignments come up. Some associate relationships are very casual – more like a network; others are more formalised so that the same group of associates become almost a virtual organisation, getting together on a regular basis and becoming very familiar with each other's skills and approaches. You may regularly work on the same assignment as particular associates, or you may simply draw upon your pool of associates (or be drawn upon by others) when suitable work arises.

- *Working with other independents*

  There may be times when you find yourself collaborating with other independent consultants for the same client. This happened to me on one assignment, when I was dealing with HR issues and another consultant had been brought in to deal with finance issues, both of us having come through the same interim management organisation. In a case such as this, you need to be able to establish a good working relationship speedily and ensure that what you are doing is complementary, rather than competitive or duplicating effort.

- *Working on joint projects*

  An example of this is another book on consultancy to which I contributed (see Bibliography). The book was produced by the Richmond Group, to which I referred earlier, and a number of its members collaborated on the final product.

What 'ground rules' might you need?

Although collaboration has many good features, there can also be drawbacks. You will need to agree on points such as the following if collaboration is to work:

- *Do you need a formal contractual arrangement, or will you simply have a verbal agreement?*

  Formal contracts may seem complex and unnecessary, but they can be valuable. On one occasion, I was working with another person and that person had to stop working because of family commitments. We had not established a formal contractual arrangement and there were some real problems that arose through differing expectations of what obligations should pertain in the event of the relationship ceasing. If you are as explicit as possible about such arrangements, in the event of a dispute, or of the relationship ending, it will be much easier to bring about a successful outcome that satisfies both parties.

What will people's roles be?

For example, who will be responsible for administration, or for billing or for production of material on any particular assignment? Will both parties be working under their own business name or will one take on responsibility for the project with the other working as a sub-contractor (at least in the eyes of the client)?

How will you communicate with each other?

Do you need a formal system of communications, i.e. weekly phone calls or e-mails, or periodic meetings where everyone can get together, or will you simply contact each other as necessary?

What about ethics?

What is appropriate and acceptable is one area where people sometimes experience difficulty. For example, one consultant I know became associated with another person and then found that he accompanied her to meetings and tried to promote his own services rather than their joint ones. So considering ethics is important if your collaboration is to stand the test of time. I will be returning to this topic in Chapter 6.

Collaboration can work very effectively, but it is not for everyone; deciding if it will be beneficial to be associated with others is simply one element in being an effective consultant. I have personally collaborated with other consultants on some assignments, and my own opinion is that the most important element is whether you and the other person/people share a similar approach to work (and life!). When you have shared perspectives and interests the working relationship becomes enjoyable and effective but, however competent others are, if you are not on the same wavelength, it can be a disservice to both you and your clients.

Final Points

This section has been about some of the issues involved in working independently. There are many rewards and benefits to be obtained from working in this way and, if you are unsure in advance, you will certainly know within a reasonably short time after starting whether it is for you. If it is, fine; if not, you may find that joining a larger practice and becoming an employed consultant suits you better.

And, as a final example, one consultant I know set up a single-handed business after several years of being employed in an HR function. She started with a combination of locum work, small HR projects and some training and, within her first year, was self-sufficient. Her business continued to thrive each successive year. In my experience, the degree of her first year's success was unusual, which is why I give her as an example of what can be done, but it does show that having good contacts and a positive outlook, as well as professional skills, make major contributions to consultancy success.

Getting a Job as a Consultant

If the idea of becoming an independent consultant does not appeal to you, you may consider seeking a job with an established consultancy practice. There are many large, medium and small consultancies seeking suitable staff, and prospects within these organisations are excellent for people who are suited to this kind of career. At the time of writing, the ten largest UK consultancies are recruiting around 3,000 consultants annually between them and, as there is around a 30% turnover each year, this level of recruitment is likely to continue.

Employment opportunities, expectations and rewards

Although consultancy jobs are well paid, high commitment, time and effort is required in return, and this commitment can be very disruptive to 'normal' family and social life. Salaries vary depending on the level of post (ranging from junior consultant to partner/director) and on the sector, with some sectors (such as finance, telecoms, high technology and recruitment) commanding higher fees and others (for example public sector and manufacturing) being less well paid. As a rough guide, in the UK at the present time, junior consultants can earn around £20,000 to £40,000 (according to one survey, those with MBAs are able to attract higher salaries, possibly from £45,000 to £85,000), senior consultants around £30,000 to £125,000 and managers/partners/directors around £45,000 to £450,000 depending on size and type of organisation. Other benefits can add from 10% to 50% of basic salary to the total package.

In the USA rates also vary with the organisation and the geographical region, but some sources indicate starting salaries, with a first degree, of between $30,000 and $50,000 and starting salaries with an MBA of between $80,000 and $140,000, plus other elements in the total package.

In addition, some of the larger firms are offering sizeable inducements to join; at the time of writing one major consultancy firm in the UK is offering graduates £10,000 'golden hello' payments – £6,000 immediately and a further £4,000 after one year – in order to join. At 21 years of age this is an excellent incentive (on top of a starting salary of almost £30,000 a year) to move into consultancy.

At the higher levels, as well as functional expertise, business and marketing skills are vital, and a good deal of the work can involve gaining new business for the organisation. Some people work for consultancy firms as a career, while others look upon it as a career step, perhaps for 3 to 5 years, rather than an end in itself.

The joys of consultancy

Seen in the September 2000 issue of **Management Today**, a short piece about one UK consultancy that rewards good timekeeping by letting staff have free breakfasts at local bagel shops (as long as they arrive at work with the food before 8.30 a.m.) and free food and drinks if they work late! So consultancy work may not be purely its own reward!

Consultancy organisations

In the Resources List you will find details of some of the larger consultancies in the UK, USA and Europe, and their contact details at the time of writing. If you are in a country not covered by the Resources List, you will need to identify organisations within your own geographical area.

The larger consultancies, which tend – in the UK at least – to have started out life as accountancy-based firms, can be split between 'strategy houses' and more functionally based consultancies; most of them are international in their activity. These two groups tend to have slightly different approaches to recruitment. There are also smaller consultancy practices that, again, recruit on a slightly different basis from the larger firms.

What they look for

The days of the generalist in consultancy, as in the Civil Service, are declining. Nowadays most jobs are specialist jobs, apart from those offered by the 'strategy houses', which often tend, still, to recruit generalists and, in particular, ones with excellent academic achievements. Such houses hire on the basis of overall brightness and the ability to pick up new skills, rather than a record of achievement in any particular discipline.

Other consultancy firms tend to look for people who are, or are starting to become, specialists in a particular function or sector, for example local government, telecommunications or accountancy. On the whole, what is required is five to seven years' postgraduate work experience (a minimum of three years is generally acceptable), which means that the ideal candidate will be aged around 27 or 28. Older people are also hired, but they generally tend to be taken on by the strategy houses and are likely to be well known as thought leaders in their specialist fields. Once someone has more than fifteen years' work experience, they are unlikely still to be on the upward stage of their career and less likely to fit easily into the typical consultancy profile found in the larger consultancy firms.

Once you have been taken on by one of the major consultancy firms, you will receive excellent training and support and gain valuable experience on a range of assignments, which will either give you a step up to advancement as an employed consultant, or give you marketable skills if starting up on your own or moving into employment in another capacity. Many people do move between management and consultancy, in both directions, and the skills gained in either field are invaluable in the other.

When recruiting, there are several criteria that are used by consultancy firms. Three are of particular importance:

- *Academic achievement*

  Firms will be looking for a good record of achievement at school and at university. This is used as an indicator of general levels of intelligence. An MBA is a good addition to your academic armoury and is mainly sought after by the strategy houses, but will rarely compensate for a poor academic record earlier on. The recruitment manager of a major consutancy practice in the UK was recently quoted as saying that it was better to do an MSc in business information systems than an MBA, because this would make applicants more employable. In the USA an MBA probably carries more weight than in the UK, but is still unlikely to compensate for practical business experience.

- *Work experience*

  In this field firms look for a demonstrable track record of success, the more business-oriented, the better.

- *Personal qualities*

  This is the area where firms will be looking for people who are articulate, have presence, can make an impact and are distinctive in some way. In addition, being a good team member and leader is important.

An excellent academic record can make up for relatively low work experience, and an excellent work record can make up for slightly poorer examination results. However, on the whole, both are needed. The strategy houses in particular are more likely to be influenced by academic results and more likely to waive the need for in-depth business experience.

How to apply

There are four main ways of applying to work for a consultancy firm:

- *Recruitment from university or business school*

  The larger firms go around selected universities and business schools talking to potential recruits. This is an excellent way for prospective employees to find out what is on offer and have exploratory discussions with a range of firms. Not all universities and business schools are included, however, and not all firms can afford to recruit in this way, so you will be finding out – in the main – about the larger consultancy organisations, although the smaller consultancies may also alert university/business school careers advisors to vacancies they have.

- *Responding to advertisements*

  Apart from the university 'milk rounds', most jobs are advertised in the media. Replying to advertisements is the main route in for most applicants who have not come in straight from the education system. The advertisements will tell you exactly what is required and whom to contact. It is particularly important that your application creates a good impression – one of professionalism, confidence and capability. You will find a little more on job applications in Chapter 14, Business Writing.

- *Using e-recruitment services*

  Nowadays there is a growing movement towards recruiting via the Internet. The worldwide market for online recruitment is currently estimated at around £650 million, and research shows that more than two million Europeans use the Internet to look for work. According to the Chartered Institute of Personnel and Development's annual recruitment survey in the UK, 47% of employers recruit through the Net. However, only 1% of recruiters appear to view it as an appropriate method for professional recruitment, so it may be a little early for it to be a major focus for consultancy jobs.

  You will find details of some UK sites specialising in e-recruitment in the Resources List.

- *Approaching a recruiter*

  There is a range of recruitment agencies that act on behalf of consultancy firms. It can be worth approaching such firms to find out if they have any current opportunities that could be right for you. You will find some agency information in the Resources List. Smaller consultancy firms rarely use recruiters, as the costs of doing so tend to be high, and they may only have vacancies once or twice a year, which does not justify retention of a recruitment agency.

- *Applying direct*

  If you are an 'experienced hire', you can also apply directly to any consultancy that appeals to you. However, the smaller ones are unlikely to have many vacancies, if any, at any particular time, and the larger agencies are quite hard to find your way around, making it difficult to get through to the appropriate person to advise you on opportunities. The human resources (personnel) department may be a starting point, but with the larger firms, it is more likely that an approach to the head of consultancy in the relevant function within that firm will be best.

The recruitment processes they use

In general, there are three elements to recruitment processes; these may all take place at one stage, or be phased over several sessions.

- *Stage one: a values-type interview*

  This is to check that you have the 'right' personality for consultancy and that you are aware of the downside to it as well as its good points. At this interview, the selectors will be looking for good oral and written communication skills, a diplomatic manner, the ability to express your thoughts clearly, good reasoning and analytical skills, confidence and, preferably, a good understanding of a particular function or sector. Your commitment to the time spent away from home and the long hours involved will also be checked.

- *Stage two: personality or aptitude tests*

  At this stage you will be given a range of tests designed to find out your own characteristics, strengths and preferences. Some of the tests are likely to be aimed at assessing your reasoning and analytical abilities and include verbal, numerical and diagrammatical tests. About half of the firms use 'assessment centres', which are designed to take candidates through a range of situations and tests, often as a group with other candidates, all designed to find out your suitability for that organisation's work and approach.

- *Stage three: an interview with a senior person*

  At this stage you will be interviewed by a partner or director of the firm; probably the person who heads the part of the organisation in which you would be working. This interview is designed to confirm that you have the ability to 'deliver' to that part of the organisation. This interview is often especially important in assessing your technical abilities, if they are relevant to the job for which you are applying.

How to apply for a job

Principles of job applications are not unique to consultancy, and there are numerous sources of information on this topic; some are listed in the Bibliography. I will simply give you a few pointers here, and you can pursue the detail elsewhere at a later stage. Points to be aware of include:

- Finding out about the organisation in advance. Do some research before applying and certainly before attending an interview.

- Doing as the advertisement says. If you are asked to complete a form, do so. Don't send a c.v. instead and ask them to refer to it.

- Sending a covering letter that shows how you meet the requirements of the job. Keep it brief – no more than one side of A4 paper – and try to use some words or phrases they use in their advertisement so it is clear that you have picked up what they are aiming for.

- Telling them what you can do for them, rather than what they can do for you. Include as much evidence as possible of your capabilities; detail achievements and quantify them if possible.

- Typing or word processing as much as possible, although this may be difficult with a form. If you cannot do this, keep it neat and in dark ink so it is easy to photocopy.

- Keeping a copy of any applications you make – form and covering letter – in case it is lost in the post and you have to send another. If you are called for interview, a copy will also remind of what you have already mentioned.

How to behave at an interview

- Arrive in good time.

- Wear businesslike clothes.

- Before you go in, take a few minutes to tidy yourself up and organise any papers.

- Remember that anyone can form an impression of you. It is not just the interview panel who may see or meet you, so create a sense of confidence, professionalism, pleasantness and ability with anyone you come across.

- In the interview aim to look confident, relaxed, interested, alert and responsive. See Chapter 12 for more on interviews.

- Look at the interviewers, listen carefully, take time to consider your answers to questions and make sure you ask some questions yourself at appropriate points.

- Give examples of your ideas and activities. The more interesting you can make the interview, the more likely it is that you will come across well.

Final Points

This part of the chapter has covered some of the issues relating to being an employed consultant. I hope you will now be able to compare the relative benefits of being independent or employed (assuming you are still motivated to become a consultant). You can now move on to the chapters covering the skills of consultancy.

Consultancy choices

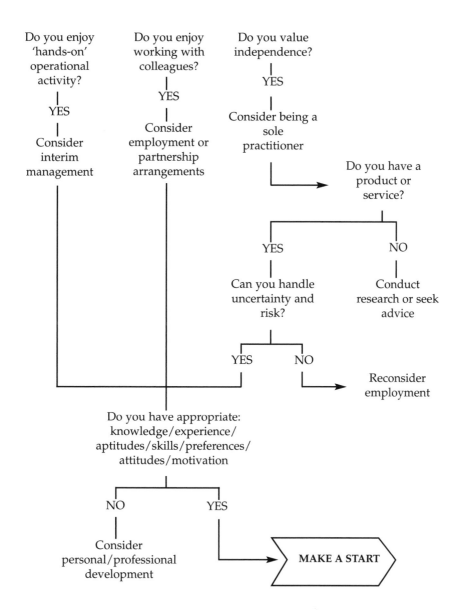

Chapter 4
Defining and Establishing Your Business

This chapter covers those skills involved in the early stages of developing a consultancy business.

In consultancy, as with most other businesses, there are a range of activities that need to take place if success is to be achieved. The activities I will cover in this chapter are: ◆Having a purpose; ◆Creating a vision; ◆Stating a mission; ◆Strategic thinking; ◆Goal-setting; ◆Tactics and planning; ◆Organising. I refer to various techniques and processes in this chapter, many of which you will find explained in Chapter 7.

Having a Purpose

In business, the received wisdom is that the first stage is to have a vision and, until recently, I would have given this to you as a starting step for business development. In his book *Awesome Purpose* (see Bibliography) Nigel MacLennan presents his model for integrating organisational/cultural behaviour and change, and this model begins with consideration of purpose.

MacLennan considers that your purpose denotes 'why you are' (compared to values, which express 'who you are' and what you stand for). To identify your purpose you keep asking the question 'why?'. In Chapter 7 I mention cause-effect chains, and the 'Why' questioning process is similar, in that you keep asking 'why' until you reach an end point that provides the 'best' reason for doing what you do. In the part of this chapter that deals with goals, you will find a point on 'real' objectives, that is the essential purpose of an objective rather than simply its apparent purpose. Questioning your overall purpose at the very first stage of your business development should help you identify why you are (or want to be) in business at all, and specifically in the particular business you are contemplating; all the other stages of activity will then follow on from that.

Associated with purpose is a sense of direction. While later stages are to do with definable results, a purpose and direction are broader-based and define the total context in which other elements are developed. And direction implies an ongoing process, which is essential in business (and in life itself) if you and your business are not to ossify and become immobilised. Having a sense of direction means that you can keep pursuing whatever you value, even though the ways in which you do so can change. Given the changes that are ever-present in the world around us, this is a vital aspect of success.

So, if you are considering a consultancy career, you might like to take your responses to the self-tests in Chapter 2 and ask yourself some 'why' questions, or get someone else to ask you 'why' questions, until you believe you know your underlying reasons for starting your business and for it having the particular focus you desire. Do make sure you keep up the questioning until you know you have the really significant reasons, not simply the surface ones. For example, money is rarely the reason for people going into business – it is more generally the tangible (e.g. houses, cars, food) or intangible (status, security, choice) things money can bring that people want. So carry on the questioning process until you are reasonably sure you have found your underlying purpose or motivation for taking up consultancy.

Creating a Vision

Some people set up their own business because they already have a vision of what they want to achieve in the future; if you are one of those people you will probably be familiar with much of what I will be saying in this section. If, on the other hand, you are inclined to start up on your own, but have not devoted much thought to this subject, I hope you will find the section helpful.

What is a vision?

The word 'vision' is used in many contexts. In its simplest form it describes the function of seeing. It can also mean an apparition; something that is conjured up by the mind (or, some would say, by forces beyond our capacity to understand) and that is different from our normal sense of reality. Vision can also mean a concept of the future (being a 'visionary'), and there is often the implication with this use of the word that, by envisaging, or envisioning, the future, it is possible to create it; most 'personal power' programmes are based on this concept.

It helps to think of a vision as having a long-term time scale (MacLennan suggests 8–25 years hence), so it informs the overall operation of your business for the foreseeable future.

As far as your business goes, having a vision is important for a number of reasons, which may include:

- Having a focus for your activity.
- Being able to state your mission.
- Being able to specify your goals.
- Achieving, and maintaining, motivation.
- Bringing about change.

Let's consider each of these:

Having a focus for your activity
There are so many options for business activity that, without a vision, you may be tempted to follow any interesting avenue that beckons. Once you have a clear vision, it is much easier to know what your business will be and how it will be pursued.

Being able to state your mission
A vision is just that – an image of what could be. You need to translate your vision into a statement of mission if you are to be able to work towards it. I will be dealing with mission statements in the following section.

Being able to specify your goals

Once you have a vision and mission, they can be translated into specific goals, or purposes, or objectives, or targets. The vision may, in itself, produce the goal, but it is more likely that you will need to work out and define your goal much more specifically than a broad conceptual vision can provide for.

Achieving and maintaining motivation

Having a clear vision is an excellent way of motivating yourself (and others). By keeping your vision in mind, you can remain focused and see the possibilities clearly, although you should be careful that you don't ignore possible obstacles in the way by seeing only the vision and nothing else.

Bringing about change

Once you are motivated and have the resources you need (which are the subject of Chapter 8), you are equipped to bring about change. If all you have is a sense of what is, then the status quo may be the most attractive option; once you have a strong vision, what *might* be can be more enticing, and therefore more likely.

How can you create a vision?

People use their senses to differing degrees and, in the conventional sense of the word, a vision relies on the visual sense for its existence. Because of this, it helps if you can enhance your visual capability in order to create a strong vision. If your visualising skills are good anyway, I hope the following exercises will come easily to you; if you think you have a poor visual sense, you may find the exercises will give you ways of strengthening your capabilities.

Visualisation

As a preliminary to the exercise that follows, here are two simple visualisation processes to help strengthen your ability to picture things in your mind:

Process 1

Picture a bird flying across a blue sky. See the bird's wings flap and notice the shape of its body, how its feathers lie and the colour of its beak. Imagine the sky changing colour and becoming dark and cloudy. See some drops of rain fall onto the bird. Now see the sun come out and see how the bird's wings glisten as the sun reflects off the rain that has fallen on it.

Process 2

Remember an event you attended within the last week. Picture the location and see as much detail as you can of the place and of any people and objects in that place. Make the picture as large, bright and colourful as you can. Now see yourself in that place at the event. Picture yourself walking around the place. Put in as much detail as you can, so the image becomes like a video recording of the actual event.

Looking forward in time

Exercise

> Now you have strengthened your visual skills, let's create a scenario for the future. This time, before you begin, I would like you to create an imaginary set of five lines on the floor. All the lines should start from one point, close to you; that point represents the present time. Each line then diverges from the others, so they have angles of around 20 degrees between each pair, and each line should be somewhere between 6 and 10 feet long if possible. The far end of each line will represent a time a few months into the future.

> Now, stand at the point where the lines converge and look at the middle line of the five. At the far end of that line, create an image of an event (for example, a holiday) that you would like to take place in the future, say somewhere between three months and a year from now.

Make your image of the event really large, bright, colourful and full of movement. Now include yourself in that image and notice how you would be behaving if you were there.

Now make an image at the end of each of the other lines; these will be alternative options for that time in the future (possibly a different kind of holiday; perhaps embarking on a new job; maybe taking an examination). Now make equally clear images of these different options and view them, one at a time, to compare how they seem to you. Again, include yourself in each picture. Notice your reactions to the different options and whether any of them are more appealing than others.

Once you have found the most appealing, walk along that particular line and stand where you had been visualising the image; notice how you feel once you have placed yourself in that appealing future. If you are not sure which appeals to you most, walk along each line in turn, standing at the end of each and noticing how it feels to be there; this should help you assess your feelings about each option.

When you have completed the exercise, you can set to work on your own 'real' vision. This time, consider your own business and think about what you would like to create that is unique to you, meaningful and worth striving for. Then turn your thoughts into a mental image that you can project out in front of you whenever you need reminding of what it is you are working towards. Make your mental picture as large, bright and colourful as you need, with movement and interest, and have it at whatever distance works best for you. When you have turned your ideas into this kind of image, you will find it is a powerful tool to keep you active in achieving success.

How can you remind yourself of your vision?

As well as keeping your vision in mind, you can also make a physical pictorial representation of it, which you can pin up in a prominent place, or have on your computer screen, as a tangible reminder of what you are working towards.

It also helps to have occasional sessions where you get into a very relaxed, meditative state and, in this state, focus again on your vision and how far you are towards its fulfilment.

Finally, you can remind yourself in words, either by repeating to yourself what it is you are working towards, or by having messages on your computer screen, or by putting up little messages or posters for yourself with phrases that will remind you of your vision and of your desire to turn it into reality.

Stating your Mission

Once you have your vision, you can begin to translate it into a mission or, as is commonly understood, a mission statement. Just as a vision relates to the long term, a mission relates to the medium term. MacLennan (see Bibliography) suggests that, to be effective, a mission must have '… a visualisable end point which is the mid-term achievable manifestation of your vision'; he suggests this point is between 3 and 8 years in the future. If your mission does not have a target, it is simply a purpose statement, which may sound good, but is hard to work towards because of its lack of definition.

The purpose of a mission statement

Stating your mission can achieve various things, including the following:

- Keeping it in your mind.
- Communicating it to others.
- Achieving a common purpose.
- Remaining on track.

Let's consider each of these:

Keeping it in your mind
While images are powerful, words may be more specific and, for some people, are the best way of keeping themselves on track.

With this process, just as you can manipulate your visual images to make them enticing, so you can vary how words sound in your mind by making them louder or softer, quicker or slower, of different tonality and pace. You can also hear your words as if they are coming into one ear or the other, or as if they are filling your entire head with sound, and you can accompany your words with other kinds of sound such as music, cheering, fireworks, or any other sound element that keeps you in tune with your mission and determined to follow it through.

Communicating it to others

Putting your mission statement into words, and writing it down, can help you communicate it to others. It is generally easier to explain a concept once you have words for it, and it will certainly be easier for people to understand words than to understand a picture that only you have in your head. Talking your mission statement through with others can also help you check that it makes sense to them and conveys your vision and purpose effectively.

Achieving a common purpose

If you have work colleagues, then stating a mission will help everyone to work together for a common end. It is important, however, that everyone signs up to the mission, otherwise there may be a loss of cohesiveness and direction. And if you have colleagues working with or for you, having them work with you on stating the mission will help them feel more involved and more committed to where the business is going.

Remaining on track

Once a mission has been stated, it is easier to check on whether you are still working towards it. A vague sense of purpose is hard to manage; a clearly stated mission becomes much easier to handle. You will also need to check, from time to time, that your mission statement still reflects your current direction and purpose; once you have written down your statement it can be easy to forget about it. If circumstances change, revisiting it is a good way of monitoring your progress and effectiveness.

Writing a mission statement

The important thing about a mission statement is that it should be a concise, focused summary of what your business aims to achieve.

A good way of starting to write your mission statement is to brainstorm about why you are in business. Take a sheet of paper, or use your keyboard and, in turn, write down any words:

- that relate to your purpose for yourself: for example you might produce words such as money, recognition, service, security, innovation, success, independence, excitement.

- that relate to the purposes you believe would be beneficial to your clients: for example, results, success, quality, value for money, reliability, innovation, resources, change.

- that relate to the purposes you believe would be beneficial to your family and/or your colleagues: for example security, teamworking, enjoyment, development, progression, variety, stimulation, opportunity.

- that relate to the purpose you believe to be beneficial for the wider community: for example contribution, common good, conservation, integration, benefit, enhancement, collaboration, resources.

You might find it helpful to have others assist you with your brainstorming, or you may prefer to do it on your own. Once you have completed the brainstorming session, select those words or phrases that best represent the elements that you feel are important.

Now you can use what are referred to as 'cause-effect chains' to assess the consequences of each of the words you have retained. Take each word, for example 'independence', and ask yourself the question: "If I had (or if I provided) this, what would it make possible?" Then write down what comes to mind – for example, in the case of independence you might feel the result of being independent would be that you had an ability to make your own decisions.

Then repeat the question on this new word or phrase: "If I was able to make my own decisions, what would that make possible?" Ultimately you will get to a point that is likely to represent one of your highest values or one of your most desired end states, either for yourself or for others.

Once you have these highest values or goals, you can select two or three that have the most significance to you, and incorporate them in your mission statement. The statement should, ideally, be a single sentence that sums up and incorporates your highest values, or your core end state, for your business activities.

Strategic Thinking

Once you have created your vision and produced your mission statement, you can turn your thoughts to the scope and direction of your business. Strategic thinking involves taking an overview and considering all the major, long-term aspects of your business. MacLennon suggests that each organisation should have only one strategy and that if more than one strategy is required, the organisation probably needs splitting into discrete entities. He has devised a new term for defining and communicating purpose, vision and strategy – the term is 'Awesome Purpose' (see Bibliography).

To start working on strategic thinking, take your mission statement and consider what its implications are for each area of your business. You can think about products, services, activities, systems, structure, location, finance, resources, staffing, support, customers, marketing, administration, networking, relationships, development, culture, image and so on. You will need to consider both your business and the environment within which it operates. Each person will have a slightly different collection of issues, and so your strategic thinking will need to be personal to you and your business.

In conducting this process you will be generating an understanding of your total business concept for each business area and how it can, effectively, be developed. Once you have your main areas of activity, you can consider each of them – and their interconnections – in a broad, long-term manner.

When you are doing your strategic thinking, you might like to use the concept of chunking (see Chapter 7). This will help you check that you are actually dealing with the major areas of your business and your overall sense of direction and approach towards them, rather than more detailed, activity-based, tactical matters. By drawing a chunking diagram, you can slot in the really broad strategic issues and then work downwards to see what sub-sections each one has and what might be parallel issues.

There are many different approaches to strategic thinking. In a recent article (see Bibliography) Mintzberg and Lampel outline ten 'schools' and discuss their evolution and interrelationships. The schools they review are:

- *Design school*

   The 'original' and possibly the 'dominant' strategy process; a prescriptive approach that uses conscious and conceptual thought and considers the relationships between internal and external factors. Predominant until the 1970s.

- *Planning school*

   Parallel growth to the design school, a prescriptive approach that uses formal steps and techniques. Linked to systems theory and cybernetics.

- *Positioning school*

   Another prescriptive approach and the major approach in the 1980s. Preceded by very early (400 BC) thinking on military strategy. Much use of analysis and calculation and a foundation for many academic and consultancy ideas and products such as game theory.

- *Entrepreneurial school*

   A visionary process, centred on the chief executive and utilising intuition, vision/envisioning and broad perspectives – often using metaphor. The process very often relates to specific contexts such as start-up situations.

- *Cognitive school*

  A psychological approach, often generated through academics. The process considers strategy as a mental process resulting in models, schema and concepts – with emphasis on knowledge structure mapping. Much research carried out, especially in the 1980s and much development into interpretative or constructivist views of the strategic process – i.e. mental processing constructs strategies rather than simply mapping reality. (Constructivism is an established area of study within the field of psychology.)

- *Learning school*

  The concept of strategy-making as learning. In this approach, strategists can be found throughout an organisation. The principle here is that strategies are emergent, and formulation and implementation are inter-related. Some links to learning theory and chaos theory.

- *Power school*

  Based in political science, this approach is based on self-interest and has two orientations: micro, where development of strategy internally is seen as political; and macro, where the organisation uses power and engages in alliances, joint ventures and networking relationships to negotiate 'collective' strategies that benefit it.

- *Cultural school*

  Based in anthropology, this is a social process, rooted in culture, which focuses on common interest and integration. This approach often resists change in favour of the status quo.

- *Environmental school*

  Based in biology, this is a reactive process emphasising the demands of the environment. There is an association with contingency theory and some claims that there are major limits to strategic choice.

● *Configuration school*

> This is a transformational process, concerned with integration. The academic approach to this sees organisations as clusters of characteristics and behaviours – that is organisational states. There is also a complementary emphasis on transformation – change as a movement from one state to another – which tends to be much promoted by consultants.

Mintzberg and Lampel also indicate that some of the schools look 'at', some look 'ahead', some look 'below', some look 'inside' and so forth, giving a multiplicity of ways to consider the strategic process. They say: "Strategy formation is judgmental designing, intuitive visioning, and emergent learning; it is about transformation as well as perpetuation; it must involve individual cognition and social interaction, cooperative as well as conflicting; it has to include analysing before and programming after as well as negotiating during; and all this must be in response to what may be a demanding environment. Try to omit any of this, and watch what happens!"

They also identify four factors relevant in the evolution of strategic management: ◆Collaboration – learning and borrowing from others; ◆Competition and confrontation – new ideas arising from market forces; ◆Recasting – where old practices are blended with new; ◆Creativity – where strategy is driven by managers' exploration of new processes.

So strategic planning can be a complex process but, at its heart, it is simply about considering the business as a whole, where you want it to be and the direction you will take in getting it there. When you have carried out your own strategic planning process you will have a strong foundation for taking your business further.

Example
In a recent survey – Glaister and Falshaw (see Bibliography) – 113 large UK companies (around half in manufacturing and half in services) were investigated to find out their nature and practice of strategic planning. Around two-thirds of the firms had a written mission statement and over 90% had a set of medium/long-term

objectives. Over one-fifth did not have a group with specific responsibility for business/corporate/strategic planning. The business plans for most of the firms did not extend beyond five years – even in those areas that would be expected to embody a relatively long time horizon. The greatest level of commitment was found with regard to specification of business and corporate objectives and aims. Although it is important to bear in mind that there was still a relatively high level of commitment to each of these activities, the lowest-ranked activities involved monitoring results against strategic plans and evaluation of strategy. This indicates that strategy formulation has more commitment, and implementation and evaluation of strategy has less.

In this study, a range of tools for strategic analysis was surveyed, and four emerged as most significant. These were:

- *'What if' analysis (using spreadsheets to try out alterations in interrelated factors and assess their consequences)*

  This process is possibly used so much simply because of its availability and ease of use. Corporate modelling and strategic planning software was used less frequently than spreadsheet analysis, perhaps because it demands a higher level of skill in its use.

- *Analysis of 'key' or 'critical' success factors*

  This relates to internal factors for the organisation.

- *Financial analysis of competitors*

  This also relates to external factors, but there seems to be a stronger (although by only a small amount) focus on the external environment than the internal.

- *SWOT analysis* (see Chapter 7)

  It was interesting that SWOT analysis was ranked quite highly, but even though external factors were perceived as important, other analytical tools, such as PEST reviews, which deal with external elements, came much further down the list.

Much less use was made of the other techniques, for example scenario planning, which has been gaining popularity in recent years; cognitive mapping; SSM (soft systems methodology) and value chain analysis.

The study also showed that the quality of analysis that was carried out in strategic planning was not always high, particularly in SWOT analysis, where this tended to "… generate long lists of descriptive items" with "… little effort to prioritise or verify points and the output of the analysis was rarely subsequently used in the strategy process."

There are differing views on the value of setting corporate strategy and carrying out strategic planning processes, and these views were echoed, to some extent, in this survey. While some attitudes were positive in these areas, there were a few responses indicating that strategic planning had encouraged excessive bureaucracy, rigidity and inflexibility of response to the changing environment.

And the overall view in this survey was that strategy formulation is more of a deliberate process than an emergent process (an emergent process being one that simply emerges over time without resulting from a definite plan).

Goal-setting

Once you have your strategic plan, you can turn it into specific goals, which will give you your blueprint for action.

Remembering the chunking concept again, you will need to consider how your goals fit with the broader aspects of your business activity. You will also need to check whether there are subgoals to each major goal you define.

There are a number of principles involved in goal-setting. You may be familiar with the acronym SMART, which is commonly used as a goal-setting process. NLP also has an approach to goal-setting, which is broader than SMART; it incorporates most of SMART's elements and adds some other, important ones. I would like to cover the NLP approach here.

NLP goal-setting (Well-formed Outcomes) process

There are nine elements commonly covered in this approach, although you could choose to use fewer, or to add others of your own if there are more you feel are important to you. The nine elements are:

● *Stating your goal positively*

   Being clear about what you actually do want. For example, "To achieve a level of income at least as high as my current salary" rather than "Not to drop below my current income level." The first is stated positively, the second negatively.

● *Having a defined context for your goal*

   Knowing when and where you want to have your goal. For example, "To work within the public and voluntary sectors" rather than "To provide services to a range of organisations." The first enables you to target a specific market; the second does not.

● *Specifying your goal at the right level or standard*

   It is easy to specify a goal, but unless you have it specified at the right level and standard you may be either wasting your efforts or failing to meet requirements.

   Example of level: "To have variety of work" rather than "To work for a range of clients." The first (variety) is the 'real' goal, whereas the second is simply a way of achieving it.

   Example of standard: "To have all my client files updated weekly" rather than "To update every file on a daily basis". The first is more realistic as a standard for most consultants, unless they are working on activities where it is vital to keep up with constant change.

- *Considering the ethical, social and political implications of your goal*

  In NLP, this element is referred to as 'Ecology' – considering the broader implications of your objectives. Gregory Bateson (a British anthropologist and systemic thinker) is reported to have said that "Ecology is the study of consequences", and considering consequences in relating to others is an important element of goal-setting.

  Example of ethical implications: "To ensure that this goal does not take work away from a colleague."

  Example of social implications: "To ensure that working at home fits with my family's interests."

  Example of political implications: "To ensure that my report does not undermine the position of the client's chief executive."

- *Weighing up the pros and cons of achieving your goal*

  One of the most important aspects of goal-setting is to consider the benefits and the disadvantages either of achieving the goal or of remaining as you are. There are likely to be both pros and cons in the situation remaining the same or in it changing, and assessing these will help you with your planning. Remember too the aspect of 'hidden' benefits (sometimes referred to as secondary gain). There are often benefits in retaining the status quo; for example you might think you want lots of overseas travel in your job, but if you stay where you are you have the company of your existing friends and associates, your name remains more constantly in front of people and you can enjoy activities that might not be available to you overseas. You may be aware of all these factors, but it is likely that some of them will be 'hidden', so that you are not aware of them unless you specifically analyse your situation and your motives.

- *Having the resources to achieve your goal*

  Your resources include time, money, support, information, skill, energy, equipment and so on. Achievement of any goal needs appropriate resources, so checking on what you need, and what is missing, is an important part of the goal-setting process.

- *Ensuring that achievement of the goal is within your control*

  People often strive to achieve goals that are not within their capacity to manage. For example: "To send a mailshot to 200 selected companies" rather than "To get a 20% response to my mailshot." The first is within your control, the second is not. Of course you can target your mailshots so they are more likely to get a response, but you cannot control the response itself.

- *Being able to measure achievement of your goal*

  This includes the usual 'hard' statistical, financial and performance-based measures and can also include the 'softer' measures, such as how people will feel, what they might say and how things could look (in other words, emotional/sensory measures).

- *Checking that the goal is consistent with your self-concept*

  If a goal is out of line with the kind of person you are (or think you are), you may well fail to achieve it or, quite possibly, sabotage your own efforts to achieve it. For example if you don't think you are a good negotiator, you may not take on the kind of assignments where skilful dealing is required. When goals are out of line with your self-concept you may either give up on them or, more constructively, you may set about expanding, or changing, how you see yourself in order to broaden your range of capabilities.

  And you should add to the above measures, a time measure; in other words the time-scale within which you wish to achieve your goal. There may be sub-sets in your time-scale so that you can assess your progress along the way.

Now you have a framework for goal-setting, you can take your strategic plans and devise as many major goals as are needed to take your business forward. Remember that you are considering major goals here, not the minor targets you need to put in place for every small area of your business activity. The minor targets are important too, but you can develop these later, in conjunction with tactical thinking and planning, once you have determined the major objectives to achieve your business strategy.

Tactics and Planning

Having set your goals (and remember that goals do need to be revisited and revised from time to time to ensure they are still valid), you can turn to deciding your tactics and doing your planning.

Tactics

Tactics are the processes you use in achieving your goals. De Bono says they are "… the servants of strategy". Unlike strategy, which operates at a broad level, tactics are the more detailed, day-to-day methods used to put your goals into practice. Once you have determined your major goals, you can devise tactics for achieving them.

Your tactical approach will need to relate to your own personal and business factors. For example, are you someone who likes to work through other people? If so, your tactics might lean towards networking, collaboration and so forth. If you are someone who has a theoretical inclination, your tactics might include a research bias and testing of specific models and frameworks for achievement.

Similarly, if your business is running on a low budget, your tactics could include taking maximum advantage of low-cost services in its start-up. If you have many potential competitors your tactics will need to relate to ways of making your unique benefits apparent.

So it is important that your tactics are suited to your own situation as well as being aligned with the other elements of your business development.

Planning

Having decided on your tactics, you can now find ways of implementing them. You will find a range of planning techniques in Chapter 7, so in this section I will simply outline three elements of planning: ◆**Work and time scheduling**; ◆**Resourcing**; ◆**Uncertainty** /risk assessment.

Let's consider each of these.

Work and time scheduling
Any assignment needs consideration of what needs to be done, and when. Techniques such as flow charts (see Chapter 7) will help you in the process of scheduling, but first of all, you need to decide what the elements of the work are.

The elements of an assignment depend on various factors, such as its objectives, client need, your own personal approach and whether or not that particular project can be separated into discrete elements. You will need to carry out this thinking for each separate assignment, as they are all likely to differ in some respects. For example, let's take my work on writing this book, and apply the elements I have just mentioned:

●   *Objectives*

    For me, the objectives of a book are to produce the required product, at the required time, in the required format. There are also objectives around style, originality, quality and so forth. All of these can be planned for, although some of the planning measures are less quantifiable than others.

●   *Client need*

    Assuming my initial client is my publisher, I have to work to contracted schedules. I also have to produce according to the 'house style' of that particular publisher. Taking the reader as the end client, I have to plan for comprehension, interest, practical application and any other elements that are appropriate for the particular reader group.

- *My own approach*

  I like to write in smallish chunks, when I have the mental and physical energy to do so. Often early mornings and late evenings are good, but other times work as well. I like the diversion of other things to intersperse with my writing, so I can maintain motivation, and I like to spend time on exercise so I maintain my energy levels. I also like to schedule roughly how many hours I need to work on each available day if I am to reach my targets for time and quantity.

- *Capacity to split into different elements*

  Books can be split into elements such as writing, researching, checking, information-gathering and so forth. I plan the writing and checking elements and intersperse the others because they are not always within my control and I often rely on others for input.

Resourcing

Another element that requires planning is the resources that will be required for an assignment. These may include financial resources, time, equipment and materials, information, staffing or support and personal resources such as energy and motivation and also any development/revision of skills needed. With my books I need to make sure I have time allocated, supplies of paper to print out text, information in various forms and a ready supply of water to drink; these are the minimum resources I must plan for.

Uncertainty/risk assessment

Nothing about the future can be certain and planning, by its nature, involves considering the future. So you do need to build in some assessment of things that could change or that could go wrong. With my books I am never sure if other urgent assignments will come up during the time period I have allowed for production, so I need to make sure I have more than enough time for the task. I also need to consider the risk of losing my computer files and make backups in case this happens.

Organising

I have devoted a separate section to organising because, although not everyone would consider it a direct part of the business planning cycle, it is an important element in allowing you to carry out your business activities efficiently and effectively. So here are a few thoughts about organising:

Organising yourself
Self-organisation is a first step. Although the following processes are about things you might organise, it is important to get yourself into a frame of mind where organisation is possible. So clearing your mind, setting aside time to organise and having a positive intention to be organised will be a good start.

Organising others
You may have other people working for you in some capacity, for example providing secretarial services, doing marketing or acting as an assistant. You may have work colleagues who share space with you, or you may have children or other dependents who need attention. In all these cases there may be elements of organisation required.

Organising space and equipment
Having a suitable work space is essential for consultants working from home. You will probably need more space than you anticipate. Assuming you have a computer, printer and scanner, a fax machine, a telephone and answer machine, you will need surface space for all of these, as well as suitable work surfaces. Add to this filing cabinets and shelving for books and other items, and there is a sizeable space requirement.

How you organise the space itself will depend on your ways of working. You will probably find, if you have not worked from home before, that your ideas of layout will change as time passes. So it is probably best not to make too many firm fixtures until you are certain you have the most suitable layout for your needs.

It is also worth mentioning the importance of suitable seating, especially if you are going to spend a good deal of time at a keyboard, and of good light and ventilation. Plants will help to maintain good air quality, and some table lamps will help with close work when natural daylight is scarce. And, if you have a large house, or work in an adjacent building, it may be worth having your phones double up as an intercom system, so you do not have to leave your desk in order to communicate with others.

Organising information

A suitable information storage and retrieval system is another vital element of home working. You will need to ensure you:

- have incoming items readily to hand.
- have a suitable work-pending system.
- have files arranged in appropriate systems.
- have easy and logical access to existing information.

Although you could have a purely manual system, nowadays most people work with a range of electronic equipment to manage their businesses.

Assuming you are using a PC (personal computer), Microsoft Outlook is simple and readily available software for recording and organising information. This will allow you to input and work with data, maintain a diary, produce reminders for outstanding activities required, receive and send e-mails and carry out other tasks. If you have complex information you wish to retrieve in a variety of different ways, then you will probably need a simple database such as Microsoft Access. As well as computer files you will need some form of information storage for documents; ordinary filing cabinets are probably the most useful for this purpose.

Whether you are using a manual or an electronic system, do make sure you keep separate files for different aspects of your work. It may be tempting to put all pending work into one large 'action' file, but this will probably ensure you never see it again! Similarly, you will need to split your computer files into sub-directories so you can access things simply. And do make sure your files have names you will remember, and check them regularly to see what needs to be dealt with.

You will need to decide for yourself what is the most suitable way of indexing your information; some examples are client files, subject files and project files. You might also find it useful to duplicate papers so that you can access the same items in different ways, or at least have cover sheets in secondary files to show you what information is kept in your main subject files.

Personal organisers are also useful for handling information. There is a wide range of small electronic organisers that can store information, run your diary and so forth. And nowadays most electronic equipment serves a range of functions, so that your telephone can double up as a pager or send your e-mails, your computer can send your faxes and your personal organiser can link you with the Internet. So keep up to date with equipment and choose the most appropriate for your needs.

Organising work

Probably the most important element in organising as a whole is organising the work you have to do; if this does not happen you will not be able to function effectively, and your present and future work and relationships are likely to suffer.

Work organisation can cover a whole range of activities. Some that you will need to consider are the following:

- *Prioritising tasks*

    You will need to decide how urgent or important tasks are, and then put them in the order you believe is most appropriate. You will also need to revise your priority listing periodically to check where on your list any item should be placed and whether any existing tasks need relocating on your listing.

- *Allocating appropriate time periods to activities and assignments*

  Slotting work into a schedule is the next step. This means deciding how much time each one requires, whether there are any particular time constraints on it (when to start, how long to take, when completion is needed) and where each activity fits with others.

- *Grouping similar activities together where possible, to maximise efficiency*

  It is often helpful to put similar activities together, for example setting aside time for a whole group of telephone calls, or arranging consecutive meetings on one subject area so you already have all the relevant papers to hand.

- *Dovetailing visits to minimise travelling time and maximise effectiveness*

  You can cut down substantially on travelling time if you arrange visits to adjacent locations so that only one journey is necessary rather than several.

- *Remembering what you have to do*

  It is important to have a way of reminding yourself of tasks otherwise, however good your system for organisation is, your memory could let you down.

- *Avoiding overload and stress*

  Finally, keep a balance, so that you can avoid taking on too much and becoming stressed by the activities you engage in. This is partly a matter of organising your workload so it is manageable and partly a matter of balancing work with other activities, such as rest, exercise, and socialising.

As with information handling and retrieval, there is a whole range of aids available to assist with work organisation, including computer software, personal organisers, time planners and many others. Once you have decided which are most appropriate for your use, you will be able to organise your work activities really efficiently.

You can be a successful consultant without having a vision, mission statement, long-term strategy, specific goals and good planning and organisation, but you are more likely to be effective if you build these elements into your activities and run your business in a coherent, comprehensible and systematic manner.

Final Points

It is well worth spending time on the preparatory stages outlined in this chapter. The more focused you are on what you want to achieve, the more likely it is that you will be successful. Everyone has their own way of creating their business, and once you have an approach that works, you will be well on your way to achieving results.

NLP techniques used in this chapter, and the sections where you can find them:

Cause-effect chains (mission statement)
Chunking (strategic thinking)
Internal dialogue (visualisation)
Submodality changes (visualisation)
Time Lines (visualisation)
Well-formed Outcomes (goal-setting)

Chapter 5
Controlling and Promoting Your Business

This chapter covers the skills involved in controlling, managing and developing your business.

In the previous chapter I covered some aspects of business development. This chapter goes on to consider some of the skills involved in starting up and managing your business.

The main elements I will be covering in this chapter are:

- Financial management.
- Marketing.
- Selling.

Financial Management

"Annual income twenty pounds, annual expenditure nineteen pounds nineteen and six, result happiness. Annual income twenty pounds, annual expenditure twenty pounds ought and six, result misery." Mr Micawber. *David Copperfield*. Chapter 12. A simple yet memorable quote, of which any business should take heed.

When you set up your business you may be able to finance it yourself, or you may need to seek startup funding; whatever the case, you will need to consider some basic financial aspects. I describe some of these in the sections that follow.

Business plan

A business plan is generally a pre-requisite to forming a new consultancy business. Your business plan will show the results you aim to achieve, the resources you need to achieve these results and the processes you will use along the way. If you are seeking finance for your business, or need an overdraft facility, your bank will almost certainly want to see some kind of business plan.

As I mentioned in Chapter 3, when I set up one of my first businesses, in conjunction with a colleague, my bank was only too happy to give us financial backing and did not ask for any kind of business plan or forecast. Looking back, it would have been better if they had done so; the market we were operating in was notorious for delays in payment and, although the business was profitable, we ran into some serious cash-flow problems that might have been anticipated if we had done more thinking in advance.

Before starting to write your business plan you will need to devote some thought to its particular purpose, as this can vary. You should consider who it is it aimed at, and whether you need it for your own planning purposes, for your bank or for potential colleagues or investors. Its focus may need to vary slightly, depending on its target readership.

Once you have decided on the purpose of your plan, you can start to produce it. Some general principles for producing a business plan are that it should be simple, accurate and useful. It should contain objectives, strategy, tactics and any assumptions you are making. It should also be presented in good condition, without errors or typing mistakes, and signed and dated.

Elements you might like to include in your business plan are:

- A management overview, giving the essential elements of the plan in very simple terms.

- Details of your business: name, location and contact details.

- What your business entails: its purpose, area and range of activity, focus and product/service range. Include your business history if the plan is for a business development rather than a start-up.

- What your competition is: who the main competitors are; benchmarking against others.

- People involved in your business: owners, staff, associates, etc. If it is a new business, provide some relevant information on your own background and track record.

- Your market: who will purchase from you, what your marketing and sales strategy is, results of any market research you have conducted.

- Financial calculations: target turnover, income and expenditure breakdowns, estimated profits and losses, cash flow forecasts, capital expenditure and stock. You might also add to this any assets you have.

- Your financial base: how you will finance your business and any external investment needed.

- Any identified risks and how you would deal with them.

- Future development: how you expect the business to grow and any projected new activities.

- Processes: how you will achieve results, your time inputs, networking activities, etc.

- Business management: how you will monitor activities, accounting and management information systems.

- Action planning: details of areas of activity, decisions to be taken, time-scales and results aimed for; any review procedures you have for updating your plan and ensuring it is fully implemented.

Each business plan will vary in its structure, style and content, depending on the particular circumstances of the business and the personal approach of its creator but, if you follow the above outline, you will cover most of the relevant topics.

A useful approach to planning comes from Colin Edwards and uses the mnemonic SUPER:

S – Is your plan Sound? Will it have a healthy start with good life expectancy?

U – Does your plan show Understanding between internal capabilities and external expectations?

P – Is your plan Practical? Do you have the resources to implement it?

E – Is your plan Exciting? Is it firmly based on your experience and expectations?

R – Is your plan Realistic? Ambition is good, but plans need to deal with reality rather than fantasy.

I have listed some books on business planning in the Bibliography. Your own bank manager should also be able to help with this process.

Funding

Once you have worked out your business plan, and know the cost involved, you can assess whether you have the funds required to set it up, or if you need to seek financial support.

If you do need additional funding it can come through a variety of sources, including a bank loan, remortgaging your house, getting a colleague to come in with you on a profit share basis or seeking commercial funding from organisations that specialise in this field.

Your bank or financial adviser will be able to offer you help in identifying suitable sources of funding for your requirements.

Bank account

You will need a separate account for your business activities. Most banks will offer free banking for a period to newly formed businesses; if yours does not offer this, do consider moving elsewhere as bank charges can be substantial depending on the nature of your business. Because there are so many options now regarding types of account, facilities and charges, it is well worth shopping around before making choices.

It is also worth having frequent bank statements – at least monthly – which will give you updates on how you are doing and remind you to check your financial affairs on a regular basis.

Records and accounts

It is essential to keep records of financial matters, partly so you can monitor your income and expenditure and partly to comply with statutory requirements.

You can do without the services of an accountant, but I would not recommend this course of action. A good accountant is likely to save you money and will certainly take some of the administrative load from you. You could, as an alternative, have a bookkeeper and do all your returns yourself, but this will probably take your time away from fee earning and may not be the best use of your resources.

Accountancy fees can vary considerably, so, again, it is worth shopping around before making a choice. If you run more than one business you may find you need separate accounts for each, and this, as I have found myself, can lead to substantial increases in accountancy fees.

Financial adviser

Your bank and your accountant can give you financial advice, but you might also consider using an independent adviser, especially if you have investments you wish to maximise while building your business. There are associations to which independent financial advisers belong, and choosing one who has this kind of accreditation is more likely to guarantee you unbiased and wide-ranging advice.

VAT

In the UK, if your turnover is above a certain level you will need to be registered for VAT. It is also possible to register on a voluntary basis if you are below the minimum level, but you will probably need to convince the authorities that your business is likely to grow to the point where it would need to be registered anyway.

Having VAT registration tends to lend credibility to a consultancy; if you are not registered it is apparent that you are operating at a fairly low level of turnover, which may give potential clients the impression that you are not good enough to be successful.

If your business is mainly with small organisations or individuals, you may find that having to add VAT is a deterrent, because they will not be able to claim back the VAT you charge them. In this instance, it will probably be better not to seek voluntary registration but to wait until you have no choice but to register.

Fee rates

There is an enormous range in the fees charged by consultants. Independent consultants often find this issue a difficult one because they do not know what other consultants charge and do not know how their potential clients may respond to different fee rates.

In general terms, much independent consultancy work in the UK is currently charged for at somewhere between £350 and £1,500 a day. Public sector work tends to be less well paid than other work, and long-term assignments are often charged for at a lower daily rate than one-off, short-term projects because they offer a higher volume of work. In a recent IMC salary survey (see Bibliography), the average daily fee rate for sole practitioners was £725 per day, with £500 as the lower quartile and £950 as the upper quartile. The IMC survey also reported that consultants in London charge, and earn, up to 50% more than anywhere else in the country.

For employed consultants, recent surveys of larger firms in the UK indicated an average charge-out rate of £1,450 per day. The average fee for the public sector was £900 per day; for finance, retail and utilities it was £1,100; and the average for all sectors was £1,000.

Research on employed consultants indicated that directors and partners averaged around £80,000; managing or principal consultants around £60,000; senior consultants around £50,000; basic grade consultants around £30,000; and assistants or researchers averaged £20,000 (all these figures being without benefits).

It is difficult to obtain comparable figures for the USA, country-wide, but some information is available. Kennedy Information estimates the average day rates for most independents as being between $750 and $3,000 per day. Other sources indicate that, with a first degree, starting salaries range from $35,000 – $60,000 and with an MBA from $40,000 – $140,000. Salaries vary with the firm and the geographical region and, as with the UK, there are signing -on bonuses and additional elements. It is worth remembering that these figures, and some of the UK ones too, are based on research that can be at least a couple of years old, so may not actually represent current rates.

In the UK, the interim management market is worth about £500 million and looks to be growing at just over 10% per annum. The average interim manager currently earns around £65k, the top 15% of all interim managers earn over £95k and the top 30% earn over £75k, with IT executives earning the most (£82k) and production executives the least (£44k). (Source: *The Russam GMS Market Research Report*, 2000).

It is important to get your fee level right. Rates that seem too high may put clients off, but rates that seem too low can make them think you are not sufficiently experienced or capable, or are short of work and therefore possibly not all that good. It is also worth revising your fee rates from time to time to keep up with market trends and with inflation.

Remember that your daily fee rate has to cover all your non fee-earning days too, so you cannot compare independent consultancy rates with what your average pay per day would have been as an employee. On average, consultants probably work around two days a week on direct fee-earning activities, while the remainder of their time is spent on marketing, planning, preparation, administration and other activities.

Tendering

In the public sector in particular, consultants are often selected by tender. This means you are asked to submit a costed bid for work in competition with other consultants. Tendering can take up a good deal of time, as there are often lengthy documents to be completed, pre-tender meetings and interviews and presentations. You will need to consider the best use of your time when deciding whether to go for tender work or to avoid it.

Large consultancies can put enormous resources into the tendering process, because this is how they obtain much of their work. For an independent, however, tendering can take valuable time away from other kinds of business development, so you do need to weigh up the pros and cons carefully.

Debt collection

One of the issues you may need to be concerned with is debt collection. The success of your business does not depend simply upon your turnover, or on your profit; it also depends on your cash flow. Most of your client organisations will probably pay in a reasonable time. However, there are likely to be some who will take an inordinately long time to pay your invoices, and this can cause you cash flow problems. It helps to have in your terms of service, and on your invoices, either a clause saying 'Payment within 30 days (or by a particular date) or interest will be charged at X%' or a clause saying there is a discounted price if the invoice is paid before a particular date. However, whatever you put, you may have problems with some organisations. It is possible to use professional debt collection agencies to help with this, but it is less expensive to do some checks on how your clients pay, and then decide whether you can afford to work for them if they are likely to take, say, three months before paying your invoices.

Personally I have never had clients who have failed to pay at all, but I have experienced considerable delays in payment from large organisations and institutions, which has caused both cash flow difficulties and wasted time on administration. In my experience, the worst organisations for payment are often in the public, or academic, sectors, and it does make me wary of doing business with some of them.

Marketing and Selling

Your business will thrive if you market it successfully. Unfortunately, many consultants find this aspect of running a consultancy hard, especially the selling side, as they do not consider themselves to be salespeople. However, if you look upon marketing and selling as letting people know about a service that will really benefit them, rather than simply as something that will make you money, you may find it easier to do.

I would define marketing as the overall process of bringing yourself, your business, your products and your services to the attention of your prospective market, and I would define selling as the process of directly encouraging the people in your market to buy from you. Whilst there can be overlaps between the two, marketing tends to be a longer-term, broader activity, whilst selling tends to be shorter-term and more focused.

Let's consider marketing first.

Marketing

There are many ways in which you can market your services but, before you do so, you need to be clear about three major things: ◆What it is you have on offer (what are your products or services); ◆What benefits your offerings will provide to your clients (what purposes your products or services will serve); ◆Where you will position yourself in your marketplace (what your target sector, function, client, value level, etc. are). You should already have clarified this when you created your vision, mission and business plans, but it will probably be useful to go over this ground again, checking that you can state clearly what your products and services are and just how they will be of value to their recipients.

To do this, it is often useful to do some shifts of perspective, mentally adopting the position of your clients to see what is important to them. I heard an interesting radio programme once (unfortunately, I did not make a note of it at the time, so I cannot say who presented it), in which someone said that, when we say, "If I were you...", what we generally mean is, "If you were me...". So when shifting perspective, really try to get into the other person's shoes, rather than simply thinking what would interest you if you were a client.

You could also do some market research to check on how your products and services will be perceived by clients. Market research can also bring you useful contacts and extend your personal network as a by-product of gaining information for future marketing. Some ways in which you can carry out market research are speaking to other independent consultants to find out their views on particular consultancy offerings, reading market reports and surveys to assess client opinions and purchasing patterns, conducting a telephone survey into local businesses asking if they would be prepared to spare a few minutes to discuss your ideas, and so forth. Major market research is time-consuming and expensive, but you can shorten the process and still get some useful feedback and ideas.

Once you know what products, services and benefits you are promoting, you can develop your marketing strategy and tactics. The next section details some of the ways in which you can consider marketing yourself. I say 'yourself' because, although it is your consultancy business you are promoting, most clients are likely to come to you because it is YOU, rather than simply because of the services you have on offer. Because YOU are the product, you need to think carefully about how you come across, as well as how your services can appeal to your target market. So here are some suggestions.

Networking

One of the best ways of marketing consultancy services is through networking. By this I mean any way in which you can come into contact with other people, directly or indirectly, and gain an opportunity to make them aware of what you do, to get leads to others who may be interested, or to obtain ideas about other ways in which you can promote yourself.

Networking tends to be low-cost, often gives you additional benefits (for example attending meetings, conferences and workshops) as well as providing the opportunity to meet others. Books on networking, including my own *Networking for Success*, are listed in the Bibliography if you would like to follow this up in more depth.

Referrals

Sometimes an extension of networking, there are two aspects of referrals I would like to mention here.

The first is about cultivating contacts with colleagues who can refer work to you when it is outside their own field of expertise, when they need additional support or when they are not able to carry out the work themselves through lack of availability. Some referrals may be free, others may come with the expectation of a commission, especially if they come via an established consultancy group, or agency, with formal provisions for payments on referral.

The second source of referrals is from current or past clients. If your clients are satisfied with your work they will probably be only too happy to recommend you to others. Asking for referrals is one way of making the most of this possibility, perhaps at the end of a successful assignment when you are discussing the project as a whole. You will probably also find that satisfied clients recommend you to others anyway, and you may frequently be contacted by new clients who have come through this route.

Referrals can be an excellent source of work, and it is useful to direct marketing efforts towards possible referral sources.

Giving talks

Giving talks on your business or your specialist area of activity will give you exposure to an audience that is likely to be interested in the services you have on offer. You may be paid for talks, but I have always thought of such activities as marketing rather than as work and, as long as they are reasonably local, I have been happy to do them free, or for expenses only.

It helps to design your talk for the particular audience, rather than having just one or two 'off-the-shelf' topics. It is also useful to check in advance the size of the audience, their previous knowledge of your subject matter and any particular areas of interest they may have.

You can take along your business literature and any products you may have on offer. As long as you do not simply plug your business, rather than give the audience an informative and interesting session, you will probably find it is productive in terms of future work. It may be a long time after the talk that business is generated, so do not expect it to produce fee-earning results immediately.

The groups I have given talks to include professional bodies, local business groups, trade associations, industry groups, women's networking and business groups and educational groups. If you visit a local library you should find many publications listing established groups, and you can contact them to see if they would be interested in a talk from you. If you can suggest a particular angle that would be relevant to their members' interests, or a particularly topical issue, that would be even better.

And if you would like to enhance your speaking skills, there are organisations that exist to develop and promote speakers (see Resources List).

Writing articles and books

This is another good way of promoting your activities. Articles placed in publications which reach your target clients can be a good source of work, and both articles and books will lend credibility to your professional activities. Again, do not expect this to be a major source of income in itself; articles may not be paid for and books, in relation to the time they take, are unlikely to compete with consultancy assignments in terms of profitability. Nevertheless they are well worth doing and can also provide you with useful items to send out with letters and proposals to potential clients.

Even through there may be other books in your specialist area, your book will be just that – your own personal thoughts about your topic – so do consider this as a way of extending your reputation, as well as an interesting activity in its own right.

Advertising

Advertising is a possible way of selling your services, but it can be expensive and, unless repeated on a regular basis, is unlikely to be sufficiently memorable or to land on people's desks at exactly the time they need what you are offering. On the whole, for consultants, advertising is more likely to be useful as a marketing tool than a sales activity. Most consultants I know do not advertise their services; they rely on word of mouth, repeat business and referrals for much of their income. If you do advertise, make sure you assess its effectiveness and ask people who enquire exactly how they have heard about you, as this will be a good guide to the productivity of your marketing and sales initiatives.

Possible places to advertise are local and national press, trade and professional magazines, telephone directories/Websites and local radio stations as well as your own website. Most of the remaining sources are likely to be too expensive, or too inappropriate, for independent consultancy services.

Press releases

Getting your name and activities into the media is a good way of marketing your business. Press releases should only be used when you have something which is really newsworthy, for example a

119

new product or development, an impressive result with a well-known client who is happy to be mentioned, or a personal achievement that is of interest (at least in your local media). It is well worth getting to know your local newspaper and radio journalists and photographers so you can contact them directly when you have a story that would interest their readers or listeners.

Press releases should be concise, have an enticing headline that sums up the main feature of your news, give full contact details and be sent to the appropriate person for the subject matter. If in doubt, enlist the service of a PR expert; you may pay to have your press releases written, but this could pay dividends in the long run.

Business stationery

Having professional-looking business stationery will help raise your profile and keep you in front of potential purchasers. It is essential to have well-designed letterheads and business cards, and it is also good to have a brochure, leaflet, or folder with inserts showing what you do. I will be covering the process of business writing, including brochure production, in Chapter 14, so here I would just like to cover the content itself.

A good brochure will show who you are, what you do, how you do it, where you do it, whom you do it for, what benefits accrue from using your products and services and how to get in touch with you. Some optional extras are endorsements from previous satisfied clients and your fee rates. Including fee rates is debatable; some people like to include them as they are then providing a well-defined product; others prefer the flexibility of individual negotiation. The choice is up to you, but I now personally prefer to leave costs out of printed brochures.

A website

Having your own website is an excellent way of marketing; it can also be used for selling if you have appropriate products and services to communicate in this way.

Your website should be easy to find and speedy to search. It should be straightforward for users to move from one page to another and find the elements that interest them; it should be updated regularly so it stays current and interesting; it should be visually appealing (and it can contain sound too, if you wish) and contain information that is of real interest and benefit to your market. You will need to register your site with all the search engines (and if you do not understand this term you need assistance in developing your site!), and it is usually more economical to use a web registration service than to attempt to do this yourself. These services also assist you in identifying key words to use in order to help people find your site easily.

Registers/intermediaries

There are numerous registers that provide an intermediary service between you and potential clients. Many professional bodies have registers of consultants, so it is worth approaching any to which you belong to check their usefulness to you. There are also independent registers, many of them now Internet-based, that will list your activities.

Many of the registers are free, but some do make a charge for promoting you. Some offer a free listing, but then charge for any expanded advertisements they carry for you. You will also find that some registers will want a commission on any fees you earn through referrals from them; this may be a percentage or a fixed payment, or whichever of the two is higher.

I have listed a few registers in the Resources section at the end of the book. There are also other intermediary facilities – for example consultancy networks often have internal arrangements for referrals. You may also come to private agreements with other consultants regarding work leads.

Final Points on Marketing

Many independent consultants find it difficult to balance fee earning and marketing. Because of the nature of consultancy, there are often periods when you are working flat out with no time to spare. If this is the case, it is often difficult to set aside time to do marketing. It is also easy to fall into the trap of thinking that, because you are so busy, you don't need to bother with more marketing, as you already have as much work as you can handle. Both of these situations are likely to result in 'feast or famine' – the consultant's constant complaint – and you would be better advised to keep your marketing going permanently, so you have potential work coming to you for the future. Now let's move on to selling.

Selling

Selling is the process of persuading potential 'prospects' to buy from you. This is an activity that many consultants find difficult and off-putting, especially if it involves 'cold calling' or approaching people with whom you have had no previous contact.

Sales tends to depend, to a large extent, on having a specific and readily identifiable product to offer. A term that is often used in sales is USP, or Unique Selling Point (or Proposition). The more readily you can distinguish your offerings from those of others, the more likely it is that you will be noticed, remembered and contacted (as long as you also build quality, value and reliability into your equation).

Your USP can come through the words you use to describe what you offer, but can also come through design elements. Many businesses use a logo, or graphic feature that represents that business. Some people extend this into accompanying words (Timothy Foster has referred to these as 'Slogos' – logos plus a slogan). Some memorable slogans, past and present, are British Telecom's 'It's good to talk', PAL dog food's 'Prolongs Active Life' and Heinz's 'Beanz Meanz Heinz'.

Once you are convinced, personally, that what you have to offer will be of value to your prospective purchasers (prospects), you are likely to get a more positive response, because your enthusiasm for what you are offering will communicate itself to people. So, the first person to sell to is yourself; when you are sold on your ideas it is easier to sell to others.

Let's consider some ways of selling your services.

Cold calling

As this is likely to be the most challenging, let's take it first. Cold calling involves telephoning people to see if they are interested in what you have to offer. You can get hold of names from published lists (available for purchase) or you can make up your own lists from directories and other sources. Do check, if you are using a directory from a membership body, that there is no restriction on its use for this purpose. The best lists to use are probably those available in public and specialist libraries listing organisations by geographical area, sector or size.

If you are going to embark on cold calling, it helps to get yourself into a confident frame of mind first (see Chapter 8 for how to do this). Talk about benefits, rather than the features of what you are offering ("This will help you save 10% of your energy costs", rather than "This is the most up-to-date system on the market"). People are more attracted by what they will gain than by a catalogue of points and processes. It is also important to:

- Check you have the correct name and title for the person you are calling.

- Select what you believe will be a good time to call that particular person.

- Find a way round 'gatekeepers', such as personal assistants who are there to filter calls; it helps to say you have been referred by someone else, so contacting another person in the organisation first will give you a name to mention.

- Check they have time to speak to you and, if not, ask when would be a good time to call them back (and do call them, rather than relying on them to call you).

- Have some inducement if possible – news of a useful publication, a discount on products, a free trial, or something similar.

- Ask for the name of a further contact if you cannot make headway with the original person.

In consultancy, cold calling will probably only be successful in a small number of cases, but it can work as long as you do your homework in selecting suitable leads to start with and have something of real value to offer.

Using agency services

If you really cannot face cold calling, you could use the services of an agency to do telesales for you. This will, however, cost you money and, unless you can show a good return, it may not be a cost-effective option. If you do use an agency service, be sure that you know exactly what they will be saying to people they contact, because you don't want misleading or off-putting information or approaches to be associated with your business. You should also make absolutely sure that, if your business is at all specialised or technical, the agency staff understand enough to be able to speak on your behalf.

Agencies can also do direct mail design and distribution for you, but the same provisos apply: make sure they know your business, vet what they do and check that the cost is not prohibitive.

Offering further services to existing clients or employers

If you have existing clients, or organisations you have worked for in the past as an employee, they are probably the most cost-effective means of making sales. Sometimes this is referred to as 'farming' rather than 'hunting', as you are gaining benefit from existing resources rather than having to constantly chase new ones.

Contacting existing client organisations to see if they could benefit from what you can offer is likely to be inexpensive and, as you already have an established relationship, will be easier and probably more productive than approaching potential clients 'cold'.

If you are going to follow this route, it helps to keep in touch with your clients even when you don't have anything specific to offer them. Contact them by phone, through newsletters or e-mails, so your name is still familiar and you can maintain an ongoing relationship. And if you can offer them things other than fee-paid work – perhaps information or maybe just being there for a chat – so much the better.

Producing a newsletter

If your newsletter simply contains broadly based information about your business, news about trends in your field, and so forth, it will probably be more of a marketing tool than a sales one. If, however, you include some specific sales elements in your newsletter, it can work for you in generating income.

Some of the things you can include to make sales through a newsletter are:

- News of new products and services.

- Discounts/vouchers/free offers to be used in conjunction with products and services.

- News of social events/open evenings to promote activities and help people network.

If you produce your newsletter as hard copy you will have the expense of producing and mailing it; if you produce it as an E-mailed document it will be more immediate, but may not be retained and may be seen as an intrusion by some people. So, again, there are pros and cons all round; it's up to you to make the most appropriate choice for your own business.

Doing mailshots

This can be a good way of making sales, but only if your selling is targeted, economic and appropriate for what you have to offer. There is generally a very low response to mailshots, even quite well-targeted ones, so if you are considering this option, do make sure your promotional material is professionally produced, that you have an up-to-date mailing list and that you have costed the activity and are sure it is likely to be financially viable.

So these are some ways in which you can make sales; if you are keen to sell in person, that's good. Otherwise, you might consider having support with this, possibly on a commission basis. The more sales you can generate the more your business will thrive – unless you over-commit yourself, which is a common consultancy problem and one to be avoided.

Final Points

Firstly, timing may be important to some clients in deciding whether to purchase goods or services. The end of a budget year may be a time when they want to use up remaining funds or, alternatively, are short of money. The start of a budget year can be good because there may be high levels of funds available. So having this information can be useful when thinking about sales; it can also be useful because some clients may want you to work in a particular period, but invoice for it in another, to optimise their own budgetary control.

Secondly, you might wish to consider taking on an assistant, or using an agency service, to do some marketing and selling for you; possibly on a commission basis so they have a vested interest in helping you sell your products and services. It is not necessarily easy to find such help, apart from expensive agency services, but it can be worth looking for if you feel you need some support in this area.

Finally, it is always worth checking that the person to whom you are speaking has the authority to commit expenditure. It is not uncommon for clients to enthuse about an assignment, virtually commit the organisation to its conduct and then turn out to have to seek final agreement from elsewhere, which is then not forthcoming. So it is worth keeping this in mind, when doing your marketing or selling, along with the inevitability of occasional organisational changes that mean that a project is put on ice, or never actually happens.

NLP techniques used in this chapter and the sections where you can find them

Perceptual positions (marketing – perspective shifts)

Chapter 6
Enhancing Your Business

This chapter covers a range of processes and issues that are important in enhancing the success of your business.

The elements I will be covering in this chapter are:

- Project management.
- Monitoring results.
- Personal development.
- Culture and divergence.
- Ethics.

Project Management

You can think of any assignment you conduct as a project. It is worth using the 'chunking' concept, which I cover in Chapter 7, so that you can consider which are total projects and which are simply sub-sets of other projects. One definition (Rory Burke) of a project is: "A group of activities that have to be performed in a logical sequence to meet present objectives outlined by the client." Burke goes on to define project management as "Making the project happen."

Project management is a way of keeping track of assignments, whether they are your own or projects you are managing for a client. The subject of project management can be quite complex and is worth exploring in some depth. I will go into some of the basic detail here and have suggested a few books on project management in the Bibliography so that you can follow up in due course.

Aspects of project management you will need to consider are as follows:

Understanding project composition

Projects have 'life cycles', which usually start from a low base, building up slowly to a peak and then declining as they reach completion. The stages of project life cycles can be defined as: ◆Conceiving; ◆Planning; ◆Resourcing; ◆Implementing; ◆Completing or terminating. Let's consider each of these in turn.

- *Conceiving/devising*

  In the conceptual stage the project's identity needs to be established, considering its: ◆Objectives; ◆Outputs (sometimes called 'milestones' – or measurable deliverables); ◆Measures; ◆Stakeholders and ◆Team members. Depending on who is involved at this stage, the project may stand a better, or worse, chance of success.

- *Planning*

  The planning stage requires identification of: ◆Activities and sequences of activities; ◆Time-scales; ◆Roles and ◆Resources required. There are many project planning techniques covered in Chapter 7.

- *Resourcing*

  The resourcing stage consists of gathering the resources needed, which may include: ◆People (and any training they may require); ◆Finance; ◆Buildings, equipment and materials; ◆Time allocation and ◆Information. If projects are under-resourced, they will stand little chance of successful completion.

- *Implementing/controlling*

  The implementation stage involves managing the project by: ◆Leading and managing any people involved; ◆Tracking and controlling quality, costs, time and performance; ◆Managing risks; ◆Producing results. You will need good process skills at this stage, including interpersonal skills to keep the project afloat as well as effective record-keeping processes. If your project is substantial, you will probably find that using project management software will be your best option, while for small projects a manual system, or even a simple wall chart, may be sufficient.

- *Completing/terminating*

  Finally, completing may involve any of the following, depending on whether the project is a one-off and whether it involves other people: ◆Assessing results and gaining feedback; ◆Winding up a team; ◆Handing over to any successors; ◆Setting the stage for any subsequent related projects. It is important, at this stage, to learn any lessons from the conduct of the project, so that future projects can be informed by your learning.

Identifying the elements of your project

The better you can define your project, the easier it will be to carry out. For example, when planning this book, I first of all had a broad outline; I then mapped out the elements and finally decided what would be contained within each chapter. As I go along, I do make alterations to my structure when I find I have more or less to say on a particular topic, when I find that certain sections fit better earlier or later, or when I need to add new elements that seem appropriate. However, having the structure at the start makes it very much easier to have an overview of what needs to be done to get started, to keep on track and to see which changes might contribute to the overall result.

Managing resources: time, information, people, money, etc.

All these need effective management if you are to be successful. Projects generally need good time management skills as they help you keep on target and avoid the Pareto Principle trap (see Chapter 7) of unnecessary use of resources; they also help other people who may need to collaborate with you, or with whom you may need to work in parallel.

When I set about writing a book, I have a deadline by which the copy has to be with the publisher; this provides a broad framework for the time involved. I then work out how many words have to be written in this time and allocate a period each day in which to write that proportion of what is needed, allowing for any days when I will be unable to write because of other commitments.

I work out what information I will need, in broad terms, and build this into my schedule, having folders and computer files for the different kinds of information I will be collecting. I ask for help from anyone who will be assisting with research and do checks on whether they are actually doing what they have agreed to.

There is not a great deal of outgoing money involved in writing, but any other resources needed, such as available space around me, a constant supply of bottled water and a telephone-free environment, is organised.

Contingency planning

Whatever the project, there may be times when things do not go according to plan, when circumstances change or when there are uncertainties that cannot be assessed in advance. All these can benefit from consideration and are called contingency planning.

By definition it is hard to plan for events you cannot predict, but there are specific contingency planning techniques to help you do this.

Example
A colleague had accepted an assignment that required two people for its conduct. Although there was no reason to expect that there would be problems, in the event, the second person had a serious accident and was unable to work for three months. Because the consultant managing the assignment had spoken to three or four others before choosing who would be the second person to work on it, it was easy to go back to this list and find a substitute at fairly short notice. This was not specific planning for the situation, but doing some homework on who could be suitable associates made the task of finding a replacement much easier.

Maintaining progress records

Keeping records of how you are doing is also important, and I will return to this topic in the following section, on monitoring results. To take the book example again, at the end of each time I work on it, I count the number of words I have written, check the time it has taken, and then add the word total, and how far I had got towards the objective number of words for each chapter. In this way I have an ongoing check on progress. It is also quite motivating to see the results, even if it is only a few hundred words at any one time.

Ensuring you have the personal qualities needed

I will be covering some of the requirements for self-management in Chapter 8. As far as project management goes, there are some specific attributes that will help you be effective:

- *Taking an overview*

  Being able to 'see the big picture' is a vital skill. Unless you can conceptualise the whole project, it will be difficult to conduct it effectively, explain it to others and motivate yourself and anyone else to work on it.

- *Being concerned with detail*

  Just as it is important to see the big picture, you must also be able to notice and work with detail on a project for at least part of the time. Even if you can delegate all the tiny detailed aspects to someone else, you will still need to be able to check that they have been done – and this needs an eye for detail. When I write my books I constantly check for grammar, spelling and punctuation, even though it will be proofread by the publisher. I want each word to be right, because slight differences can totally alter the sense and meaning of what is being written.

- *Motivating yourself and others*

  Keeping yourself and others on track is important, and the more you can make the activities seem interesting and valuable, the more likely it is that things will go well.

- *Avoiding becoming sidetracked*

  Sometimes you can get stuck in a project, when you don't know what to do next; alternatively you may find yourself spending more time than you should on the aspects you really enjoy and putting off the less appealing aspects to another time. Each of these should be avoided, where possible, otherwise you will find your projects can go over schedule in time and cost and your reputation as an effective consultant could be affected. To overcome being stuck, it helps to have a break and allow your mind to refresh itself, discuss the issues with someone else or simply come back the next day when you may have a new perspective on the matter. And to avoid spending time solely on the elements you enjoy most, keep focused on your goal and consider giving yourself a reward for dealing with the less interesting aspects of your task.

Monitoring Results

This is an element of consultancy that is often overlooked. It may be because of lack of time; it may be because of uncertainty of its value. Whatever the reason, it is worth paying attention to assessment of effectiveness, as this is the foundation for future success.

Monitoring results utilises feedback processes, such as those I mention in Chapter 7. They provide ways of comparing results with goals or predictions, so you can see what variations there have been, measure how far you have gone and assess whether any remedial action needs to be taken. You can also consider trends in your business environment and see whether you are responding to them, or simply following a pre-set path without real sensitivity to current requirements.

Some of the ways in which you can monitor your results are as follows:

Comparing results with expectations

This is a simple exercise and relies on you having set measurable targets to start with. Assuming you have done this, you can then compare these with the actual results you have obtained to see whether you are on track.

Some of the things you could assess in this way are turnover, response rates to advertising, number of clients, number of fee-earning days and average fee rates over the period.

You can also compare different periods and map overall trends, so you can see whether you have constant growth, cyclical activity, seasonal variations and so on. If you map out your progress as you go along, on a chart or using your computer, you will be able to see at a glance how your business is performing on any of the indicators you select. Using colour is a help in this process, so you can easily distinguish one element from another.

You are likely to find that using this process will help you review which indicators you need to have in place, so, to some extent, it is a self-correcting system.

Getting feedback from clients, colleagues and others

Another way of measuring your performance and success is through feedback. You may receive this unsolicited, or you can ask for it directly or indirectly.

Feedback from clients is probably the most useful, as it directly impinges on your fee-earning relationships. However, it is also useful to talk to colleagues, suppliers, friends and family to get their opinions about how you are doing; sometimes feedback can come from the most unlikely of sources and yet prove invaluable.

Getting ongoing feedback from clients is helpful and, at the very least, it is worth having a 'wash-up' session after a project in order to exchange views and ideas. And I do mean exchange, because clients can be helped (see Finale) to be better users of consultancy services if you are also open with them about how your relationship with them has gone and how easy or otherwise it has been to work for them.

Conducting surveys

Once you have a reasonable number of clients, it is possible to use this technique to assess their opinions about your work. You should be careful about this approach, as it can seem a little detached. Also, many people dislike filling in questionnaires or forget to do so, so your results may not be representative of your client group as a whole.

If you are going to survey client opinion, you will need some expertise in survey design. There are many good books on this subject, and I have listed some in the Bibliography as well as mentioning surveys again in Chapter 7.

Assessing your own responses to your activities

Although you can measure results against targets, this is often a numerical exercise, far removed from personal feelings and values. Another way in which you can assess your effectiveness is by checking personal measures such as the following:

- A sense of satisfaction.
- A belief that you have given value.
- A feeling of confidence.
- Knowledge that your development has been enhanced.

These kinds of measures may not be as quantifiable as some, but they are valid nevertheless. If you enjoy what you are doing and believe you are fulfilling a useful function, you are more likely to remain motivated, be responsive to your clients and produce results that are appreciated.

Personal Development

Your performance as a consultant is only as good as your current skill level, and because the world changes, your skills need to move in accordance with such change.

In the world of work, the term CPD, or Continuing Professional Development, is used to indicate that people who practise a particular occupation need to update their knowledge, skills and performance if they are to continue to be successful. To this end, most professional bodies nowadays have a formal requirement for CPD from their members, and they monitor adherence to this requirement, usually on some kind of sampling basis.

Assuming you have carried out a process of monitoring and evaluating your performance, you should have identified areas where personal and professional development would be helpful. Your aims then could be to address these areas and target them with selected and appropriate development processes.

It may also be that you wish to extend your business activities into other areas in the future and, because of this, need to extend your expertise in specific ways, which would be another use for CPD.

Some of the things you can do to update and develop yourself are:

- Learn from assignments conducted.
- Read, listen to audiotapes or watch films and videos.
- Discuss issues with colleagues.
- Attend courses.
- Prepare talks, presentations, training sessions, articles or books on your subject.
- Coach somebody else.
- Join in e-mail discussion groups.
- Attend meetings of professional bodies.
- Research new topics.
- Have peer development sessions, undertaking action learning or similar activities.
- Have a mentor or personal coach to assist you.

It is also helpful to keep a learning log, to monitor your progress and results; such logs are also a requirement for many CPD programmes run by professional institutes. A learning log involves identifying your learning need, describing the processes selected to address the need, exploring the learning gained from the development processes and then setting new targets for development. You can either create your own log, or you can use existing formats available from many professional bodies and published learning materials.

It is well worth taking the time to develop yourself, as your consultancy business will only be as good as the resources you put into it, and your major resource in this context is yourself.

Culture and Divergence

As a consultant, you will come into contact with many people, some of whom will have similar backgrounds, ideas, values and ways of working to yourself and some of whom will be very different. In earlier chapters I covered ways of establishing good working relationships with others; in this section I would like to mention a few of the broader issues that can affect consultancy assignments and relationships.

Stereotypes

Many people have very stereotyped views about other cultures; they also tend to group together people who are, in practice, very diverse. For example, Europe is made up of many different countries, as are the Gulf states, South America and Africa, to give but a few examples. The USA is made up of different states – culturally it is very disparate. Yet people from outside these areas often consider them each as single entities. As an example of this, the British Tourist Authority often had requests from Americans for information on 'English' locations when they actually meant to include Scotland and Wales also (that is, they meant Britain, but thought of it as England).

So when dealing with different cultures it is important first to be clear about the actual area or organisation you are considering, and second, to be careful to deal with individual countries, areas or organisations as such, and with individual people within them as such. If you carry around stereotypical thoughts you are likely both to offend people and to limit your chances of successful interactions with them.

Values and ethics

As I mentioned earlier, ethics are not universal, but relate very specifically to the culture in which they exist. A recent television series in the UK on 'Disgust' found that, while there was some evidence for the universality of certain responses, most reactions to 'disgusting things' were socially conditioned, so that babies and very young children did not show the same responses as adults, but learned them from older members of their society. There was one unfortunate clip from an old documentary film showing a young child being progressively conditioned to be frightened of a friendly dog.

In the same way, values and ethics tend to be socially conditioned, so that what is acceptable and valued in one society, or even in one organisation, is condemned in another. Some years ago, a student on a course for women returners to work said she had been invited to a job interview at an advertising agency and offered the position as long as she felt she could 'rough up her appearance a bit'; she declined the offer! Similarly, in a multi-national company, I trained a senior manager in image management, and offered the usual tips on business dressing. At the same time, his new boss – temporarily seconded from Italy – couldn't understand why there was any emphasis on formality when in his country casual (although often very expensive) clothes were more frequently worn.

So, as a consultant, you will come across many differing values and ethical stances. You will have to make up your own mind about how to respond to them. I have already mentioned the codes of ethics of professional consultancy bodies. One of the elements commonly found is an injunction against accepting inducements of any form. And yet in some countries it is reported that the only way of getting things done is through bribery, even in government departments! If you work with people who have very different principles from your own, you will need to consider carefully what your position will be.

Time

Another fascinating area of divergence is that of time. Both individuals and cultures have differing approaches to time, and you should understand both your own time 'orientation' and that of the people with whom you are working if you are to function effectively.

There are two major differences in time orientation. The first is a belief that time is important – and limited; that punctuality matters; that tasks have to be time-bounded; and that time management is a valued skill. The second is a belief that time is flexible; that it is more important that a task is done well than that it is done on time; and that the moment-to-moment experience of life matters more than a structured and controlled way of functioning.

Different cultures often tend to demonstrate one of these approaches in preference to the other. In the Western world in particular, time matters. In the UK, and probably even more in the USA, it is considered professional to be on time and disrespectful to be late. Time-management systems are top sellers in the management world, and sayings such as 'Time is money' abound. In many other cultures this approach tends to be different and there is a more fluid and flexible approach to business, and to life. You need to know which you are dealing with if you are to be successful, and if the approach differs from your own you may well have to adapt if you are to be successful.

There is a fascinating book on the nature of time, called *The Dance of Life* (see Bibliography), which should be required reading for anyone working in different cultural contexts.

To assess your own time orientation, you might like to do the following little 'test', just see which of the two sets of statements best describes you:

Set One	Set Two
• I am generally on time for appointments.	• I am quite often late for appointments.
• I look at my watch frequently.	• I rarely look at my watch.
• I am irritated when others are late.	• I don't mind, on the whole, if others are late.
• I am usually aware of time as it passes.	• I am rarely aware of time as it passes.
• I manage time very well.	• I manage time fairly poorly.
• I generally complete tasks in time.	• I am often late with tasks.
• I am good at estimating what time is needed for tasks.	• I am poor at estimating what time is needed for tasks.

If you agree with more statements in Set One than in Set Two, you are time-conscious and probably what is referred to in NLP as a 'Through time' person – someone who reviews time and sees it from a detached perspective. If you agree with more Set Two statements you are less time-conscious and probably what is referred to as an 'In time' person – someone who is immersed in their total time experience. If the latter is the case, and you intend to be a consultant, you would probably benefit from some time-management lessons and possibly some NLP training in how to alter your time 'orientation' on occasions when it is important for you to manage your time well. And, whatever your own time orientation, you may well benefit from learning to understand people from cultures where attitudes to time are different.

Proximity and formality

Different cultures have differing ways of considering how people look and behave, and I will be covering Impression Management in Chapter 10. Some cultures require a more formal appearance, and this can relate to the clothes you wear (dark suits or dresses with jackets), your manner (sitting upright; using restrained gestures) and your language (in the UK, using 'Mr' or 'Mrs' rather than first names; in France, '*Vous*' rather than '*Tu*'). Other cultures have a less formal, more casual approach to all these things.

Another element of behaviour is how close people stand to each other. The 'personal space' element can vary considerably; in some cultures people are happy to stand very close to each other, while in others a greater distance is considered appropriate.

Yet another element is eye contact. In some cultures looking at someone directly, especially looking into their eyes, is considered open and assertive, while in others this kind of eye contact is considered impolite or confrontational.

Remember, too, that in some countries it is considered inappropriate to make physical contact with women, so offering to shake hands should be avoided in such cases.

And be careful about discussing personal matters; there are wide cultural divergences here too. For example in some countries it is taboo to discuss earnings, while in others they are discussed openly; in some countries it is considered impolite, or demanding, to comment on people's possessions or family, while in others this is welcomed. So you do really need to know your environment before venturing into social interactions.

On the whole, American business people tend to be less formal than the British and also tend to be more direct, while the British are often more diplomatic.

Business culture

While most of the comments I have made here relate to regional or ethnic cultural differences, there are enormous differences too in organisational culture. When we use the term 'culture' in a business context we are usually referring to the sum total of all the norms, conventions, behaviours, expectations, attitudes and so forth that are characteristic of, and displayed by, people within those organisations. Because business culture tends to be developed over time, it can become entrenched and can take a long time to alter, which is why change-management programmes are big business and can involve lengthy time periods and substantial effort and resources to implement.

When you work in a client organisation, you are well advised to do your research in advance and be sensitive to any manifestations of cultural identity. Some of the things you can look out for are:

- Equality or differentials.
- Openness or secrecy.
- Formality or informality.
- Innovation or traditionalism.
- Receptiveness or insularity.
- Co-operation or conflict.
- Independence or teamworking.

Bearing in mind that having things in common is often the foundation for good relationships, once you notice the cultural components of an organisation, you will be able to adapt to it in whichever ways are most appropriate to make you acceptable valued.

Two anecdotes

* Almost thirty years ago I worked on a consultancy project in Scotland, helping a national newspaper deal with organisational change. In those days, being a woman on this kind of project was a strange experience. Firstly, women were not so frequently found in consultancy in general, so my presence was probably unexpected to many people there. Secondly, women were not often found in this kind of job in Scotland, especially the part of Scotland where the newspaper was based. And thirdly, women were rarely found in the print industry, especially visiting those parts of the business that were seen as predominantly male preserves. So it was difficult for people to know how to treat me, because the organisational culture was such that my presence there conflicted with many of their long-established practices and attitudes.

* As Director of Personnel and Administration at the Arts Council of Great Britain, I appointed a new secretary who happened to be male. Even in the relatively unconventional environment of the Arts Council, many visitors simply assumed he was the boss and I was the secretary. Cultural norms are hard to eradicate, and my comments about stereotypes are borne out by this example.

Ethics

Finally in this chapter, a brief exploration of ethics in consultancy. What is ethical depends on many factors, including the culture in which you are operating, the rules of professional bodies to which you belong, the consequences that may follow and your own personal values and beliefs.

Over the last year or two there has been a series of television programmes in the UK called 'Hypotheticals'. In each programme in this series, a different group of fifteen or so people – all 'experts' in their fields or representing particular relevant interest groups – are led through scenarios that relate to a particular field of ethics. Topics have included euthanasia, abortion, human tissue, cloning and foreign policy.

The programmes are very thought-provoking and often contentious. A particularly interesting point about them is the divergence of opinion among people who are all prominent in their own fields. You might think that is only human nature demonstrating its variety but, as the issues are specifically ethical ones, it does show that ethics is neither universal, nor static, in its application.

So how do you decide what is ethical in consultancy? You do not have to reinvent the wheel, as the major professional consultancy bodies have their own codes of ethics to which members are expected to adhere. Even if you are not yet a member of one of these, you can still see copies of their codes and use them to inform your own thinking. Whether or not you use an established set of ethical guidelines, here are a few issues that are commonplace within consultancy – you might like to consider these, and your own stance on each of them, when you embark on a career in consultancy.

Ethical issues

- *Professionalism*

  Maintaining high standards of conduct, integrity, objectivity, impartiality, transparency/openness, respect, dignity, independence, loyalty, trustworthiness and honesty. Keeping accurate accounts. Not selling products and services that are not needed and not colluding with inappropriate requests.

- *Confidentiality*

  Respecting the information you obtain from clients, colleagues and others. This might be internal business information, personal information on individuals, information on competitors and so forth. Not using confidential information for personal gain or third-party gain. It is also important to remember that concealing certain information might also be regarded as a criminal activity; for example if you know that someone in a client organisation is behaving fraudulently, or otherwise illegally, but you do not reveal this information, you could be held liable as an accessory to their actions. So this issue can be fraught with difficulty for the unwary.

- *Conflicts of interests*

  Avoiding being in situations where you either have a prior interest that might conflict with a work assignment, or where you take on work for competing clients. Disclosing personal interests where these might be relevant. Knowing where your loyalties lie.

- *Boundary management*

  Being able to define, and stay within, an appropriate consultancy role. Avoiding personal/professional relationship conflicts.

- *Poaching*

  Avoiding luring staff away from clients or colleagues.

- *Ability*

  Knowing your own capability and only accepting work that you have the capability to do. Telling people what your limits of ability are. Not making misleading claims or misrepresenting yourself or others.

- *Vulnerability*

  Safeguarding the interests of clients, colleagues and any other stakeholders, and not putting these at risk.

- *Consequences*

  Assessing the consequences of your actions, or inactivity, on each of the people involved.

- *Inducements*

  Neither giving nor accepting inducements in relation to assignments.

- *Legality*

  Acting within the law.

  When considering the ethics of a course of action, it is important to think about the issues involved, how the situation arose, whether you have contributed to the situation and whether it will go away on its own or needs to be resolved.

  The IMC in the UK (and similarly elsewhere) has produced a brief document with ethical guidelines and useful questions to ask yourself, to test for possible ethical dilemmas and methods of resolving them. A point made in this document regarding ethics is that you should consider whether you would be happy to explain your behaviour to your family, friends, colleagues and the media.

Some examples of ethical dilemmas faced by consultants I know are the following:

- Having pressure exerted to slant the findings of a report.
- Being asked to put in high, or low, tenders, so that a competing bid is accepted.
- Being asked by a member of a board to provide evidence of incompetence on the part of a senior manager.
- Having to make personal advances to a member of staff in order to gain basic contact details of staff who were essential to the conduct of the assignment.

And of course there are countless other examples that every experienced consultant would find commonplace.

Final Points

This chapter has raised a range of issues that you will need to consider if you are to embark on a successful consultancy career. You will have to make up your own mind on how to approach them, but help is to hand. One of the advantages of consultancy is that it can offer very cohesive and supportive networks and associations that do act to the benefit of new and experienced practitioners alike.

NLP techniques used in this chapter and the sections where you can find them

Time orientation (time)

Chapter 7
Consultancy Techniques

This chapter considers some of the techniques and approaches used in consultancy. There are three elements to this chapter: ◆Generic consultancy techniques; ◆Underlying concepts; ◆Specific techniques.

Many of the topics contained in this chapter are used generally within the business world as well as in consultancy. Some of the concepts and techniques have readily definable origins and attributions, and some are trademarked processes. There are numerous books written on these topics, and I have referred to some of these in the Bibliography.

Generic Consultancy Techniques

Information Collection

Information collection is the foundation for much of a consultant's work. It is important to ensure that information is actually valuable. A distinction may be made between data and information; generally data is considered to be the raw material, whereas information is material that has been manipulated to be useful. For example, a list of all the stationery suppliers in the country is data, but the details of those suppliers within your own area and carrying products that are useful to you, is information. You can utilise the second list of suppliers, but need to work on the first before it can be useful.

Elements of information
To be useful, information needs to have certain attributes; it needs to be:

- Relevant   – appropriate for your needs.
- Up to date   – as timely as possible.
- Comprehensive – sufficiently wide in scope for the purpose.

- Reliable   – 'correct' and stable.
- Available   – readily usable.
- Accessible   – easy to find.
- Comprehensible – understandable.

Use of information

Information is required in many situations in consultancy. Some that spring to mind are

- Setting up your business.
- Marketing and selling.
- Financial management.
- Client relationships.
- Project management.

Information-gathering processes

There are numerous ways of gathering information; some you may find useful are:

- Discussion.
- Questionnaires and surveys.
- Library and information bureau searches.
- Company searches.
- Internet and intranet searches.

Analysis

Having accessed your information, you will need to work out how to use it to best advantage. Analysis of information can be conducted in different ways, depending on your purpose and your time and resources. The word 'analysis' can seem to imply a mechanical process, but there is more than one way to assess the information you hold. A useful distinction can be between 'finger-in-the-air' techniques and 'number-crunching' techniques. I like to think of the first as 'intuitive' analysis and the second as 'numerical' analysis. They can both have their place in consultancy processes, as I will go on to explain.

Intuitive analysis

Using intuition for analysis means gathering as much information as is appropriate and then simply making a personal judgement about its implications. You may feel this is 'unscientific' and unverifiable and, to an extent, you could be right. Really effective consultants, however, will often tell you they 'have a gut feeling' about a situation, they 'can't put a finger on it but know...', or make other, similar, observations. It is rather like a sixth sense and is an invaluable asset.

Animals have a very well developed sense of intuition. Dogs, for example, can give advance warning of their owner having an epileptic fit, so action can be taken to prevent injury. I had a dog that knew when a thunderstorm was about to arrive and became very depressed and lethargic. Car drivers develop this kind of sense and can tell when the driver of a vehicle in front or behind is about to make an erratic move. And consultants often 'just know' that a situation should be handled in a particular way.

Intuition may not be something that is in any sense paranormal; it relies on awareness and responsiveness to minute cues that people give out – and I will be giving you ways of observing and reacting to such cues in Chapter 10. For now, it is useful simply to register that intuitive analysis (and decision-making) is an asset, not a second-rate method of working.

Numerical analysis

Using numerical methods of analysis is another technique that can be used on its own or in conjunction with intuition. Numerical methods are more likely to go down well with clients, who may be apprehensive about the use of intuition on its own, although buying in intuition may sometimes be better value than buying in mathematical analysis.

There is a variety of computer programmes suitable for carrying out statistical analysis, and there are also many books and other publications this topic. At least basic numeracy and IT skills are necessary to use analytical techniques.

Diagnosis

Diagnosis becomes possible once sufficient information has been gathered and analysed. Of course, it is possible to diagnose a situation and then gather and analyse information in relation to it, but it is generally more helpful to keep an open mind until the facts have been collated and analysed. I am reminded of situations which often occur in employment contexts, where over-enthusiastic managers diagnose a 'problem employee', only later to ascertain the reasons for the person behaving as they did – reasons which bore little, or no, relation to the apparent problem. Had the facts been gathered and sifted earlier, premature action could have been forestalled and possible litigation avoided.

Diagnostic issues
In consultancy, there are many issues which can be diagnosed from information gathered; some common ones are:

- Dysfunctional organisational structure.
- Poor financial control.
- Interpersonal conflict.
- Lack of quality control.
- Weak management.
- Safety risks.
- Marketing inefficiency.
- Poor communications.
- Tactical misjudgment.
- Lack of vision.
- Non-competitiveness.
- Unresponsiveness to customer demand.
- Failure to adapt to new technology.
- Insularity.
- Fear of change.

Of course, the consultant's diagnosis may differ from that of the client, which can give rise to some interesting exchanges of opinion.

Problem-solving

Problem solving comes into many areas of consultancy. You may have your own problems, such as how to find work, whether to take on support staff and what to do about conflicting demands on your time. You may also have problems to deal with in your work assignments, such as how to introduce change while maintaining staff morale, how to produce an effective development pro-gramme on a low budget or how to streamline production processes when the organisation is limited by outdated facilities and technology.

Problem-solving elements include the following:

• Defining the issues.
• Collecting information.
• Evaluating the information.
• Generating ideas.
• Producing options.
• Selecting the most suitable course of action.

You can tackle these stages on your own, or ask colleagues to help you with the process. It is important in problem-solving to main-tain an open mind and not prejudge the issue. You can sometimes find that the most unlikely solutions emerge, which would not have stood a chance if you had not been open to exploration and innovation.

Problem-solving methods, some of which are covered in the following sections, include logical analysis, brainstorming, mindmapping, trial and error, free-association (coming up with associations from 'trigger' words), metaphor use (taking an object or idea and seeing how its attributes can throw light on your prob-lem), visualisation (imagining possible solution states in order to move forward), shifts of perspective (considering the problem from another person's point of view) and personal advisers (tak-ing imaginary characters and asking them how they would solve the problem).

Another useful aid to problem-solving is allowing your unconscious mind to help you. Just as you can wake up just before your alarm clock rings by deciding in advance when you will get up, so you can go to sleep and allow your mind to get on with its own process of analysing the factors and creating ideas. You can also do this in a waking state by defining the problem you need to solve and then getting on with other activities, while your unconscious mind continues to work on the issues. It may sound slightly unfocused as an approach, but it very often works. You have much information and knowledge in store and, when you free your mind from structured constraints, you may be surprised at just how much it can achieve for you.

Decision-making

Making decisions is important both in your own life and in your clients' projects. You may need to make decisions about how much time to allocate to particular work assignments, when to take a holiday, what to wear to a presentation and how to reinvigorate yourself after a long period of concentration and effort. You may also need to decide matters such as what information to collect, which aspects of an assignment are most significant and what proposals to recommend to your client.

Decision-making steps include:

- Defining the issue that needs a decision.
- Deciding whether to consider the issue/make the decision alone or jointly with others.
- Specifying options.
- Applying criteria in order to assess each of the options (including their short- and long-term consequences and any risks involved).
- Taking a decision.
- Making a commitment to the course of action required.
- Evaluating the decision taken in the light of subsequent experience.

Various techniques may be used in decision-making; I cover some of them in later sections of this chapter.

One final input to decision-making is that outlined in Action Profiling, which was originally developed by Warren Lamb in the early 1930s. In Action Profiling, which is a broadly based psychometric approach, three progressive stages of decision-making are considered:

- **Attention** – where you collect facts, generate alternatives and consider the issue from different angles.

- **Intention** – where you evaluate issues, express determination and build resolve.

- **Commitment** – where you move forward and check on progress being made.

Before moving on to the specific techniques used in consultancy, I would like to outline some of the topics on which much of this book is based.

Underlying Concepts

Neuro–Linguistic Programming (NLP)

NLP originated in the early 1970s, based on earlier thinking and research, and is still developing and growing as a field. NLP has its origins in role-modelling – studies into how extremely successful people get their results. NLP's approach is that performance is competency-based and that, by analysing the elements of performance (objectives, behaviour, thoughts, feelings and beliefs), it is possible both to enhance one's own skills and to transfer skills from one person to another. There are many descriptions of NLP, but a couple of popular ones are 'The Art and Science of Excellence' and 'The Psychology of Achievement'.

Accelerated Learning (AL)

AL originated around the 1960s, rooted in Suggestopaedia – an earlier approach to language learning – and is very much focussed on the needs of the individual learner, the creation of an environment where people can learn, and the responsibility of a trainer to generate learning states in people who need to enhance their development.

Both NLP and AL offer ways of understanding people, enhancing motivation and performance, overcoming problems and improving relationships. NLP has applications in many fields including business, health, education, therapy and sports; AL is also used in different fields and is particularly useful in developmental work. Books on both disciplines are included in the Bibliography.

Systems Thinking

Systems thinking is a precursor of both NLP and many of the analytical processes mentioned in this book. Although there were some individual instances of systemic processing many centuries ago, systems thinking as we know it has more recent origins. Cybernetics, explained by Norbert Wiener as 'the science of communication and control' deals with how systems function, whether biological, social or mechanical. Later developments were ◆General Systems Theory, ◆Systems Analysis, ◆Second Order Cybernetics (which includes the relationships between systems and their observers as well as between elements of the systems themselves) and ◆Socio-technical Systems Theory.

In the systems approach, an organisation is seen as a network of interdependent elements or components. A closed system is one that automatically controls and modifies its own activities or operations, through responding to data generated by the system itself. An open system has to be supervised by external forces, or people, taking into account data about the system's operations and making interventions to modify inputs so that the system can function effectively.

An important element in systems thinking is the influence of one element on another. To this end, feedback loops are featured strongly, showing the effect of activity or inactivity on results achieved. Feedback is the term used for assessment of past activity, and feedforward the term used for assessing the impact of anticipation of future events on present activity.

Specific Techniques

The techniques that follow have been grouped, in order to give you an idea of their applications. They can, however, all be used in many contexts and for many purposes, so if you feel that one belongs in a different section, or that the groupings are very artificial, please use the techniques in any way you wish.

Context defining

Chunking

This is an NLP term, which has been borrowed from information technology. Chunking enables you to consider an issue in perspective, or in a broader context. An issue frequently faced by consultants is clients seeing only particular elements of a situation. It is very easy, when you are immersed in a business situation, to be acutely aware only of the aspect that is closest to you. It is important, however, to be aware both of the broader picture and, conversely, of the details of the issue. In this way a much more informed conclusion can be reached about implications and about any necessary action.

The graphic approach to chunking involves taking the issue that is of concern and putting it in a box in the centre of a sheet of paper; it is helpful to use a flip chart or whiteboard if doing the exercise with a group of people. Once the issue has been noted, another box is drawn above the first one; this denotes whatever that particular issue is part of – what is broader than that issue, or encompasses it. Next, the component parts of the issue are drawn in boxes below the original box, and finally any comparable, or parallel, issues are placed in boxes to the side of the original one.

In this way, a picture can be built up of the issue in context, and its relationship to other elements can be noted and explored. People often see issues in isolation and chunking is an excellent way of showing the broader context.

Chunking may be used across a wide range of business situations: project planning, teambuilding, negotiating, product development and so forth. Although it is a very simple concept, chunking works well with people at all levels, including senior management teams, to help them think through issues and put their ideas and concerns in perspective.

Chunking diagram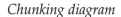

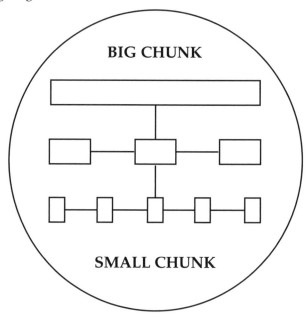

One approach to chunking that has been applied to consultancy in particular is the 3M mapping process (Cope, *The Seven C's of Consulting*; see Bibliography). Using this approach to a consultancy assignment, three elements are defined: ◆**Meta** (large chunk analysis) – for example core outcomes; ◆**Macro** (medium chunk analysis) – for example the broad actions that need to be taken; and ◆**Micro** (small chunk analysis) – for example the small items that need to be considered. This provides a simple but elegant way of handling projects.

Idea Generation and Creativity

Brainstorming

Brainstorming is a technique that is helpful when a group of people come together to consider an issue. It can also be used very effectively by individuals.

The steps involved in brainstorming are simple.

- Define the issue to be considered. Set boundaries so everyone works to the same objective.

- Select your brainstorming group. A mixed group will give differing approaches, knowledge and perspectives.

- Ensure everyone present understands the process and any constraints that apply (for example time). Give information in advance or check, when people are present, that they understand.

- Provide relevant equipment, for example a means of recording such as a flip chart, whiteboard, magnetic board or Post-it® notes.

- Have a facilitator. An external facilitator is often helpful to avoid domination by those with vested interests in particular outcomes. Facilitation ensures everyone contributes and is valued.

- Arrange the environment and equipment so that it is easy for everyone to contribute. Try to ensure comfortable seating, avoid interruptions and have seats in a circle or semi-circle to help interaction.

- Invite ideas. Each person should suggest ideas, which can be recorded without comment, criticism or evaluation. Ideas do not have to be 'sensible'; often the most outlandish produce most innovation.

- Explore and sift ideas. Once all ideas have been generated they should be discussed, and any which do not seem relevant should be discarded. (You may still wish to keep a record of the others in case they are of use subsequently.)

- Finally, evaluate and reorganise the remaining ideas. The remaining ideas can be organised into a structure and taken forward for action.

Mindmapping

Mindmapping is a process developed by Tony Buzan, although similar approaches have been developed by others. Mindmapping is like brainstorming, but is somewhat more structured from the outset, while still being a lateral thinking process. Mindmapping, like brainstorming, can be carried out by one person or by a group.

The precursors to mindmapping are the same as for brainstorming – a suitable environment, a facilitator and so forth. To use mindmapping, take a large sheet of paper, write the topic to be considered in the centre of the sheet and leave lots of space for additional information. Alternatively, you can use the technique with magnetic boards, Post-it® notes or similar tools, although written maps are more common.

Assuming you are working with a group of people, once you have the central topic in place, you ask the group to specify one aspect of the topic, then ask for subsets of that topic, and then subsets of each subset, before starting on another topic. Each time you explore a topic in this way you draw lines between its elements, resulting in treelike branches. You can also put in dotted or coloured lines between elements of different branches to show the connections. The subsets may be represented by circles, or the lines themselves can represent the sub-elements. You can use graphics instead of, or in support of, words in a mindmap; you can also use different colours to add interest and to highlight connections.

Mindmap

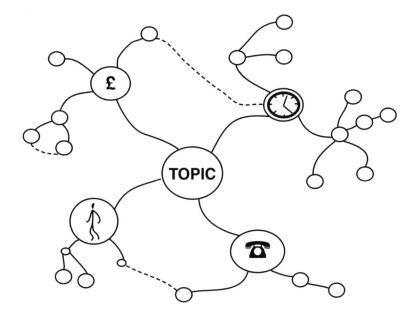

Meta-planning

Meta-planning is a term used for group assessment of ideas, where thoughts can be brought together and worked on in a collaborative way.

With meta-planning, people within a group are divided into smaller groups and then each of these subgroups is asked to come up with ideas. Once each group has produced its own ideas, all the groups present their ideas to the whole group so that each idea can be considered, discussed and compared with others. Post-it® notes or magnetic boards are useful for the presentation of ideas. The result is a complete picture of the thoughts of each of the subgroups involved. When they are combined, further ideas and actions are usually developed.

Venn Diagrams

This technique, devised by John Venn, uses circular shapes to represent different 'sets' or elements of a situation or idea being discussed. Where elements overlap, the shapes are drawn so they overlap; in this way it is easy to see the interconnections between the different parts of the subject under consideration and the sub-elements created by the areas of overlap.

Venn diagrams can be output on a computer and are helpful in showing, pictorially, the results of discussions on a topic.

Venn diagram

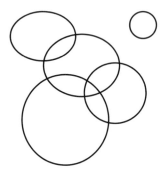

Storyboarding

Storyboards use graphic techniques to aid thinking and analysis. With this process, a situation, issue or problem is analysed through the use of pictures and associated words. Storyboarding can also involve brainstorming and other processes to achieve its results.

To create a storyboard, drawings are produced of each of the different stages of a process. More than one process can be considered simultaneously, with a different 'storyline' being produced for each. The pictures may be sketches, cartoons or whatever the person or group working on the issue finds appropriate. Words may accompany the pictures, and there can be subsets of each picture, showing various elements of each stage. As the process moves on, the pictures can be moved around and rearranged to form different scenarios and sequences, and the advantages of one storyline over another can be explored.

Storyboarding is used a good deal in the entertainment and advertising industries, but is equally useful within business consultancy. And storyboarding can make excellent use of metaphor: for example a team may be asked to produce drawings that represent their concept of the organisation (perhaps one person will draw a castle and another will draw an octopus), or they could be asked to come up with words or drawings to illustrate their team (for example they could consider what kind of animal, car or food the team would be and represent it pictorially).

Storyboards

Pinboarding

This is a process whereby ideas are put up on a board – possibly with pins, although it may just as easily be done with magnetic boards, plastic film that clings, Post-it® notes or any of the various trademarked products available to use in this way. The advantage of pinboarding is that ideas can be moved around, grouped, replaced and used very flexibly.

Delphi technique

This technique may be used to generate ideas where future situations or trends are uncertain. Developed by the Rand Corporation and named after the oracle at Delphi in ancient Greece, the process relies on asking 'experts' for their opinions and ideas about specified future events or issues.

Carried out informally, the technique could simply involve gathering a group of relevant people together and letting them discuss the issues and come up with ideas. In this way both individual and group opinions may be gathered. Carried out formally, however, the technique involves questionnaires that are sent to the experts and then analysed. Further questionnaires are then sent in order to assess those people's detailed responses to opinions expressed by members of the group, until a conclusion is reached. The group does not have to meet in this approach; communication is simply through questionnaires, which are then processed to glean any trends in opinion.

Quality circles

Often used in Japanese companies, and now common in other parts of the world, quality circles consist of a group of people from an organisation who meet to consider how to improve quality (often in production, but also in services and other functions) through discussion and generation of ideas.

Focus groups

Focus groups are used in many contexts, from market research for product development to organisational change management. As a consultant, it can be helpful to be skilled at facilitating focus groups, or at least recommending their use when appropriate. A focus group is simply a small number of people who get together, with a facilitator, to consider a topic. Often there are several focus groups within the same organisation, or as part of the same process, so that their findings and recommendations can be contrasted and compared.

Analytical and Planning Techniques

Flow charts and network diagrams

Flow charts and network diagrams are often used for planning purposes and for project management, where it is important to work out which activities are required, and how they relate to each other.

Both flow charts and network diagrams are diagrammatic representations of activities, systems and processes, showing their interconnections over time. Flow charts are predominantly linear processes, although parts of them may be recursive and go in loops back to particular starting points. Network diagrams may sometimes be more complex than flow charts.

There is now software available to produce these aids, so they can be used whenever the need arises.

Flow chart/Network diagram

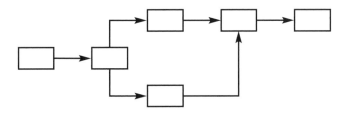

Critical Path Method (CPM)

This process is helpful in analysing, planning and scheduling projects, especially large-scale ones. The process provides a means of determining which activities are 'critical' in the overall project and how to schedule all activities within the project so that it can be completed on time and at minimum cost. Devised by Remington Rand Univac in 1957, the process enables you to model the effects different project time cycles have on costs.

Critical path analysis is usually carried out in graphic form; although it can be done in other ways, a visual representation makes the whole process much easier to see and to work with. Assuming you represent the process graphically, each activity is given a unique identifying symbol (usually a letter or a number) and a time for completion. If the activity is dependent on another activity having been carried out, its preceding activities may also be listed.

Each activity is then represented in some way. Originally, activities were drawn as circles, each with its identifying symbol and time inside the circle. Sequences of activities were represented by arrows connecting the circles, with the arrows pointing towards the succeeding activities. The word 'start' was put at the beginning of any sequence and the word 'finish' at the end of any completed sequence. The result is a number of different paths from start to finish. Each path can be timed by adding up the individual times contained within it. The critical path is then the one that takes in all essential activities and their associated times, and it shows the minimum time necessary to complete the total project.

To shorten project time, the critical path needs to be reduced, which is done by shortening activities along the critical path. It has been suggested (reported by Levy, Thompson and Weist) that only around 10% of activities in large projects are critical; you might like to consider this figure when planning your own projects.

An alternative way of drawing this kind of chart has the arrows as activities and the circles as events, but the overall concept is the same.

Nowadays, however, critical path analysis has become more of a generic term for a range of processes that assess activities and time. Much of the analysis is carried out by computer, and the most typical diagrammatic form is rectangular boxes, joined by horizontal or vertical lines, indicating the major elements of a project, their inter-connections and their related activity and time components.

See the illustration of a Gantt chart (page 171) for an indication of how a critical path diagram may look.

PERT charts

PERT is a way of handling projects. The letters PERT stand for Program Evaluation and Review Technique, and the method was developed by the US Navy and Booz, Allen and Hamilton consultants.

PERT considers two elements – events and activities – and represents these elements pictorially: events by circles and activities by arrows. The activities are timed, usually in weeks, and an arrow between two circles has a time-scale attached to it, showing how much time each activity will take before the event takes place. Because the circles may be joined in different ways, PERT analysis is often represented graphically in the form of a network diagram rather than a linear one.

TOTE diagrams

Another technique, used a lot in NLP and based on systems thinking work by Miller, Gallanter and Pribram, utilises flow chart principles.

A TOTE is the name given to a kind of trial-and-error process, whereby you adopt one course of action, test its results and, if it is not as successful as you would like it to be, adapt it until you achieve the results you require.

The letters in TOTE stand for Test – Operate – Test – Exit. The process is simply to test one course of action and, if it is acceptable, to exit the procedure. If the course of action is not acceptable, an 'operation' can be carried out, which is an alternative means of achieving an end. The feedback gained in the TOTE process can be used to speed up or slow down the rate of progress.

Tote diagram

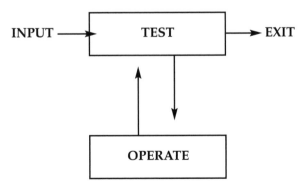

Cause-effect chains

A cause-effect chain is produced by writing a problem or goal on a piece of paper. You then draw one or more arrows from that issue, going to the right. At the end of each you write in one or more consequences of achieving that goal, or solving that problem, or dealing with that issue. You then continue the process, making further arrows showing the consequences of each subsequent stage in the process.

You also repeat the process in reverse, putting one or more arrows towards the original point showing what would have to precede achievement of that result, and continue to the left with prerequisites for each preceding step. The result is a chain of consequences giving ideas for analysis and decision-making.

Cause-effect chain

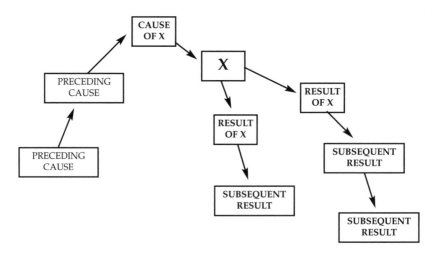

Fishbone diagram

Fishbone diagrams are a way of helping to analyse problems and assess their elements and links between these elements. The fishbone diagram was developed by Professor Kaoru Ishikawa, of Tokyo University, reputedly after he had observed a fish skeleton sitting in a container near a table where he was eating in a restaurant.

A fishbone diagram consists of a horizontal line, with the issue to be considered in a box at the right-hand end of the line. From the line, you draw straight lines above and below at about 45-degree angles to the horizontal line. In a box just above or below each smaller line, you write one reason for occurrence of the issue. From each of these smaller lines, you place other lines at 45 degrees, each containing the reason for each of the points on the first set of lines.

This approach allows you to see the problem as a whole and to see the relationship between its component parts; it is similar to the cause-effect chains described above.

An adaptation of the fishbone diagram is solution-effect analysis, where you place the possible solution in a box on the left, draw a horizontal line from it towards the right, and then put shorter lines at 45 degrees from the horizontal, and further lines at the same angle from them, each with a possible consequence of that solution. This will allow you to see the possible effects, and inter-relationships of effects, of that course of action.

Ishikawa or 'fishbone' diagram

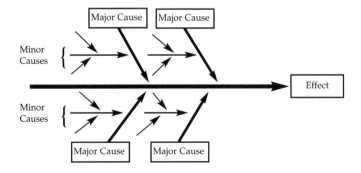

Solution-effect diagram

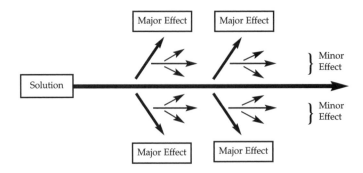

Matrix diagrams

Matrix diagrams are a very common way of representing issues. A matrix has two axes, vertical and horizontal; their intersection produces four quadrants. A matrix can be used to show the different results achieved from different combinations of the elements.

I find it helpful to have people design their own matrices, or to work with them in designing ones which relate well to their situations. To do this, simply take two different issues that are relevant in the situation being reviewed and put each on one axis; this gives the four quadrants, which can then be analysed in relation to the real-life situation that exists.

Matrix diagram

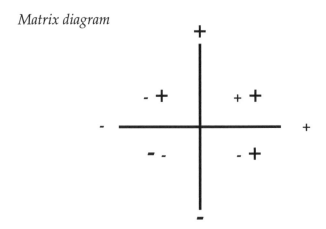

Gantt charts

Another technique that is especially useful in project management is the Gantt chart, designed by an American, Henry Gantt, at the time of the First World War. A GANTT chart has vertical columns and horizontal lines. The first column lists the activities and the other columns represent time periods.

As each activity is listed, a horizontal bar is drawn across all the time columns that relate to it – so if the columns were months of the year and an activity was due to begin in March and continue until June, the bar against that activity would run across the March, April, May and June columns. Other activities are similarly indicated, so it can easily be seen where there are many parallel activities, where there are quiet periods and so on. A normal office day planner is a kind of Gantt chart.

Underneath each bar, you can also put a second (parallel) bar; this is to show the actual progress of the activity. So if the March activity did not actually start until April, and continued until July, the bar for progress would begin later and extend further than its estimated time. If you put the actual times taken in a different colour, this also gives you a very clear way of showing comparisons between estimated and actual activity times and indicates the overall progress of a project very simply and effectively.

Gantt chart

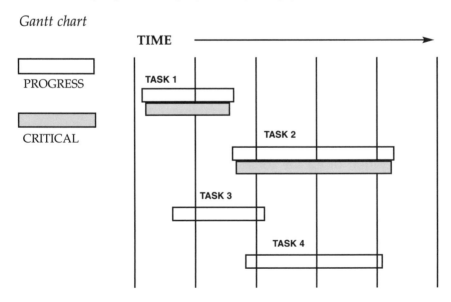

171

Force-field analysis

Developed by Kurt Lewin in the early 1950s, force-field analysis (or, as it was referred to initially, field-force analysis), is helpful in understanding the pressures operating either for or against a change. Force-field analysis may be done conversationally, but is usually better done visually by putting its various elements on to a flip chart or other device.

The principle behind force-field analysis is simple. In any situation, there are likely to be forces operating to support a particular situation or process and other forces operating against the situation or process. The driving forces will support movement towards a desired state, while the restraining forces will act to maintain the present state. The present state itself is an equilibrium between the forces for change and the forces resisting change.

Forces can exist in:

- The environment (social, political, economic, technological, ecological, and so on).

- The organisation (mission, objectives, strategy, culture, values, and so on).

- Groups within the organisation (departments, business units, representative groups, informal groups, and so on).

- Interactions (roles, styles, alliances, conflict, and so on).

- Individuals (objectives, expectations, needs, temperament, behaviour, and so on).

Consideration of all the forces, assessing their reasons for existence, direction, strength, relative importance and scope for modification, is the force-field analysis. The analysis is usually carried out by representing the various forces in a diagram, including the present situation, the desired outcome and the forces both for and against the change to the desired state. It is important to check where the balance of weight is, allocating values – where possible

– to each of the factors, and then work to reduce the opposing forces and increase the supportive forces and make the desired state more attractive. In this way, a change process may be introduced and managed more effectively.

In organisational contexts, it seems that reducing restraining forces works more effectively to begin with, as simply enhancing the driving forces may increase resistance to change. Often, in change-management programmes, the attitudes of those involved within the organisation, especially the managers, can hold back proposed changes.

Force-field diagram

FORCES AGAINST CHANGE

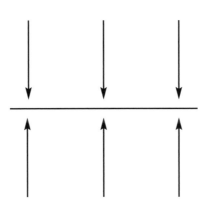

FORCES FOR CHANGE

SWOT analysis

SWOT analysis is similar to force-field analysis in that it considers both positive and negative aspects of a situation.

The letters SWOT stand for Strengths, Weaknesses, Opportunities and Threats. They are generally represented in a matrix form, usually on a board or flip chart, although the process could be done simply through discussion.

SWOT diagram

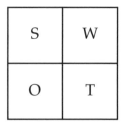

S	W
O	T

PEST review

It is important, in consultancy, to take both an overview of situations and issues and a detailed view of their component parts. Chunking gives you the principles of how to put issues into perspective, and the PEST process allows you to consider some specific elements of the broader picture and take them down into detail if you wish.

The letters PEST stand for Political, Economic, Sociological and Technological. By considering all these environmental issues, you can analyse a situation and assess which factors need attention and how the different factors relate to each other.

Critical incident technique

People often overlook things that are influential in their success. Critical incident techniques allow the exploration of organisational and personal effectiveness through the analysis of 'exceptional' occurrences.

To use this technique, the people involved in the analysis are asked to think about any incidents that stand out from their normal day-to-day activities. The incidents may be ones where an excellent result was achieved or ones in which an unsuccessful result was achieved; for example an exceptionally successful presentation or a disastrous negotiation. By building up information on a series of such incidents, conclusions may be drawn about what approaches are more, or less, effective in achieving results.

Morphological analysis

With this process, an idea, issue, problem, system or entity can be considered in the search for an outcome, for example the creation of a new product or a solution to a problem. To carry out this analysis you need to list the elements of the issue, subdivide each of the elements into its smallest parts, represent the parts in a matrix or other form that can connect them, and consider all of the possible combinations of these parts (or as many as is feasible).

The elements may be represented on pieces of paper or Post-it® notes, which can then be re-arranged or grouped in different ways. They can also be placed on cards with a pin through the centre, around which the cards can be rotated to form different combinations. It is also possible to represent the elements in a three-dimensional cube, with smaller cubes within it. Morphological analysis can be carried out on a computer; as a little example it is possible to create anagrams from combinations of words – you put in the original words and the computer breaks them down into their component elements (the letters) and re-arranges them in a multitude of ways.

Pareto Principle

One of the issues faced by consultants, in common with many other practitioners, is how to allocate time and resources appropriately. Pareto put forward the idea that it is possible to use the ratio of 80:20 in many situations to explain and expedite activity; this is sometimes called the 'law of diminishing returns', whereby most of your results are achieved by a small percentage of your effort, the remaining results taking substantially more of your resources, including time and effort.

Examples of this thinking are:

- 80% of your results are achieved with 20% of your effort.
- 20% of your clients produce 80 % of your income.
- 80% of your response comes from 20% of your advertising.
And so forth …

Cartesian coordinates

This approach, derived from ideas put forward by René Descartes in the 1600s, is used in counselling and therapy and is applicable to business as well. The approach is based on the analysis of positives and negatives as options in problem-solving.

The simple way of doing this analysis is to have two entities, A and B, which relate to each other in a cause-effect manner. Let's take a common business issue as an example – the impact that developing and launching a new product has on the staffing resources required in the organisation. The analysis, at its simplest level, would then take this form:

> A   =   new product
> B   =   staffing

If A, then what would happen to B?
Possibility: If a new product were introduced, the result could be improved job satisfaction.

If A, then what would not happen to B?
Possibility: If a new product were introduced, staff turnover would not increase.

If not A, then what would happen to B?
Possibility: If a new product were not introduced, staff might become bored.

If not A, then what would not happen to B?
Possibility: If a new product were not introduced, staff might not develop new skills.

Of course there could be many more possible outcomes, but this shows the questioning technique and how pros and cons can emerge differently if you pose the question in a different manner.

Scenario planning

Scenario planning has been used for 25 years, starting life in Royal Dutch/Shell. It is used to help in strategy development. To work with it, three or more different, and plausible, scenarios of the future are taken. The intention is to identify prospective events and the driving forces that might produce them, enabling the organisation or industry to understand how its underlying dynamics could move it from its present state to different future states. The process is useful in situations where the external environment can change in major ways that are not predetermined and that are outside the control of the organisation doing the planning.

Wally Wood, in *So Where do we Go From Here*, says that scenario planning should probably be called scenario learning, because if you simply pick the most probable future scenario you are 'almost certainly doomed to fail'. So scenarios enable you to determine 'whether a corporation's established filters are blocking important information that, if withheld, will be valuable or harmful' (quoted by Simpson).

Some key factors in scenario planning are the following:

- It needs a 'champion with enough power to effect change' or the effort will be wasted.

- Scenarios must not be too broad ('staff people tend to create these') or too narrow ('operating people tend to create these'); they need to be 'strategic, not futurist'.

- It needs to take account of issues, not all of which can be quantified.

- You need to allocate sufficient time to it – probably a minimum of three months and sometimes six months or longer.

- There should be a diversity of participants and inputs (Schwartz), including some external ones to avoid introspection.

- It is important for both the individual and the organisation to learn – and to unlearn (see also Kurt Lewin's change management model of unfreezing, changing and refreezing).

- It must be connected to strategy.

- It must take account of continuous, ongoing changes in circumstances.

- It is an aid to good business judgement, not a substitute for it.

- You must have a process to move from scenario to strategy.

Some elements to consider in scenario planning are customers, markets, products, services, business processes, asset providers and other stakeholders, social values and government policy (GeoPartners Research). The scenarios created may simply be future possibilities, or they may be 'ideal' possibilities (in NLP terms, 'desired future states'), which may lead more easily on to strategic planning.

Nowadays, 'e-scenarios' are becoming popular. In the wake of the developing 'knowledge economy', whole organisations can take part in scenario thinking. With dedicated Internet chat rooms, it is possible to have fast exchange of ideas, even between people working in geographically different locations, at different times of the day and across time zones. Web-based scenario development uses virtual teamworking to achieve organisational involvement and coherence.

Personal Assessment

Psychometric tests

For those consultants working within the human resource field, it can be useful on occasions to use tests of personality, aptitude, attitude, motivation and so forth. Most tests require training, and many are licensed products requiring purchase, or payment of royalties.

Some of the contexts in which psychometric tests may be used are:

- Recruitment and selection.
- Teambuilding.
- Conflict resolution.
- Market research and sales.

Some commonly used teambuilding tests have been designed by Belbin, and Margerison and McCann. Commonly used personality tests have been designed by Saville and Holdsworth, Myers Briggs, and Cattell.

Example

While working at Ashridge Management College, I conducted some research into the characteristics of computer programmers and systems analysts. I was trying to assess whether there was a particular personality profile for each, and to this end, I used the 16PF test across a number of companies. I also tested the managers of the IT departments and asked them to rate each of the staff against a number of performance criteria. I expected to find a consistent profile across the companies, so that highly rated people demonstrated similar personality characteristics. The actual results, with hindsight, were probably more predictable. Those people who were rated as good performers by their managers had similar profiles to the managers themselves (different in each company), not necessarily to other people doing similar jobs in other companies.

As well as the commercially available pen-and-paper/hand-and-keyboard tests, there are also some NLP approaches to psychometric assessment (although they are rarely described in such terms). These tend to rely more on subjective assessment than standardised instruments, but are nonetheless extremely valuable in providing practical information for a range of purposes. I will be covering these approaches in more depth elsewhere, so will just mention them briefly here.

The two NLP measures are:

- Meta-model analysis.
- Meta-programme analysis.

Meta-model analysis is based on the work of Bandler and Grinder, NLP's best-known originators. The Meta-model is a linguistic tool that facilitates understanding of how individual people function. The Meta-model relies on the use of very precise questioning to elicit underlying (deep structure) experience.

Meta-programme analysis is about ascertaining people's motivational and other operating patterns. This approach uses conversational techniques to elicit information about a range of polarities, such as whether someone is internally or externally focused; whether they are concerned with detail or generalisations; and whether they make decisions rapidly or after lengthy consideration. See Chapter 11 for more on this topic.

Repertory grid/personal construct theory

Developed by George Kelly in the 1950s as a methodology for exploring 'personal construct' systems, repertory grids are helpful in analysing people's personal approaches to situations. Although they emerged from psychoanalytical contexts, repertory grids can be useful in business consulting as they help both the consultant and the client understand how people's attitudes, preferences and needs can vary.

To produce a repertory grid, you can take any issue (or indeed any person, object or other class of experience) and then ask questions about it – questions that have two polarities and the possibility of a range of responses between each. Each of these sets of opposing polarities is called a construct. Single issues can be explored in this way, and it is also possible to compare and contrast responses across issues or contexts.

As with any form of questionnaire design, the structure and wording of these grids may influence the response given, so the person designing them needs an awareness of how their design can influence the ways in which they are completed – and therefore their usefulness.

Fact-finding and opinion assessment

Questionnaires and surveys
This is a specialised topic, but one that you may well find useful. Questionnaires and surveys are used in consultancy in many ways, including:

- Staff opinion and morale assessment.
- Staff performance assessment.
- Customer opinion and need assessment.
- Project success reviews.
- Research projects.
- Change-management reviews.

A few elements to consider in questionnaires and surveys are:

- Issues to be included.
- People to conduct the research.
- Support of management and any other stakeholders.
- Target group to be questioned.
- Size of sample taken – whole group or subset.
- Validation and testing of questions.
- Format.
- Question design.
- Significance of responses (statistically and in personal terms).
- Follow-up sampling.
- Scoring (manual or computerised).
- Interpretation.
- Feedback.
- Publication of findings.
- Implementation of findings.

If you do want to produce a questionnaire or conduct a survey you would be well advised either to do some reading or take a course that will give you the relevant techniques, or work in association with an expert in these fields. There can be pitfalls, including the possibility of bias in the results through badly designed instruments and procedures, so these tools need a professional input.

It is also important to remember that, when you conduct some of these kinds of research, people's expectations are raised regarding implementation of findings. If you do not intend, or are not able, to take action as a result, or if you do not intend to feed back the findings to those involved, you should be prepared for possible negative reactions and possibly lowering of morale as a result.

Final Points

This chapter has covered many of the concepts and techniques used in consultancy. There are, of course, many more, and it is worth exploring these in order to have a broadly based knowledge of the field.

A few additional concepts that are worth some reading are:

- Knowledge (intellectual capital) management – with its associated measurement issues.
- Customer relations management.
- Total Quality Management (TQM).
- Business Process Re-engineering (BPR) – or Business Process Analysis (BPA).
- Emotional Intelligence.
- Just in Time (JIT) and its counterpart JTL (Just Too Late!).

NLP techniques used in this chapter and the sections where you can find them

Sensory acuity (intuitive analysis)
Metaphor (problem-solving)
Visualisation (problem-solving)
Perceptual positions (problem-solving)
Personal advisers (problem-solving)
Unconscious processing (problem-solving)
Chunking (chunking)

TOTE diagrams (TOTE diagrams)
Cause-effect chains (cause-effect chains)
Meta-model analysis (psychometric tests)
Meta-programme analysis (psychometric tests)

Author's note: I have credited the originators of techniques where I have been able to determine them.

Chapter 8
Self-Management

This chapter will show you how to maintain a positive outlook and sense of balance while engaged in business.

Being a consultant, especially an independent one, requires excellent self-management skills. If you can handle yourself well, it helps create a sense of confidence in those with whom you deal. So this chapter will cover the following topics:

* Confidence.
* Motivation.
* Emotional control.
* Positive thinking.

These topics are linked so, although I will describe them separately, the techniques you can use to enhance them are shared and overlap considerably. Let's start with some brief descriptions of each of these topics:

Confidence

If you are confident in yourself, others are more likely to be confident in you. It takes confidence to promote yourself, compete in tendering processes, give presentations, deal with senior people and specialists, justify your proposals and publicise your successes.

Some people seem naturally confident and at ease in any situation. If this describes you, this chapter may give you some ways of helping others to be confident. If, on the other hand, you feel your confidence could be boosted at times, I hope this chapter will enhance your skills in heightening it.

Motivation

Motivation is about getting yourself going – starting and continuing activities; maintaining energy despite challenge; keeping going in the face of adversity. One of the questions you will need to ask yourself, if you are considering a career as a sole practitioner, is how you will motivate yourself.

If you are a naturally self-motivated person, this is unlikely to present a problem; it may well be the reason you considered embarking on this career in the first place. Personally, I find it very easy to maintain my own motivation and will always initiate things rather than rely on others to start first. However, some consultants find self-reliance hard and need other ways of keeping their motivation levels high.

If you think you may have difficulties in motivating yourself you should first of all ask yourself whether you would be better off being employed, perhaps in a larger consultancy practice, or whether you need to build a really good support network early on to ensure contact and support. Once you have determined that you are in the role you enjoy, you can then work on building your motivation through the kind of activities I will be suggesting.

Emotional control

Being able to manage your feelings is a vital skill in consultancy. There are many situations where your emotional control may be challenged, either directly or indirectly. You may come across demanding people; you may run into personal conflict; you may be put under pressure; you may be intimidated; or you may have things going on in your personal life that are at odds with your responsibilities at work. In all these situations, it helps to be able to manage your feelings effectively.

Positive thinking

Allied with emotional control, positive thinking is an asset. Being able to look on the bright side, to remain focused on your goals, to understand the good intentions behind other people's seemingly negative behaviour and to imagine a beneficial result in all that you do. These are key skills in consultancy.

You may be surprised that I use the word 'skill' in this context, but how you think (and how you feel) can, to a very large extent, be managed. When you direct your thoughts in a positive way, not only are you more likely to achieve results, you are also more likely to remain healthy in the process. The developing field of PSI (psychoneuroimmunology) teaches that what goes on in your mind is inter-related with what goes on in your body. So positive thoughts and feelings produce biological reactions that keep you well; conversely, negative thoughts and feelings create an environment where disease (dis-ease) can flourish.

These four elements – confidence, motivation, emotional control and positive thinking – all contribute to your ability to manage yourself. Let's now move on to ways in which you can enhance your skills in these areas.

Self-management skills

There are two major ways in which you can develop; the first is through experience and the second is through imagination. Many years ago I took on a new job. In meetings, I found I was observing my behaviour and I thought, "This is interesting; it's not really me." In other words I was almost role-playing – taking on a part that I believed was appropriate. Many years later I find that the behaviours that were so unusual for me then are now part of my everyday activity; they have become incorporated into my self-image and they are no longer role-playing.

The process I have described took many years, however. If you were to develop your consultancy skills solely through this kind of process, which is what many consultants do, it would be a long time before you were competent. There is an alternative, however, and that is to supplement real-life experience by using your imagination.

Your mind is capable of taking suggestions and acting as if they were real. This is very apparent with phobic behaviour, when, for example, a person is 'afraid' of snakes, heights, public speaking and so on. The person's mind presents them with scenarios, scenarios that seem very real, and the result is that their behaviour is affected by their mental processing. Sometimes what goes on in a person's mind is really disabling and they do not know how to get out of their 'mind set'.

The mind does not work in isolation. In order to produce behaviour, feelings are also involved. So the person who is afraid of heights may begin by feeling sick, giddy or anxious. The feelings then link to behaviour, which might be changes in breathing, immobility, running away or a whole range of other responses. The mind and body work together.

Another factor, to which I have already referred, is the close link between mental and physical health. Negative mental states can lead to physiological changes that can result in various kinds of ailments such as high blood pressure, headaches, stomach aches and digestive problems, as well as accident-proneness, poor sleep patterns, irritability and difficulty in concentrating. Long-term, even more serious illnesses, in particular auto-immune responses and cancers, have been linked to negative thoughts and feelings.

That's the bad news. The good news is that, just as your mind can create 'dis-ease', it can also create positive states, which lead to enhanced performance, better health and improved relationships. I will be considering relationships in Chapter 10; in this chapter I will give you some ideas on how you can develop your self-management skills through using your thoughts, feelings and behaviour in positive ways. The kind of techniques I will be covering are now in common use in many fields, including sports, where top sports people use them to enhance their performance; education, where students use them to improve their studying and exam performance; and health, where health practitioners and patients use them to support, or replace, traditional medical processes.

So, what are these techniques and how can they be of use to you as a consultant?

Self-awareness

The first step is to become aware of what you are doing at any particular time. It is difficult to plan a journey if you do not know where you are starting from – you cannot set a direction, map out a route or estimate your journey time unless you know where you are to begin with. Similarly, to adopt more effective behaviour, you need to know how you are doing at present.

So the first thing I would like to suggest is that you consider self-observation as your initial process. You can use self-observation in any situation, although, because it involves an element of detachment, it is probably more appropriate to use it in situations where you do not wish, or need, to be immersed in the experience. If you are at a concert, enjoying a relaxing bath or sharing reminiscences with an old friend, self-observation may take you out of the experience and distance you from your immersion in sensory stimulation. The best times to use self-observation are when you need to monitor what you are doing or when you want to assess how you behave in a specific context.

Let's take some examples that are relevant to consultancy. Here are some situations where it can be helpful to use self-observation. Think about each one and consider what your 'rating' might be in each. High self-awareness means you usually are conscious of what you are doing and how you are coming across, and low self-awareness means you usually do not pay attention to yourself in such situations. Please note that I am not making any connection here between self-awareness and the *kind* of assessment you make of yourself. You may be critical, accepting or praising of yourself; this is not relevant here. The only question you are being asked is whether you actually do notice things about yourself.

Situation	Generally high self-awareness	Variable self-awareness	Generally low self-awareness
• Meeting new people			
• Making a presentation			
• Telephoning a prospective client			
• Dining with colleagues			
• Driving your car			
• Chairing a meeting			
• Negotiating a contract			
• Giving feedback to an associate			
• Announcing delays in schedules			
• Asking for assistance			

'Dissociation'

If most of your ticks are in the 'generally high self-awareness' column, you probably spend a good deal of time in what is called, in NLP, a 'dissociated' state. Being dissociated means being detached, so that you can observe yourself as if you were at a distance – the 'fly on the wall' situation.

Dissociation is useful as it allows you to monitor yourself and be aware of what you are doing at any given time. This is particularly helpful in those business situations where you need to really be in control of yourself. For example, in a negotiation, it helps to know if you are frowning when you are unsure of your bargaining power, whether you look directly at the other person when you do not agree with what they say, or whether your voice pitch rises when you feel challenged. These movements and sounds may be picked up by the other person, who then has better information about how you are thinking and feeling. Even if they are not picked up directly, the other person may well sense them at an unconscious level, and the interaction can be affected by such non-verbal 'signals'.

Another example of when dissociation is useful is during presentations. When you are presenting to others it is helpful to know the tone of voice you are using, where you are looking, whether you are using any repetitive movements, how fast you are speaking and similar aspects of your behaviour. Understanding what you are doing enables you to check whether your actions are appropriate for the people with whom you are interacting or whether you are losing them, irritating them or enthusing them.

'Association'

If most of your ticks are in the 'generally low self-awareness' column, you probably spend much of your time in an 'associated' state. This is the opposite of dissociated and means that you are so immersed in your experiences that you do not step back and evaluate them. There are advantages to association. For example, if you are really enthused about something, your excitement and motivation may well spread to other people, making them more positive and enthusiastic. But if you stay in an associated state when someone is being critical of you, or when you are anxious about speaking to someone, then your behaviour is likely to be simply reactive, rather than calculated and managed, and you may be a 'victim of your emotions'.

It is worth practising both association and dissociation, and especially dissociation, to help you manage yourself more effectively. Practising dissociation is particularly important in the context of this section of the book, as it will enable you to be more self-aware, which is a foundation of good self-management.

So, how do you practise dissociation? Here are some suggestions, which I hope you will find interesting and easy to do:

191

● *Running commentary*

The first way is to give yourself a running commentary on what you are doing. For example, in a meeting you might tell yourself how you are sitting, who you are looking at, what tone of voice you are using and so forth. Each time you go through this process you will gain useful information that you might otherwise have missed. Do your commentary silently, in your head; otherwise people around you might think you are a little strange!

● *Bleeps*

If you have a clock or watch that can bleep (or a 'stand-alone' timer) you can set it to go off, say, in fifteen minutes' time. If you set the timer for at least this time ahead it will get over any tendency you may have to 'clock-watch' in anticipation of it going off. When it bleeps, notice yourself, looking out for the things I mentioned in the paragraph above – your appearance, voice, eye contact and so forth. You can also use the telephone or a pager for this purpose and check what you are doing each time you hear the sound of someone calling you.

● *Using colleagues*

An alternative is to brief a colleague to interrupt you periodically with a request to observe yourself. You might ask the person to do this at random, or to do it if they notice you doing something that they think you might benefit from observing. This is a good way of getting feedback too, as you can then compare your own self-observation with the observations made by your colleague to see how similar or different they are. If they do differ, you might discuss the differences with your colleague to check on whose perception was most useful at that particular time.

● *Catching yourself out*

Finally, you could rely on your own 'unconscious' processing to notice things. Rather in the way it is possible to decide to wake up at a certain time in the morning and then do so regardless of whether an alarm clock has been set, it is possible to 'programme' your mind to notice your thoughts, feelings and behaviour when there is something worth being aware of. To use this process, simply keep the thought in mind that you will be alert to things that are useful to observe, and then trust that your unconscious mind will let you know when there is something to notice – it really does work.

Now you have some ways of using self-awareness and observation, let's just go over some of the things to which you might pay particular attention.

- *Posture*

Noticing your posture is useful because there is a good deal of difference between a 'positive' posture and a 'negative' one. If you want to come across as confident and in control of situations, it helps to have an upright, open, balanced and flexible posture. So notice whether you sit, stand and move easily and comfortably. Check you are not hunched up and that you are not holding tension in your muscles. Allow your head to move freely on your neck, your shoulders to drop, your arms to move easily and your spine to lengthen and straighten without rigidity. Such a posture will allow you to maintain composure, move easily and create an impression of coordination and freedom.

- *Gestures and movements*

Noticing your gestures is important, as you might otherwise develop irritating mannerisms or use movements that could appear condescending or insulting. Different cultures have different attitudes towards particular gestures, so if you are operating in an international arena it is worth checking whether there are any particular gestures you should avoid in the countries you visit. I have already covered some elements of cultural difference in Chapter 6. Some particular gestures that are best avoided are ◆Repetitive ones, such as constantly turning a ring or fiddling with your watch strap;

◆Noisy ones, such as jangling keys in your pocket or tapping a table with a pen; ◆Ambiguous ones that could be misinterpreted, such as pointing a finger at someone or clapping your hands to gain attention.

● *Facial expression*

Noticing your expression is also important as it gives distinct messages to other people. So it is worth checking whether you look ◆Serious; ◆Relaxed; ◆Amused; ◆Bored; ◆Interested; ◆Enthusiastic; and so forth. Notice whether you are focusing on your own thoughts or paying attention to other people around you; when you are engaged in your own thoughts you are likely to appear defocused and detached as you may be looking into the distance or away from the other person. A mobile and responsive face is a great aid to social interaction. Remember that, even though you think you may be conveying a particular emotion or reaction, other people might interpret your manner differently, so be watchful for any signs of how others actually perceive you (without misreading their reactions!).

● *Voice*

Noticing your voice is helpful as it allows you to check that you are speaking in a manner appropriate to the situation. You can check your volume, speed, tone, rhythm, pitch and projection. Good voice usage and projection depend on effective breathing and use of your vocal cords, facial cavities and diaphragm. If you think your voice or projection could be improved, there are aids to this such as books, tapes and voice teachers. (See Bibliography.)

● *Appearance*

Noticing your appearance is also important. There is a whole subject called Impression Management, which I will cover in Chapter 10. At this point it is simply worth remembering that the visual appearance you create through your clothes, hair, accessories and cosmetics can make a major impact on others. So checking your hair is brushed or combed, your clothes and shoes remain clean, your nails are cleaned and any cosmetics are re-applied as necessary will all help you maintain a positive and professional image.

Control of thoughts and feelings

The next step in self-management is being able to control your thoughts and feelings. People often say they are victims of their emotions and that people make them feel bad, angry or upset. However, the truth is that you are very much the 'owner' of your thoughts and feelings, and by managing them effectively, you can be much more successful.

So how do you do this? It is useful to know that thoughts and feelings have structures, and once you understand their structures, you can – if you wish – change them to get different results. Let's take some examples of how to change the structure of your thoughts and feelings.

Example 1
Suppose you have been to a meeting where you became annoyed at the behaviour of certain people who were present, but did not challenge them or explain your own responses. At the meeting you became irritated with the people, and after the meeting, you became annoyed with yourself for not having responded differently. What could you have done differently, either during the meeting or afterwards? Let's consider some options.

- You could have taken some deep breaths so that you had more oxygen available to maintain your physiology. This would also have given you time to consider the situation and to evaluate your choices.

- You could have shifted your perspective so that you imagined what it was like for the other people. In this way you could have gained a new understanding of how they might be responding, and you could also have gained a different view (dissociated) of how you yourself were coming across to them. Once you have a different perspective on things you can choose whether to take a different course of action.

- You could have interpreted the behaviour differently, so that you represented it differently to yourself. It is very easy to have just one explanation of events but, by assessing them in a different way, it is possible to come to a different conclusion. For example, a leaky roof may be perceived as a disaster, or it can be assessed as an ideal opportunity to change your decor for the better. The shift of interpretation allows you to find room for a positive outcome to an apparently negative occurrence.

- You could have changed your 'internal voice' to a more pleasant one. Often, when things seem to go badly, we have a conversation in our head that steadily makes us feel negative, upset, depressed, apathetic and so on. The kind of internal voice that has this effect often has a complaining, whiny, angry or some other rather negative tonality. By changing the tonality of the voice it is possible to stop the negativity and substitute something more positive. All you have to do to achieve this is to imagine a more positive-sounding voice saying more constructive things. For example, instead of an irritated voice saying you should have spoken up, you could have a comforting voice saying you did well to keep out of conflict, or an enthusiastic voice saying you now have the opportunity to do it differently next time.

- You could have remembered a time when you handled a similar situation very well. As you recalled the situation, imagining it in great detail and seeing your surroundings, hearing any words spoken and re-accessing the feelings of doing well, you would have taken on the physiology you had at the time (the posture, breathing, facial expression and so forth). By re-living the past experience you give yourself a way of remembering that you can handle things well and a way of re-accessing the feelings that go with such effective self-management.

So these are some examples of changing structures; as long as you maintain the same structure in your responses you are likely to get the same resulting thoughts and feelings. By changing certain elements in your habitual responses, you enable yourself to get a different result.

Example 2

Suppose you have to make a presentation to a potential client, but are a little anxious in case you do not come across well; a number of very senior people will be present and you know you are competing with other consultants who are likely to be quite experienced at this kind of event. What could you do beforehand to ensure the occasion goes well? Let's consider some options:

- You could picture the scene, putting in lots of positive images of a welcoming environment and interested people. By making your mental images big, bright, colourful and active you will bring interest and anticipation to the event.

- You could imagine the sound of conversation; hearing interested questions, lively comments and positive intimations of future contact. By making the tonality of the sounds positive and pleasing you can create an impression of enthusiasm and enjoyment.

- You could give yourself the sense of being there and doing it well; by imagining how it would feel to be making the presentation in a confident, competent and creative manner, being relaxed yet energetic, calm yet enthusiastic, composed yet motivated.

- You could say positive things to yourself in your mind, using statements which use the present tense (for example: "I am sounding clear and concise"; "I am conveying my meaning effectively"; "I am dealing with questions in a straightforward manner").

All these approaches give your mind the impression that things are going well so that, when you come to the event itself, it will seem familiar and you are pre-disposed to carry it off in a positive manner.

Generating Enthusiasm

The preceding sections have dealt with the different techniques you can use for self-management; finally, here is another way of creating and maintaining energy, enthusiasm and motivation. This technique gives you a sense of a future where you have achieved the goal you desire.

You can do this exercise – which is an extension of the exercise I described in Chapter 4 – in your head, but it is often much more powerful to walk it out, physically, as I will now explain.

Step one

Choose a goal, a particular objective you have that can easily be defined – for example handling a negotiation well, driving a new car or sorting out your filing.

Step two

Mark out an imaginary line on the ground. You can do this in any reasonable-sized room, or you can do it outdoors. The length of the line does not matter too much as long as it gives you reasonable space to move along several steps; somewhere around ten feet would be a good length. The end of the line closest to you will represent the present time, and the end of the line furthest from you will represent the future.

Step three

Stand on the end of the line that represents the present time. Look towards the other end of the line and picture yourself there, having achieved the goal. If you are good at visualising you will probably be able to see yourself clearly. If you think you are not good at visualising, simply get a sense of being there at the end of the line, having achieved the goal. As you picture yourself, notice how you will be looking, what you will be doing, how other people will be reacting to you and so on. Get as vivid an image as possible of all these things. This is likely to form a compelling picture that will draw you towards it.

Step four

Walk slowly along the line towards the point where you were picturing yourself in the future. As you move along the line, notice any sensations or awarenesses; you may find you have an increasing sense of excitement, satisfaction, energy or other feelings. When you reach the end, stand in the spot where you had pictured the future. You can either remain facing the direction in which you have been walking, or you can turn around; it depends on how you were picturing yourself initially – with your front or your back to the beginning of the line. Notice how it feels to be achieving your goal. Become aware of your thoughts and of the feelings in your body.

Step five

Now, with your back to the point at which you originally started, walk back along the line towards the present time until you are at the beginning of the line again; at that point turn around again so you are in your original position. As you move along the line you will be bringing back to the present time all those personal resources that you had in that imagined future. This will keep you aware of your capabilities and remind you of the sense of achievement you have generated. You will also be able to see, again, the image of yourself in the future, behaving in the way you have now experienced.

Step six

Back in the present, review the process. If you wish, you can now repeat the exercise, either as before, to strengthen your motivation, or adding in further steps to give you more information. Some of the further steps you could add are: ♦Taking a few steps beyond the future point and turning round so you can look back at your achievement from a time even further into the future; ✦Noticing which is the first step you have to take towards your goal, (the physical step on the line represents the actual step in real life), and then noticing succeeding steps that move you further towards it; ✦Moving to the future point and noticing what is the last step you took before you reached it, then working backwards checking what each preceding step had been; ✦Stepping off the line at any point you wish in order to observe yourself on the line from a detached position, rather as if you were someone else watching you.

Doing this exercise will help you motivate yourself as it makes achievement of your goals seem more real and attainable. You also create real feelings as you move along the line, and your mind will remember those feelings as if they have already happened.

Final Points

This chapter has given you a few ways in which you can manage yourself well and, in the process, enhance your self-concept and self-esteem. There are many, many more techniques that are helpful in this respect, and if you feel sufficiently enthusiastic, you can follow up this introduction to them and enhance your self-management skills even further. You could even teach them to others, as I suggested at the start of the chapter.

NLP techniques used in this chapter and the section where you can find them

Association/dissociation (self-awareness)
Internal dialogue (running commentary)
Unconscious processing (catching yourself out)
Perceptual positions (control of thoughts and feelings)
Reframing (control of thoughts and feelings)
Internal dialogue – self-talk (control of thoughts and feelings)
Anchoring (control of thoughts and feelings)
Submodality changes (control of thoughts and feelings)
Time lines/new behaviour generation (generating enthusiasm)

Chapter 9
Managing Work Effectively

This chapter covers additional self-management skills that are particularly useful in consultancy.

Having explored some of the basic self-management skills in the previous chapter, I would now like to turn to those personal skills that help in the overall management of your consultancy business:

- Memory enhancement.
- Time management.
- Stress avoidance.

Memory Enhancement

A good memory is a real asset to a consultant. Being able to remember your clients when they call, even if you have not been in touch with them for some time, really helps. Many years ago my own memory needed enhancing considerably – as the following anecdote illustrates. I was in a supermarket on a Saturday, fairly focused on the task in hand. Someone spoke to me, and when I looked up, he said, "You don't remember me, do you?" I had to admit I didn't. He then said "I interviewed you for the job you are starting on Monday." That was a good case for learning some memory-enhancement skills! So what can you do to improve your memory?

Believe you can do it

If you believe you will not remember things, you probably will not remember them. On the other hand, if you convince yourself that you are capable of remembering, you are likely to put more effort into doing so, and thereby to become more successful. So it is worth repeating to yourself statements such as "I have a good memory", "I am good at recalling people's names and faces" and "Every day I am improving my recall of things".

Intend to remember

Having the intention of remembering also fixes things in your mind. When you meet someone new, tell yourself you are going to remember the person's name and face. When you travel a particular route, tell yourself you will be able to retrace it another time. When you have appointments in your diary, tell yourself you can remember them even before opening the page. By putting yourself in 'memory mode' you make it easier to recall things and store them in your memory.

Understand memory training principles

There are various principles that underlie effective recall. Numerous books have been written on the topic, and I have referred to some of them in the Bibliography. Here are a few of the commonest elements in memory development:

- *Distinguishing between short- and long-term memory*

  There is a difference between recalling things in the short and the long term. Short-term memory is relatively easily brought about, as long as you decide to remember, as I mentioned above. To remember things some time after the event, however, requires a little more preparation. To commit something to long-term memory, it helps to go over it a few times so that it becomes lodged in your mind.

  Suppose you have to remember some details about a person – perhaps their name, where they live and how old they are. Once you have this information to hand, repeat it to yourself once or twice. An hour or so later do the same again; then the same next day. Then a week later repeat the information to yourself. If you wish, do it again after a month. By repeating the information at intervals, it becomes more permanently installed in your memory. If you do not do this, it is likely that you will not keep the information in your head for long, so repetition, at intervals, is important.

Unless you use memory-retention techniques, much is lost in a short time. Colin Rose (see Bibliography) refers to work by Hermann Ebbinghaus, who conducted the first scientific experiments on memory in the late 1800s. Ebbinghaus found that forgetting could be plotted on a graph (the Ebbinghaus Curve of Forgetting), and this indicates that around 40% of information is lost after 20 minutes, 70% after 24 hours and 80% after a month. It should, however, be remembered that Ebbinghaus experimented with nonsense phrases, which eliminate everything that is vital in preserving memory, so when elements that support retention are provided, memory is greatly enhanced.

- *Using association, exaggeration and humour*

If there is something you want to remember, using these three things – association, exaggeration and humour – will help you retain the facts. For example, suppose you want to remember a client's interest in motorcycle racing. You could note a feature of the person's face and then make a link with racing – maybe the person has lines on their forehead, which you could imagine being a racetrack. You could then use exaggeration and humour to imagine that between these lines are hundreds and hundreds of tiny cyclists, all wearing brightly coloured suits and making funny sounds as they speed along. When you see the person next you should recall the images and remember the connection.

Another way of remembering is to make an association between the person's name and the activity (motorcycle racing), so that when they telephone you the sound of their name will recall their interest. For example, if the person is called Mike you could think 'Mike - Bike' to make that link. It may take a little while to become proficient in this, but practising it will add greatly to your ability to remember information well.

- *Stimulating different senses*

NLP shows how to utilise the different senses, and I will be returning to this topic in Chapter 11. In relation to memory, it helps to engage all the different senses in order to enhance an experience and retain it in your mind for longer. For example, suppose you want to remember a particular meeting – who was there, where people were sitting, who said what, etc. You can stimulate each of your senses in order to do this.

So go through the senses one at a time to bring the experience to life. I list them in a particular order here, but you should start with whichever sense you find easiest to access and then move on to the others in whichever order you prefer.

First, your visual sense: picture the meeting, and make your image large, bright, colourful, moving and clear. Really see all the detail in that image – people, objects, furnishings and so forth. Then your sense of hearing: memorise the sounds, recall each person's voice, with their vocal characteristics such as intonation exactly as they were. Add in any other sounds, such as papers rustling, teacups rattling and extraneous sounds such as doors shutting or aeroplanes overhead. Then your sense of touch: put in any physical sensations, such as the feeling of the chair on which you were sitting, the pen in your hand, the degree of warmth and so forth. Remembering you emotions at the time will strengthen the process – perhaps enthusiasm, perhaps curiosity, perhaps anticipation. Finally, add any taste or smell sensations: maybe you had just had some tea and a biscuit, and perhaps there were some flowers on the table or the scent of marker pens being used. Once you put together all these sensory elements, you will be bringing the event to life and the more you replay these elements in your mind, the easier it will be to recall the actual occasion.

- *Use a memory system*

  There are several of these, mostly utilising principles of association in order to work; I will mention just two of them here.

- *Memory pegs*

  One system involves using numbers and linking each number with an object that rhymes with it. A common way of doing this is as follows: one-gun, two-shoe, three-tree, four-door, five-hive, six-sticks, seven-heaven, eight-gate, nine-vine, ten-pen. You then take the items or activities you wish to remember and list them in sequence; for example, you might be driving to a meeting and want to remember to raise two additional issues when you arrive but, because you are driving, you cannot write them down as you think of them. Let's suppose the issues are as follows: ♦Discussing car-related arrangements; ♦Sorting out who will chair the following meeting. Taking the rhyming example, you could do the following: one-gun – imagine a car's tyres being shot at with a water pistol filled with glittery paint that colours them in dazzling colours. This should help you think of the car-leasing topic. Two-shoe – imagine a giant shoe filled with minute papers and tiny chairs. The combination of the two should help you remember to check who will chair the meeting. The association technique should help you remember the topics, and the more you can exaggerate and use humour in your imagined scenarios, the easier the items will be to remember.

- *Numbers into words*

  Another system involves remembering numbers by turning them into words, as words are generally more memorable than figures. This system is a little like shorthand, in that consonants are used, but not vowels. To translate, you equate each number from 0 to 10 with a letter; letters with the same phonetic sound are interchangeable. Zero translates to Z or S; 1 translates to T or D, 2 translates to N, 3 translates to M, 4 translates to R, 5 translates to L, 6 translates to J or Ch, 7 translates to K or G, 8 translates to F or V and 9 translates to P or B.

Examples: 8430 becomes furry mice and 410201 becomes red sunset; you can put whatever vowels you like in with the consonants, as they do not count.

This system is excellent for remembering telephone numbers and financial details. A good way of practising it is to read car number plates and turn them into words.

Time Management

Managing time is an important skill for anyone in business. It is only too easy to allow the unimportant activities to dominate your time, or to spend unnecessary hours adding final touches of which only you will be aware. I mentioned the Pareto Principle in Chapter 7; there are a number of other principles involved in effective time management and, by utilising these, you should find your effectiveness substantially enhanced. Let's take the principles in turn and find out which ones could add most to your success.

Relationship to time

How you relate to time influences what you achieve in it. I have already mentioned a little about this in Chapter 6 and would like to develop this further here. Take a few moments to consider your usual state of activity.

Would you describe yourself as:

A   Generally in a rush, with too much to do and lots of things unfinished?
B   Usually able to get most things get done and to stay in control of your activities?
C   Normally unhurried, seeming to have plenty of time to do everything you want?

If you have an appointment are you generally:

A   There on time or early, and feeling uncomfortable if you are delayed?
B   On time, but able to accept delays without too much concern ?
C   Often late and not particularly bothered if this is the case?

If you have to plan a project, do you:

A   Find it easy to see the time it will take and how different elements will fit together?
B   Find it hard to plan for what to do first, as everything seems to be important?
C   Make a good start, but find some aspects difficult to put into perspective?

Those people who are well organised, able to work to deadlines and punctual seem to have an inbuilt mechanism for controlling how they work. Of course time management can be learned; that is the purpose of this section of the book. But some people do seem to have the ability to manage their time almost instinctively. So why is this?

Before we go on, here is a little exercise for you; it may seem strange, but do bear with it for a few minutes. Please do each of the following as quickly as you can:

1.   Think of an event that happened a few months ago. As you remember the event, become aware of where you are imagining it (not where it actually was, but where your mental representation of the event is). Point to that spot.

2. Think of an event that occurred a few days ago; again point to the spot where you are imagining it.

3. Think of an event that will take place in a few days' time; again point to its spot.

4. Think of an event that will come about in a few months' time; again point to it.

If you had any difficulty in doing this, you may find it useful to know some places to which other people point when doing this exercise. Some of the examples are: ◆In front; ◆Behind; ◆Above; ◆In their head. The events may also be perceived at different distances and angles, for example: "Six feet in front of me"; "A couple of feet to my right"; "Just next to my left ear".

Assuming you have locations for the four events, draw an imaginary line between all four of them and notice where the line is and what its shape is. Your line may be any shape; some people have spirals, some straight lines, some jagged shapes and so on. These lines are called 'time lines' and are one example of how NLP can work with a physical representation of time.

There are two main types of time line that people working in NLP have identified; there are others, but these two seem to be fairly distinct patterns. The first is a line that goes from back to front, passing through where the person is standing; this is referred to as being 'in-time' – not on time, or punctual, but in your own time line. The second is a line that goes from left to right at a distance in front of the person; this is called 'through-time'. These are NLP concepts I mentioned previously in Chapter 6.

Although a generalisation, certain patterns of behaviour have been attributed to people who tend to be in-time or through-time. In-time people seem to be immersed in their activities and not so able to separate out past, present and future, or to work with time planning and estimation; they are often late for appointments and find their tasks run behind schedule. Through-time people tend to be more detached from their activities, able to see them clearly, work out how long things will take and be good at monitoring time as it passes; they are generally punctual and reliable.

Knowing what your tendency is will help you enormously in time management. If you tend to think of yourself as a poor time manager, you may find it helps to envisage your activities and, if possible, 'project' them in front of you, or actually draw them on a chart. Seeing what you have to do, and noticing the connections between things, can help make you feel less associated (see Chapter 8) with the tasks and more able to take an objective view of what needs to be done and how and when.

Objectives

Having clear and well-defined objectives helps you avoid time spent on irrelevancies; the more you can focus your efforts on what your main purpose is, the more streamlined and directed your activities will be.

I have covered goal-setting already in Chapter 4, so please look at that section again if you need reminding of how to set objectives.

Standards

I mentioned Pareto in Chapter 7, and Pareto's principle applies very much to time management. It is easy to put in unnecessary effort in order to achieve the additional 20% of results that take up the additional 80% of time; the skill is in knowing where to stop.

So one underlying question here is, "What standard is actually required?" By aiming too high it is possible to achieve excellent quality, but at the expense of other activities that could have been completed in the same time. A good test for performance is whether the additional input will actually be noticed. You may be aware that a report could be improved by the addition of a further two charts, or that a presentation could have included just one more slide; however, those on the receiving end may not miss the additional elements (and could, indeed, be pleased by the relative brevity of your offering).

So checking what standard is really needed, as opposed to what is possible, is one way of keeping down activity, and thereby time.

Prioritising

Setting priorities is another essential element. There will probably always be competing demands on your time and it is necessary to know which to respond to, and when. There are many systems for setting priorities and a simple one has two elements – urgency and importance. Urgent things need to be done quickly, but may not need to have much time spent on them. Important things need to have adequate resources devoted to them, but may not need to be done at once. So a good classification system allows you to consider both of these elements independently.

One commonly used system for setting priorities has four categories: ◆Urgent and important; ◆Urgent but not important; ◆Important but not urgent; ◆Neither urgent nor important. Your priorities will generally be to do the tasks in this order – and you can label the categories A,B,C,D or 1,2,3,4 or UI,U,I,X or whatever you prefer. The important thing is to label each task according to one of these categories and then carry them out in that order. You do not have to physically label each task, although it does help, but it is important to label them mentally, so you know, as each one comes up, how you will respond to it.

Once you have set your priorities, then you should keep to them unless unexpected occurrences make it essential to change course.

Making lists

Lists are an invaluable aid to time management and they can be used for a variety of purposes. Some examples of lists are the following:

- What to do today.
- What to do tomorrow.
- Whom to telephone.
- Whom to write to or e-mail.
- What to purchase.

It is generally helpful to make a new list of activities each day and to have some system for marking, on that list – possibly with highlighters – what are the most important things to do. One good way of doing this is to have your list on Post-it® notes; in this way you can rearrange your activities if you choose and you can simply take away the notes relating to those activities you have completed. It can be very encouraging to see your lists decreasing or your notes diminishing.

If your lists seem to increase rather than decrease, it may be necessary for you to re-evaluate your priorities. It could be that you are still not getting to grips with your main objectives, or it could be that a major priority is to take on assistance rather than attempt to do everything yourself.

Dealing with time-wasters

What people consider to be time-wasters varies considerably; here are some of the things people commonly list.

- Unexpected visitors.
- Telephone interruptions.
- Slow reading.
- Not delegating appropriately.
- Putting things off.
- Unnecessary or delayed travel.
- Unwanted mail or e-mail.
- Misfiling, not filing or mislaying papers.
- Clutter obscuring current work.
- Dealing with papers more than once.
- Dealing with unimportant and non-urgent things.
- Excessive socialising during work time.
- Too high standards.

Time may be wasted actively or passively; active time-wasting is when you choose to spend more time on things than they deserve, and passive time-wasting is when you allow things to take up time unnecessarily. Of course some things may seem to be a waste of time, but can actually be very fruitful; however, one of the skills in any business is identifying those things that really are unproductive and then avoiding spending time on them.

There are many different ways of dealing with time-wasters; here are some thoughts on the list above.

- *Asking visitors to re-schedule meetings with you*

  Allowing people to take up your time when you are busy diverts you from things you need to do. Suggest a different time when you will be available so they feel you are not putting them off completely. You can also discourage unwanted visitors by: ◆**Putting** up a 'do not disturb' sign, or some other means of indicating you are busy; ◆**Telling** them at the start of a conversation that you only have a specified time available; ◆**Avoiding** all the usual signs of encouragement (smiling, nodding and so forth – I will be dealing with this further in Chapter 10).

- *Putting your telephone on to answer machine or voicemail or diverting it elsewhere*

  Remember that answer machines still mean the calls need dealing with, so only do this when you really need uninterrupted time.

- *Going on a rapid reading course*

  There are many courses available on rapid reading; there are also courses on a different approach to information assimilation. These latter courses have names such as Photoreading and Quantum Reading (often trademarked titles), which give ways of assimilating information extremely rapidly, without necessarily having conscious awareness of everything you have read.

- *Delegating where appropriate and feasible*

  If you cannot delegate because you cannot afford the staff, consider taking on agency services for some of your activities; many activities can be outsourced, and this can be a helpful way of dealing with overload.

- *Doing things as soon as possible*

  Dealing with things quickly means you do not have to spend time remembering what they are about at some later time. It can also give you a great sense of satisfaction to know they have been done, as well as avoiding the feeling of being submerged when you see piles of tasks waiting to be completed.

- *Cancelling non-important travel or taking work or reading on journeys by public transport*

  Travelling is time-consuming and can also be mentally and physically exhausting. If you do have to travel, public transport can give you a possibility of resting, or of catching up with unfinished business.

- *Having, and using, an effective filing system*

  Searching for 'lost' items is time-consuming and irritating. There are many ways of filing things so they are easily retrievable, and you may want to design your own system for your particular needs. Whatever system you use, putting things away regularly will help ensure you have a tidy work space and can locate items quickly and easily.

- *Tidying up*

  Again, this helps with ease of access to information. A tidy space can also help some people – if they cannot see any clutter, it keeps their mind focused on the task in hand. Putting away those things you are not working on at the time is a good discipline and is likely to help you concentrate better on what you need to do.

- *Handling each item only once if possible*

  Continually returning to the same piece of paper means you are not being as efficient as you could with your time. If an item cannot be dealt with there and then, have a system for putting it somewhere accessible for when you can deal with it. Don't be tempted to put it in a large pile of miscellaneous

213

papers where you will keep seeing it without taking action on it.

- *Keeping to your priorities and focusing on important and urgent items*

   I have already mentioned priorities in this section, but however much you intend to keep to them, it is easy to get diverted for a variety of reasons. Keeping your priorities in mind will help your effectiveness considerably.

- *Keeping social activities to a minimum during work time*

   If you are not naturally a sociable person, this may not be an issue for you, but many people like to spend time with others at work, as well as during out-of-work hours. Small amounts of time spent socialising can soon eat into your productivity, so keep track of the time you spend in this way and aim to reduce it if it is high at present.

- *Working to realistic standards, rather than idealistic ones*

   A quote attributed to Lord Marks is "The price of perfectionism is prohibitive". While maintaining high stadards is admirable, anything beyond reasonableness tends towards Pareto Principle effects, as I have mentioned earlier.

Attitudes

I mentioned relationships with time at the start of this section; another important issue is your attitude towards the things you have to do. No matter how much you prioritise, set standards and organise yourself for work, your attitudes can still get in the way of achievement. In the previous chapter I talked about positive thinking, and that is an important aspect of time management. Being able to think positively about the tasks you undertake will keep you on track, so it is worth analysing your attitudes towards those things you have to do and then taking steps to motivate yourself to do them or, alternatively, choosing to stop doing those things you are not motivated to do and instead devoting your efforts to activities about which you can feel more positive.

I know myself that if something remains uncompleted for a few days, when I have had the choice about doing it or not, it is probably something I do not really wish to do. This knowledge enables me to make a decision about how I will deal with it, and with similar kinds of activity in the future.

Time diaries

An excellent way of checking on your time-management skills is to keep a diary for a couple of weeks before starting a time-management improvement programme, and then keeping one again for a couple of weeks after you have been using time-management techniques for a month or two. A simple time-management diary would be structured like that in the illustration below. In the example, each activity has a column heading and along the left-hand side there is space for each fifteen minutes of the working day. You simply put a tick in the relevant column each fifteen minutes – just mark the heading that has taken up most of your time during that period; you don't need to put in every single thing you did in the time.

Time diary

Time Diary							
	Meals	Travel	E-mail	Meetings	Telephone	Presentations	Preparation
7.30 a.m. – 7.45 a.m.							
7.45 a.m. – 8.00 a.m.							
8.00 a.m. – 8.15 a.m.							
8.15 a.m. – 8.30 a.m.							
8.30 a.m. – 8.45 a.m.							
8.45 a.m. – 9.00 a.m.							
9.00 a.m. – 9.15 a.m.							
9.15 a.m. – 9.30 a.m.							
9.30 a.m. – 9.45 a.m.							

When you complete your first diary, you may well be surprised at what is taking up your time, especially when you look at how long preparatory work can take. For example, many training consultants say it takes them four to five days' preparation to produce one day's training. It will also be interesting for you to see how the time spent during the period when you kept the first diary compares with your subsequent activity when you do the second diary.

Scheduling

Most people have certain times of day when they are at their most productive, either physically or mentally. It is worth checking on this for yourself so that you can schedule activities for times when you can do your best at them. To check on personal effectiveness levels you can keep another diary, or you can combine this analysis with the activity diary I referred to in the previous section.

For an effectiveness diary, I suggest you put thirty-minute segments in, then, each day, you simply put a letter and a number in each space. A good coding system is: M1 for high mental energy, M2 for reasonable mental energy, M3 for low mental energy; P1 for high physical energy, P2 for reasonable physical energy, P3 for low physical energy. If you prefer you could have four categories rather than three for each (mental and physical), or you could use symbols instead of letters as your code. An example of the structure of a diary is given below.

Personal Effectiveness Diary							
	Mon	Tue	Wed	Thu	Fri	Sat	Sun
7.30 a.m. – 8.00 a.m.							
8.00 a.m. – 8.30 a.m.							
8.30 a.m. – 9.00 a.m.							
9.00 a.m. – 9.30 a.m.							
9.30 a.m. – 10.00 a.m.							
10.00 a.m. – 10.30 a.m.							
10.30 a.m. – 11.00 a.m.							
11.00 a.m. – 11.30 a.m.							
11.30 a.m. – 12.00 p.m.							

You will find that once you have kept your diary for a couple of weeks (making sure that period is fairly typical for you, and not a time of very high stress or unusually low activity) you will be able to find your own energy patterns. You can then make use of this information by scheduling tasks that require high concentration at times when your mental energy is likely to be highest and tasks that require high physical energy in times when your physical energy is highest. This should enhance your effectiveness and also increase your feelings of motivation and enthusiasm.

Stress Avoidance

This subject is generally called stress management, but it is better to avoid stress than to have to deal with once it has arrived. So here are a few ideas for avoiding stress, which I hope will be helpful:

- *Maintain a balance*

  Consultancy often involves long hours of work, extensive travel, uncertainty and risk, handling other people's emotions and relationship problems and many other potentially stressful elements. So being able to balance these with more positive factors helps keep you in a good physical, mental and emotional state. Where possible, try to balance work with other activities, and, whether or not this is possible, keep a sense of perspective on work activities so they do not assume too great an importance to the detriment of your general well-being.

- *Keep fit and healthy*

  The better shape you are in, both physically and mentally, the easier it will be to cope with whatever life events you undergo. So have a healthy eating pattern with regular meals, sensible-size portions, plenty of fresh food – especially fruit, vegetables, grains and pulses – lots of water, and low quantities of processed foods and high-fat foods and little or no caffeine and alcohol. Avoiding smoking will also help maintain a healthy state. Take regular exercise, especially aerobic exercise to boost your metabolism, and consider practices such as the Alexander Technique to help your overall balance and management of your physiology. Have adequate sleep and rest, including specific times for relaxation processes that will enable you to change your brainwave patterns in positive ways, leading to both relaxation and creativity.

- *Manage your workload*

As an employed consultant you may have less opportunity to control your workload, although it is always possible to use time-management and administration skills to help manage pressure. As an independent consultant you are more in charge of your own affairs and have more choice about when, where and for how long you work. Of course the bills need to be paid, but, in the long term, being selective about assignments and sensible about working patterns will mean you can carry on for longer and be more effective in what you do.

- *Avoid negativity*

Using some of the techniques I have already referred to in Chapter 8 will help you have more positive thoughts and feelings. Keeping your mind focused on positive mental images, having pleasant and supportive internal voices, using sensory stimulation to retain positive emotions and making shifts of perspective to keep things in context will keep you in a brighter state and one where external irritations can be managed effectively.

- *Retain control*

Stress often arises when we are feel we are not in control. If you think of cause and effect, when you put yourself 'at cause' you can be in control, but if you put yourself 'at effect' you are not in control. If you are at cause you may be under pressure, but you know you are in charge of your thoughts, feelings, behaviour and responses. If you are at effect you may feel that you are being pushed around by others or at the mercy of external forces. To retain control, firstly remember that you can manage your own life, even if you cannot manage those around you, and secondly, use assertive behaviour in order to make sure your opinions and needs are heard and respected. When you can assert your own rights and thoughts and allow others to do the same, it is easier to maintain a sense of direction and a positive approach and to keep on track whatever happens.

Stress can result in a myriad of dmental and physical symptoms, such as sleeplessness, irritability, loss of concentration, indecisiveness, aches and pains, accidents, headaches, stomach pains, indigestion, backache and depression. It can also give rise to mood swings, unpredictability and relationship problems. It is very much in your interest, and that of your family, friends, colleagues and clients, to avoid stress and adopt a balanced and healthy lifestyle.

Final Points

Remembering things, using time effectively and avoiding stress can add significantly to your success as a consultant. A good memory will please your clients, colleagues family and friends, who might otherwise feel overlooked. Good time management will make your work easier and more productive. Stress avoidance should help you live a longer and healthier life. It is not always easy to do these things well, but it is well worth working at for everyone's sake.

NLP techniques used in this chapter and the section where you can find them

Sensory awareness (stimulating different senses)
Time orientation (relationship with time)
Sub-modality shifts (avoid negativity)
Shifts of perspective (avoid negativity)
Perceptual positions (avoid negativity)
Cause-effect management (retain control)

Chapter 10
Building Effective Relationships

This chapter will give you ways of starting and continuing relationships with other people.

In consultancy, much of your time is spent in dealing with other people. Whether they are clients, colleagues, suppliers or anyone else, having the skills to relate well to other people is a mainstay of consultancy effectiveness.

There are different stages involved in relating to others. The first step is to create a positive impression, the second is to help the other person feel comfortable with you and the third is to enable both you and the other person to gain something from the encounter. When these elements are present, it is likely that you will develop a pleasant and mutually beneficial relationship with another person. I would like to consider the first two of these aspects of relationship building in this chapter – Impression Management and rapport – and will turn to the third element in the next chapter.

Impression Management

'Impression Management' is the term given to the process of consciously paying attention to the impact you may have on other people. I believe it is impossible to not make an impact; the only question is what kind of impact you have. A little anecdote will illustrate this.

Many years ago, before closed-circuit television was called video, I was asked to film a training session for a small company that ran courses for sales and marketing staff. Never having used a video camera before, I was given some advice, which consisted of one simple rule: "Never move the camera quickly, or it will be difficult for viewers to watch what is going on." I followed the advice to the letter. Unfortunately, at one stage during the session, a person at one end of the long table around which everyone was seated stopped talking, and a person at the other end began to speak. I moved the camera slowly towards this person, but before I reached him, he stopped speaking and the person at the other end began again. This continued for several minutes and I never caught up with either of them. When the film was played back everyone laughed at the lack of sophistication in the camera technique. I decided the next session would be filmed differently, and only videoed selected activities – people looking bored, fidgeting and so on. When this film was played back it gave a completely distorted impression of what had, actually, been a very good session. It taught me that there is no such thing as complete objectivity and that impressions can be managed.

So what do you need to pay attention to in order to create a positive impression? Three elements are generally considered: ◆Your appearance – what people see when they look at you; ◆Your voice – how you sound when people listen to you; ◆Your words – what people understand when they take in what you are saying. All these things create responses in others, and these responses are often feelings, attitudes, beliefs and opinions about you. So paying attention to how you look, how you sound and what you say will help you come across in a positive and professional manner.

Let's consider each of the elements of impression management – and they all apply equally to men and women, apart from making allowances for any differences in what men and women wear.

Your appearance

In consultancy, a reasonably conventional appearance tends to be the norm, although some people can get away with looking different, informal and more individual. It is, however, easier to depart from convention once you have an established reputation, so unless you have reason to believe you will be well received however you look, it is worth paying attention to what is likely to be the most appropriate way of dressing.

For men, this generally means wearing a suit. Dark colours tend to convey more of a feeling of authority than light colours, although in very hot weather lighter colours may be acceptable. In some countries, where the climate is very hot, lighter clothes may be worn most of the time, but it is still worth checking what is conventional as the opposite applies in other hot countries.

For women, co-ordinated separates, or a dress and jacket, are most often seen as appropriate. Again dark colours convey more authority.

There have been some moves towards informality in clothes, and many organisations are now operating 'dress-down Fridays', when people can wear whatever they like. However, not everyone feels comfortable in casual clothes at work and clients may still not approve of such a dress code, even if some consultancy organisations favour them.

Austin Reed, the outfitters, has been assessing global trends in business dress. They indicate that "… far from taking the world by storm 'dressing-down' has already been overtaken in some countries by 'dressing-up' as companies reinstate *Smart* codes, or customers choose to stick with what they're comfortable with for work" (report in 'Smart' by Roger Tredre). In California '… many of the original dot.com entrepreneurs are now dressing smart again.' And one writer (Benjamin) says, "Men and women want to stand out from the crowd, so the real big-hitters are opting for suits." There is also some indication that economic factors have an influence; Anne Merle Sabbath says, "When the economy is good, people loosen up. Now we're tightening up, we're going back to formality." Austin Reed perceive the overall trend as more flexible, where smart, casual and smart-casual are interchangeable. The main reason for this is the impact of culture and climate on dress – 'dress-down' began in the warm climate of California, but other locations have different requirements and traditions, which are more powerful than passing fashionable trends.

So there is still a degree of variation in what is considered appropriate. The best advice I can give you is to do some research into what is conventional in the organisations – and countries – in which you will be working.

> *Example*
> One young woman consultant I met recently had been told that she looked too unapproachable because she favoured black suits or black dresses with white blouses, and was asked to wear more colourful clothes to help clients relate to her better.

As well as clothes, grooming is also part of your total image, so it is worth paying attention to that too. Consider hair, skin care and cosmetics and make sure you are always presentable; take a few moments to brush or comb your hair before a meeting and to touch up any make-up you may be wearing. Also consider shoes, tights, ties, scarves, belts, watches and jewellery and make sure they are clean and fit well.

With clothes, accessories and cosmetics it helps to coordinate them with your own colouring and proportions, so they complement you rather than dominate or look insipid. There are many books available on this subject (see Bibliography), so I will simply mention a few principles here.

- *Colour*

    Colours that complement your own natural colouring tend to work best. So, if you are dark-haired you may well look best in deep colours, and if you have light hair you may look best in lighter colours; if you have a warm (reddish) colouring you may look best in warm (yellow-based) colours, and if you have a cool (blue toned) colouring you may look best in cool (blue-based) colours. If you have muted skin tones you may look best in soft tones, and if you have a bright colouring with lots of contrast between your skin and hair colouring you may look best in clothes with colours that have a lot of contrast between them. This principle holds for clothes, hair, accessories and cosmetics.

- *Shape and scale*

Matching what you wear to your own proportions works well. So if you are tall and heavy-boned you can wear chunky clothes, with bold designs and large accessories, whereas if you are small and light-boned you will probably look best in neat, tailored clothes with classic lines and unobtrusive accessories. Similarly, if you are angular with long limbs, you will be best in clothes with straight, geometric lines, while if you are more rounded you will look best in clothes with a softer cut.

Of course, if you simply want to make a dramatic impression, you can ignore these suggestions and wear whatever you think will create an impact but, for professional credibility, it is probably best to work with your proportions and body line, rather than against them.

- *Optical illusions*

Whatever your colouring, shape and size, you can create differing effects through some strategic selection of items. For example, turn-ups on trousers will shorten your apparent height: bright earrings will draw attention to your face and away from any 'problem areas' such as hips; cutaway shirt collars will make your neck look thicker and your face look rounder; and a belt matched to the colour of your blouse will make you look longer-waisted (longer top half in proportion to bottom half).

By focusing attention on one area, you take it away from another, and by counteracting your body line with different shapes you can affect the apparent balance.

- *Accessories*

   As well as how you look personally, your accessories and accoutrements, such as briefcases, pens, mobile phones, your car and your business stationery, also affect your impression on others. Having classic and understated accessories will give an impression of competence (and also conventionality), while trendy, colourful accessories can create an impression of being up to date (or 'off the wall'). So choose carefully and remember that everything has an impact, and it is up to you to manage that impact for better or for worse.

Having considered how you look, let's now turn to how you sound.

Your voice

Some people's voices are naturally appealing, some project well so they can be heard clearly at a distance, some have a hypnotic effect, some sound authoritative and powerful. Learning to use your voice well is a distinct asset in consultancy, so how do you set about enhancing yours?

The first thing to remember is that your voice is influenced by your physiology – for example, men and women's vocal cords are different, so the pitch of their voice differs. In addition, your posture can affect voice production; if you sit hunched up with your arms crossed and your chin close to your chest, it is unlikely you will be able to expand your lungs enough to provide sufficient oxygen with which to speak and project your voice.

Your state of health can also affect your voice. If you have a sore throat, congested lungs because of smoking, a dry mouth from overindulgence in alcohol, or are tired, run-down or stressed, your voice is likely to suffer. So keeping fit and healthy will also enable you to use your voice well.

There is also a cultural element to voice. In some languages, tonality is more varied than in others, leading to a more rhythmic and varied sound. I found it interesting, after moving to Wales, that, at a Welsh language class, those people whose families spoke Welsh had a natural intonation which meant that when they learned to speak the language it sounded right, whereas others in the class struggled to achieve a rhythm and pitch that was unfamiliar to them. Tonality is an essential element of interesting voice production, and by changing your voice tonality, you can indicate emotion, question, variety, humour and whole range of other elements that can make you a more appealing and influential speaker.

And finally, remember that your voice and physiology needs warming up if it is to function well. Use some vocal exercises, do some facial exercises (make faces, yawn, etc), and do some breathing exercises to allow your whole vocal structure to work effectively. I have included books on these elements in the Bibliography.

So there are many factors that underlie good voice production; once you have understood the basic factors you can enhance your own voice for effective business use. As a consultant, you are likely to use your voice in differing contexts. Let's take a few and see what they require.

- *Speaking on the phone*

    When starting a conversation, remember that the first few seconds are often lost while the other person tunes into your voice, so begin with something fairly innocuous that does not have to be remembered.

    Remember to speak clearly and articulate words so that every part of them can be heard. Speak at a reasonable pace so that you can be understood; do not speak so quickly that your meaning is lost and do not speak so slowly that the listener is tempted to finish your sentences for you.

    Your voice reflects your emotional state, so by getting into a positive frame of mind before you speak, you are more likely to come across as enthusiastic and interesting. If you smile, it alters the shape of your vocal cords and your voice sounds warmer and friendlier.

- *Talking face to face*

  Face the listener for most of the time, so you convey a sense of interest; it is also easier for people to understand what you are saying if they can see your mouth as you form your words (especially if they are hard of hearing). Speak at an appropriate volume for the distance at which you are standing; you may have a very quiet or a very loud voice, so get some feedback on this, as you might sometimes be speaking at an inappropriate volume for the person you are with.

- *Giving presentations*

  Project your voice so everyone can hear. Put variety and interest into your presentation by varying your voice volume, speed, pitch and rhythm. Look at people when answering their questions, as your voice will carry to them more directly and they will feel you are talking to them personally (in a large group, anyone in the proximity of the person to whom you are speaking will feel that you are talking to them).

- *Running meetings*

  Give authority to your voice, without sounding overpowering, by speaking clearly and concisely and pausing from time to time to make sure people have taken in the points you are making. Look at the person to whom you are speaking, while glancing at the others to make sure everyone feels included.

- *Negotiating*

  Maintain a firm, positive and receptive tone of voice, which will help you avoid sounding too dominating or too appeasing. Look at the other person/people while you are speaking to give the impression of being confident and assured. Remember that changes in pitch may change the sense of what you are saying; in the UK, for example, if your voice remains level or goes down at the end of a sentence it indicates a statement, and if it goes up at the end of a sentence it indicates a question, so you may sound uncertain and less assured if you allow your voice to rise at the end of a statement.

- *Coaching/mentoring*

  Use a positive voice tone and allow time for points to be absorbed. Use language that allows the other person to come up with their own ideas. Keep as neutral as you can, so that your own ideas, attitudes and body language do not exert undue influence. Use questions and questioning tones so that you spark off new thoughts and help the person to evaluate their own ideas.

These are just some of the contexts in which you may find yourself, as a consultant. Each of them may require differing skills and differing vocal abilities, so having flexibility in your voice is a real asset. Let's now move to the third element in this section; what you say.

What you say

Although what you actually say needs to depend on the context, the topic and the purpose of the interaction, there are a few general principles that you can consider.

- *Relevance*

  Do make what you say relevant to the matter in hand. Of course you can begin conversations with an ice-breaker, which can be unrelated to the main subject of the discussion, and of course you can intersperse conversation with anecdotes and small conversational points, but on the whole, it is important in consultancy to keep to the point and show that what you say is considered and appropriate.

- *Balance*

  A balanced opinion is likely to carry more weight than a biased one. Showing you can weigh up the pros and cons of a situation and come up with a reasoned and reasonable solution will give people confidence in you. Similarly, if you can show you have weighed up the pros and cons of what others are saying and can base your reactions on a rational analysis, you are more likely to be seen as fair and objective.

- *Judgement*

   Using good judgement in what you say is also important. You can have all the facts in a situation, yet make a poor judgement of their implications or outcomes. Being able to back up what you say, or recommend, with reasoning and rationality is a help to clients who can then understand why you are making particular recommendations and suggestions. Often judgement can only be assessed with hindsight, but a good track record of well-assessed situations will hold you in good stead.

- *Questioning*

   Using well-formulated questions will help you understand situations and will help your clients and colleagues analyse their own thoughts and behaviour. There are various questioning techniques that are useful, including the following: ◆Open and closed questions (open to draw people out and closed to obtain very specific information); ◆Hypothetical questions (to work with ideas and imagination); ◆Meta-model questioning – an NLP technique developed by Bandler and Grinder – see Bibliography (to give you precision in eliciting information); ◆Three-level questioning (level one is questions about facts, level two is questions about feelings and meanings and level three is questions about values – the deeper you go, the more fundamental information you gain about a person); ◆Clean language questioning (where you use neutral language to ensure you do not impose your own thoughts and beliefs on the other person). See the Bibliography for books on some of these techniques.

Before leaving Impression Management, I would just like to mention one final topic, which merges all the other elements.

Presence and charisma

Presence is a hard term to define, yet most people seem to know what you mean if you say someone has 'presence'. It can be to do with physical appearance; a very tall person, for example, may seem more 'visible' than a shorter one. It can be to do with voice; a person with a voice that projects well can come across more positively than one whose voice is weak. It can be to do with authority; a person who is perceived as powerful can seem to have more presence. It can be to do with seriousness; a person with gravitas may be seen as carrying intellectual weight. However, all these elements can be reversed and a person can still have presence.

Charisma differs from presence in that a charismatic person is one who holds an attraction for people; who seems magnetic, exciting, dynamic, intriguing. A person can have presence but not be charismatic, and vice versa.

Working on both presence and charisma will help you come across as authoritative, interesting and enjoyable to be with. Here are some of the things you can do to develop these attributes.

- Adopt an open, upright, balanced and flexible posture.

- Wear clothes that are somewhat distinctive, while remaining within whatever convention is necessary.

- Speak clearly, project your voice well and vary your intonation to add interest to what you say.

- Adopt assertive, confident behaviour so you appear at ease with yourself and with others around you.

- Take time when you speak; pauses can add effect as long as they are not too lengthy.

- Generate an element of curiosity; find ways of intriguing people so they want to know more.

- Be interested in other people and discuss things that interest them.

- As you go about your activities, imagine that you extend your own personal presence throughout the space around you (a technique developed by John Heron – see Bibliography). This can enhance your presence and make you seem more accessible and integrated with those with whom you are dealing.

Example

A large management consultancy firm was bidding for an assignment and wielded a team of one senior and two junior consultants for a presentation. During the presentation the senior consultant, who fronted the team, made some comment at which one of the two juniors turned to the other and screwed up his face. The team did not win the work, and when they asked for feedback on their presentation they were told that, if the senior member of the team did not have the confidence of his own juniors, he could not expect to inspire confidence in clients. The junior member learned an excellent lesson in interpersonal skills and the team learned a lesson in cohesiveness and the importance of impression management.

I hope you have some new ideas now about how to manage your own impression on others; there is a saying: 'First impressions last', so make yours memorable and positive and you can create an effective basis for your own activities. Let's move now to the next element in building relationships – rapport.

Rapport

Rapport is the basis of effective relationships and is the term used to describe what happens when people are getting on well together.

There are probably some people with whom you feel an immediate affinity and others with whom you believe you will never see eye to eye. In consultancy you can, if you are working alone, choose which clients you will work for (as long as you can afford to be so selective!). However, if you are employed by a consultancy firm, or if you need the fee income, there may be times when you find yourself approaching, or working for, or with, people with whom you do not feel an instant companionship. There are ways you can improve your relationships with people even when you do not seem to have much in common, and I will be giving you some ideas on how to do so in this section.

Before we continue, however, take a little time to think about some people you get on well with; pick two or three people in each of the following categories:

- People with whom you felt an immediate affinity when you first met them.
- People you have known for a long time and with whom you feel very comfortable.

What I would like you to do is consider, for each of these groups, why you think you do get on well together. List these things for each of the people you have chosen. Then look at the listings and see if you can determine any pattern in what you have written.

Some people I spoke to mentioned the following elements in their lists:

- A shared sense of humour.
- Similar interests.
- Having a similar appearance.
- Having similar childhood experiences.
- Doing similar work.
- Having a common purpose.

Whatever pattern you have found in your relationships, the chances are that those relationships that work well are based on some kind of commonality – you and the other person share something in common. It is interesting how we tend to gravitate towards people who are like ourselves in some way – there seems to be an almost magnetic force at work, drawing us to similarly inclined individuals. So, when there is a natural affinity, it is easy to relax and feel comfortable with someone. But what about those people who do not immediately strike you as sharing any of the things that matter to you?

In these cases, what you can do is create a situation whereby you become a little more like the other person. What you are doing by using this process is giving the impression that you have more in common with the person than you think you do, and the result tends to be that it becomes easier to form a relationship with that person. I say 'more than you think you do', because it is common that, once you really get to know someone, you do find you have things that enable you to relate well to that person after all. So what has to happen to make rapport-building possible?

The first thing is to identify a way of being a little more like the other person. This does not mean mimicking them, because this is likely to cause offence, but it does mean showing, in some way, that you have some common ground. So the first thing you can do, which is very simple, is to adopt a similar physical stance to the other person; make yourself look a little like them. This may sound odd, but it does work; what you do is to adopt a similar posture, or a similar facial expression, or similar mannerisms. And similar means just that; if you use exactly the same physical stance, you will be 'mirroring' the person, which is unnecessary and blatant. You only need to be *a little* like them for the technique to work.

So, you might sit in a relaxed manner if they are doing so, you might use similar gestures, or you might nod as they do, or smile as they do. The art is to do the minimum necessary to adapt your behaviour to theirs, and it is often the very subtle things that are effective. This whole process is called 'matching' and you can see it at work in everyday life; just watch people together and, if they are getting on well together, you will find they are actually sitting, standing or moving in similar ways. Practising this will help you become more aware of how other people behave and give you more flexibility in how you behave also.

Physical matching is just one of the ways in which you can create a shared experience with people. Other things you can do are match their interests by talking about topics that interest them, match their voice patterns by speaking slowly or quietly if they do, or match their emotional state (for example excitement or interest) through your voice tonality and rhythm. You can also match their beliefs, although this might be somewhat unethical if you do not actually share them. Other things you can match are their motivational and activity patterns by, for example, boosting their sense of independence if they are very self-motivated, talking about goals if they are results-oriented or considering obstacles if they are focused on problem areas. I cover this latter aspect more in the next chapter.

So there are numerous ways in which you can match another person, and this rapport development activity is not only a good way of relating well to people, it is also a precursor to influence because it is easier to influence somebody who already feels at ease with you and on the same wavelength.

Having considered the various techniques and approaches for establishing good relationships, how can this be applied to consultancy in practice? There are a number of stages at which you will need to be in contact with others, and the main people for you to consider in consultancy are likely to be clients, colleagues and suppliers, although, of course, there will also be friends, family and more casual acquaintances. Let's take clients here; you can adapt the following suggestions when interacting with others.

Stages at which you will need to deal with clients can include the following:

● *Initial contact, either from you or from them*

This may be through a telephone conversation, letter, advertisement, or something similar. This will be the opportunity for you to make an impression and to begin establishing a relationship. At this stage, you are unlikely to have much, if any, information available about the particular client, so your rapport-building skills will need to be fairly broadly based.

If you are advertising, you can think about the range of client issues and types and aim to direct your copywriting towards what you believe will match your client needs. This may be quite focused if you are aiming at a very specific client group, or it may be wider if it is a fairly general promotion of your services. Think about the person reading the advertisement and aim to match their thinking and requirements; this will mean considering the benefits to them, rather than the features of what you have on offer.

If the contact is by letter, then again match the content and style to that of your client. A letter will be directed to a specific client, so the more research you can do in advance about the organisation and, preferably, the individual to whom the letter is addressed, the better. Match their concerns by referring to current issues they are involved in; match their ways of working by using words that are used in their sector; match them personally by using language that will reflect back anything you know about the recipient as an individual.

If the contact is by phone, you can match the person throughout the conversation. You can begin with a statement designed to catch their interest, continue by picking up their interests and concerns and responding to them, and also match their language by using similar patterns (e.g. if they talk a lot about the future, you can do the same, or if they use a lot of 'visual' words [see page 247], you can do so too; you can also match the pitch of their voice).

Example
There have been many occasions when I have telephoned an organisation and then adapted my voice pattern to that of the person who answers. I find this often means that I speak in a higher pitch, or at a faster or slower pace, depending on the vocal patterns of the person answering.

- *First meeting*

  This is your chance to build credibility and develop the relationship. Remember about impression management and select something to wear which is either designed to match the client (e.g. a dark suit if they dress formally) or designed to match the client's expectation of you (e.g. something slightly unconventional if they expect you to be a person who comes up with very individual solutions to problems). Continue with the general matching techniques I have already discussed, including physical matching by sitting or standing in similar postures and matching the client's speech and language. Do remember to match at a minimal level, as anything more will appear blatant and can be embarrassing, irritating or provocative.

Example
Many years ago I did a good deal of work with IBM and once had occasion to visit one of the IBM sites to discuss a possible assignment. Remembering their nickname of 'Big Blue' – because the male employees were expected to wear blue suits and white shirts – I chose a blue outfit to wear rather than another colour. This particular dress code is now largely a thing of the past, but it illustrates the principle of considering what is suitable when dealing with others.

- *Proposal*

  At this stage, you can reinforce the client's impression of you and show how you can really meet their needs in a practical way. In a written proposal, you can respond to the client's needs by putting in specific elements that will convince them that you are the right person for the job. This is likely to mean responding to their specific concerns, matching any particular ways of thinking and using language that fits with their own way of speaking or writing.

- *Interview/presentation*

  This will build on your proposal, and on any initial contacts or meetings, and will provide an opportunity to back up any written proposal in person. Again, remember appearance and manner. Match people where possible by varying your style to fit in with the different people present. In particular, listen to how questions or comments are phrased by those involved in selection, and aim to match their language, manner and interests. If doing a PowerPoint® presentation, or using slides of some kind, incorporate the matching into their production, for example by using symbols that relate to the client's business.

- *Project/assignment conduct*

  This will involve you in ongoing contact with your client and you are likely to deal with many more people at this stage. You can use your rapport-building skills with each person with whom you deal, enhancing your relationships and making a successful outcome more likely. So, remember to pay attention to each person you meet, picking up their feelings about you, about the consultancy project, about their jobs and about their organisational context and responding to them accordingly. If they are positive and enthusiastic, you can be outgoing and lively; if they are apprehensive and cautious you can modify your behaviour to be quieter, listen carefully and show you understand their concerns. By matching in different ways, you can demonstrate to each person with whom you come into contact that you are acknowledging their own thoughts, feelings and reactions; you then stand a much better chance of developing good relationships throughout the project. Do be careful to do this with sensitivity; it is one thing being responsive to individuals, it is another to come across as a person who simply puts on an artificial face and manner to enhance your own position. It is a fine line to walk, but one that really produces results if you manage it effectively.

- *Review/follow-up*

  This can provide an opportunity to exchange feedback and establish a base from which the current project can be assessed and future relationships developed. Continue the approach you have used up to now and, if you wish to gain more work from the client, use the opportunity to demonstrate your awareness of future issues and your ideas for their ongoing success.

Final Points

Starting and continuing effective relationships is fundamental to business success. In consultancy, much of your activity will be with other people – clients, colleagues and others – and the more you can develop good interpersonal relationships with them, the more likely you will be to develop a successful practice.

This chapter has covered ways of creating an image and developing rapport. These skills need practice, and an aid to this will be noticing the fine detail of what you, yourself, do and what others do. I have mentioned matching people's appearance, which relies on noticing the details of their posture, gestures and expressions; I have also mentioned matching people's expectations and interests. A good way of enhancing your skills in this latter direction is to read advertisements and then consider what you would write or say in response to them.

Here are a few examples of statements from recruitment advertisements; have a look at them and decide what is really wanted and how you could respond in a way that met the advertiser's needs.

"Would you like your senior management team to recognise how you can make the most valuable contribution to your organisation's business?"

"We need a new approach to an established order."

"Are you ready for a challenge?"

"We'll look to you to set the pace."

"Our line managers will be relying on you to advise them."

"It will be down to you to spot the issues that need addressing and devise inspired action plans."

"You'll be sensitive to the needs and issues of serving a diverse workforce."

"You'll analyse needs, design solutions, deliver results and evaluate their impact."

I hope this has given you some food for thought. In the next chapter I will be showing you how to refine your communication and influencing skills to meet the individual needs of people with whom you come into contact.

NLP techniques used in this chapter and the sections where you can find them

Tonality changes (your voice)
Rapport (rapport)
Matching (rapport)

Chapter 11
Facilitating Change Through Influence

This chapter will help you create change in both individuals and organisations.

The topics covered in this chapter include:

- Positive influencing.
- Working with people's motivational patterns.

Positive Influencing

Influence has many elements. In the previous chapter I discussed ways of gaining rapport and adapting your behaviour to fit in with others. This is the first step towards influencing and is, in fact, a subtle way of influencing in its own right, as you are enabling the person to become more comfortable with you.

You can continue the matching process by what is called pacing. Pacing simply means continuing to notice a person's ongoing 'state' and behaviour and matching as these alter. So if you are speaking to someone on the phone and that person is talking quite slowly, you could slow down your own speech a little in order to match them. If they then speed up a little, perhaps because they are talking about something that really enthuses them, you can match their increased speed; if they slow down again you too can slow down a little – this is very simple pacing.

Matching and pacing are precursors of influence, because the more you are on someone's wavelength the more likely it is that they are open to being influenced by you, and the more you match and pace them the more they may feel comfortable with you. Then you can move into influencing.

The influence stage is where you 'lead' the person instead of following them. With matching you will have been following what the other person does; in leading you switch roles and initiate behaviour and then observe whether you are now being followed. So, for example, if you are in a railway carriage and you look out of the window, it is likely that people sitting near you will also look out; they are following your lead, and this is what influence is all about.

Through influence, you can give people confidence, motivate and energise them and enable them to achieve results; you can also improve your own results by influencing, when you need to work with others in order to achieve a goal. In consultancy, much of what you do involves influence, and with good influencing skills your effectiveness should rise considerably. This chapter deals with some general principles of influencing and the following chapters will extend this concept into specific business-related contexts.

The word 'influence' is sometimes used as a verb, so you can say, "I influenced the client to devote more resources to marketing." It is sometimes used as a noun, so you can say, "I had a good deal of influence on the decision to devote more resources to marketing." Although the word is used in these different ways, it is really a process activity, not an entity (the NLP term for treating a process as an object is 'nominalisation'), so it is helpful to think of the elements involved in the process of influencing, rather than to treat it as a commodity that you either do or do not have.

I like to think of influence as a process of facilitating change and you might like to take a few moments now to think about what influencing means to you.

There are many situations in consultancy when you may wish to exert influence at both macro and micro levels – for example:

- Promoting yourself to potential clients.
- Negotiating fees.
- Getting people to invest time, resources and effort in achieving results.

- Persuading a team to adopt proposals that will benefit them.
- Getting a persistent caller to keep conversations short.
- Encouraging two people with differing perspectives to understand each other.
- Delegating work.

It is possible to influence through power; however, I think influence works best through more collaborative means. Once you find what makes a person want to act, then you have a really effective tool for change.

There are a couple of points worth remembering about influencing. The first is that you need credibility if you are to exert influence because, unless you can demonstrate that you are worth listening to and that you have interesting and useful ideas, you may be ignored or seen as simply out for what you can get yourself. So credibility and standing are worth working for.

The second point is that people are likely to be sceptical about attempts at persuasion unless you can answer two important questions: "So what?" and "What's in it for me (WIFM)?". Remembering the importance of these questions is fundamental to success. In other words, when you try to influence someone you can imagine that the question in their mind is why they should take the course of action you seem to be suggesting. And, even if your attempts to influence are covert, it is still likely that at some point people will want to convince themselves that they are doing the right thing, so it helps to have the answers to these questions.

And the answers come via benefits. Once you can demonstrate benefits to the person, you have something of value to them and they are more likely to be open to suggestion. So, before trying to influence, work out what might be of benefit to them. Knowing people's motivational patterns will help with this process, and I will be dealing with these in the second part of this chapter. Once you have worked out a good approach, you will be able to provide an incentive for any course of action you are hoping to get accepted.

There are many ways of influencing, and NLP in particular offers some interesting approaches, some of which I would like to cover here.

Role-modelling

An excellent way of influencing people is by example. This is the way most children (and animals) learn, and it can be applied very effectively to business situations. By using yourself as a role model, you can demonstrate how things can be done and the results that can be obtained. This kind of influence may be overt or indirect. If it is overt, which works well in coaching or mentoring situations, you will be pointing out how and why you do certain things and also showing how other people respond to what you do. If it is indirect, you will simply be providing the opportunity for people to watch and listen to you and get a feel for what you do; the more they are in contact with you the more they are likely to learn from your example. This is an excellent way of using consultancy to help others develop; not only does the job get done, but other people can learn a wide range of skills in the process.

For example, while I was writing this book, I had a couple of people wanting to role-model how I did it. With the first person, much of what I was doing was discussed explicitly; with the second the process was more about observation and assimilation. Conducting this process has facilitated enhancement of other people's ability to write – particularly in respect of feeling more positive about the process and being able to just get on with it, rather than procrastinate.

You can also use other people as role models, pointing out how they can be used as examples of good practice. And, of course, remember that the implication here is that a role model is a positive example; if your behaviour is not appropriate, that too is likely to be picked up and can affect others' responses towards you. So adopting a detached perspective and observing what you do will help you monitor your behaviour and its likely impact on others.

Time shifts

Another way of influencing is through the use of time shifts. What this means is that you can take someone into a past or future time (or, if you are being creative, a parallel or an imaginary time) so that they can gain a different perspective on, and new information about, situations.

Time shifts can be done conversationally. For example, saying "When you have had your meeting you will know what the options are" helps the person to imagine looking back, knowing they are aware of what their options are, rather than being in the present not knowing what options might be open to them. Time shifts can also be done physically by getting a person to walk along an imaginary line on the floor towards a future event, as I have explained in earlier chapters. It can also be used to go back in time, but forward tends to be more constructive, and I would not encourage you to take people back in time unless you have had more training in these techniques. The time shift process helps people to experience events and ideas in their mind and have an opportunity to assess their implications.

This technique may sound a little strange to those who are unfamiliar with it, but it is very effective for both individual and team-work, particularly in relation to goal achievement and change management. In consultancy, you can take whole teams along time lines very effectively when doing work on vision, goal-setting, teambuilding, change management and much more besides. It gives them an opportunity both to experience the significance of proposed changes and to discover how their individual perceptions differ from or match those of their colleagues.

Example one
One participant on a facilitation skills course I ran recently was from a major financial institution. I saw him a couple of weeks later and he said he had used some time-line work with a customer, to help that person assess a couple of alternative courses of action. The customer had found the process very enlightening and was able to assess his business activities in a new light.

Example two
I had been approached by a woman who had run a very successful business for several years and was now contemplating a complete change of direction; she was quite uncertain whether the new venture would be a good decision. I invited her to create two lines, one leading to the new venture and one resulting in the

245

continuation of her present business. While she was very happy to see herself in the new role, and to move along the line to experience it, as soon as she saw herself at the end of the other line, remaining in her present business, she felt quite depressed and didn't even want to walk along that particular line. The process took only a few minutes and was enough for her to decide that the change of direction would be appropriate and fulfilling.

Indirect language

Most of us use indirect language from time to time. When you say to someone, "Would you like to make a cup of tea?" you aren't really asking if they would enjoy the activity, you are asking them to do it. And when a salesperson says to you, "Would you prefer to receive our literature through the post or on-line?" they are implying that you will accept their material, hiding their assumption in the supposed choice. So indirectness is a feature of everyday life.

Another aspect of indirect language is the use of metaphor and analogy. Sometimes tackling a situation directly is the best way, but at other times using parallels can be helpful, either to distance the discussion from the actual situation or to give a new view of it. Skilful use of metaphor is a real asset to business communication, and there are many books devoted to this specialist topic (see Bibliography).

The use of indirect language is a major aid to interaction. This kind of language needs to be practised until you are really skilful at using it. Once you are familiar with its principles you can apply it, with excellent results, to many consultancy situations, especially those where people are nervous about change or uncertain of their own abilities. NLP uses indirect language a good deal, and much of the derivation of this usage is from Milton Erickson, a very well-known therapist, who used language patterns to excellent effect, very often to achieve hypnotic, or trance, states.

A trance state exists when a person's focus of attention narrows to exclude everything outside their immediate point of experience. It can happen, for example, when they are reading a book, listening to music, running a race, memorising a telephone number or watching snow fall (and being 'entranced' by heavy snowfalls while driving can make the process even more hazardous than it already is). Sometimes, when you use indirect language, the person to whom you are speaking will enter a light trance state because, in order to allow their mind to make sense of your words, they will momentarily detach themselves from their current experience. This state can, in itself, be an excellent medium for learning, for relaxation and for achievement. If, however, you are to use this approach effectively, it would be helpful to do some specific training in language skills, so you enhance your ability to lead people into changed states. As I have already mentioned, in consultancy, having this skill is a very useful addition to change-management techniques and general facilitation of development in both individuals and teams.

Sensory language

Another way of influencing is to use sensory language. Sensory language involves using words that relate to each of our senses: seeing, hearing, feeling, tasting and smelling. When you use sensory language you make an experience more vivid, more enticing and more memorable; without sensory language descriptions become static, colourless and less appealing.

To use sensory language, you simply include words that express the different senses. Here are a few examples with the sensory words highlighted in bold and explained in brackets.

- Let me **show** you what I mean.
- It **looked clear** enough.
- They **saw** the **light**.
- Is there a **glimmer** of hope?
- Have you had a **glance** at the report?
- I was a bit **hazy** about the details.
- Can you **picture** the changes?
- It could be a really **bright** future.
  (*Visual words highlighted.*)

- They **sounded** surprised.
- It **rang** a **bell.**
- Would you **give me a call**?
- She got a **buzz** from that job.
- They were a bit **rattled** by the speed at which it had happened.
- **Tell** me about it.
- It was **crying out** for attention.
  (Hearing words highlighted.)

- I **told myself** it was the right thing to do.
- I **thought** about what had happened.
- I **debated** the consequences.
- I **considered** the proposals.
- I had various **ideas** about it.
- I was **minded** to make the change.
- I wish I hadn't **talked myself** out of it.
  (Internal hearing/'self-talk' words highlighted.)

- He was **struggling** to **keep up**.
- I wondered how it **came across** to them.
- Do you **grasp** the concept?
- They **felt** quite **submerged** by the changes.
- They **weighed up** the options.
- I was **touched** by their concern.
- They had a **long way** to **go**.
  (Tactile/feeling words highlighted.)

- It left a **sour taste** in my mouth.
- I couldn't **swallow** the thought of it.
- It took time to **digest** the proposals.
- My **stomach churned** in anticipation.
- He **bit off** more than he could **chew**.
- It was **flavour** of the month.
- They **lapped up** the suggestions.
  (Taste words highlighted.)

- I **smelled** a rat.
- She had **a good nose** for the story.
- They were onto the **scent** in no time at all.
- Did you get a **whiff** of what was happening?

- They had an **acrid** exchange of words.
- The atmosphere was **sulphurous**.
- They wanted a **fresh** approach to the situation.
  (Smell words highlighted.)

When you use words of this kind, at least two things are possible. The first is that you can bring your conversations to life and help people to really understand what an experience is, or can be, like. The second is that you can match your words to those of the people you are with, making it more likely that you will relate to them better (see the previous chapter for more on matching).

It isn't a question of people only using one kind of sensory channel; often there will be several used by the same person. The art of effective communication is to identify the moment-to-moment use of language and adapt your own speech to that of the other person as they talk. This is an acquired skill and is one that is well worth practising.

Sometimes sensory language can be exceptionally easy to notice. On a course I ran some years ago, one person said, "We've **seen** a lot of **talk**." Not all language is as obvious as this – or as explicit about how a person is translating one sensory medium into another – but it is fascinating to listen out for such language patterns and then use your skills to influence through their use.

Now let's move on to motivational patterns.

Working with People's Motivational Patterns

Knowing people's motivational patterns, and how they respond to particular situations, makes it easier to influence them. With people you know well, you probably already have insights into how they function, but with new people you have to work it out. One way of doing this is through conversation – listening to how people speak and asking questions to elicit responses. Often you will be able to find out a good deal in this way.

It is important to remember that people may demonstrate different motivational patterns in different situations, and may also change over time, so you do need to make your interventions relevant to the particular circumstances. There are numerous patterns that you can observe and work with, and I would like to introduce you to a few of those that will be useful to you in consultancy. These and other patterns are explored in more depth in other books, and I have referred to some of these in the Bibliography.

Each of the patterns that follow has its applications. None of them are intrinsically good or bad, but each one may be more or less appropriate in a particular situation.

1. *Self-reliant (internal)/dependent (external)*

- *What they are like*

  People who are self-reliant tend to make decisions easily, have strongly held opinions and standards, work well under their own direction and need little, if any, support or feedback from others (they may, in fact, see any intervention as interference and be irritated by it). The converse of this is people who are more dependent on others when it comes to making their minds up about things. These people thrive on support, example and external validation.

- *How to find out who falls into each category*

  Self-reliant people talk about their own views and ideas a good deal and they voice their opinions even when they are minority ones. Dependent people often refer to others' opinions and need to consult before coming to a decision. If you are not sure from their general behaviour, you can ask a question such as, "How do you know whether this plan will work?" A self-reliant person will say something like, "I just know" or "I will be able to tell if it is working", whereas a dependent person will probably say, "I will see how people respond to it" or "We will be able to tell how people get on with the new approach". In other words the first person has their own way of assessing, whereas the second person relies on external responses.

- *How to relate to them*

  In order to relate well to self-reliant people, and influence them, you will need to acknowledge their personal ways of doing things and show that you are responsive to their opinions. With more dependent people you will need to lead by example or tell them about how things have worked well for other people or organisations.

- *Consultancy implications*

  Self-reliant people often gravitate towards management posts. If the top managers in a client organisation are self-reliant, they may find it hard to understand why others aren't self-motivated and don't simply 'get on with the job'. If the top managers are dependent people they may find it hard to take decisions and might want the agreement of everyone in their team before proceeding; they may also become over-dependent on you as a consultant and seek your approval for even small changes and interventions. Self-reliant people tend to undertake responsibility easily, but they can have their own ways of doing things, which might not fit with the best outcome for the organisation as a whole. Dependent people may need extra support and encouragement, but they may be more open to new ideas and, given support, can be invaluable team members.

Example

Two chief executives I worked with at different times were at opposite ends of this continuum. One was so self-reliant that it made it almost impossible for others to give that person advice or feedback; the other was so dependent that strategic and operational decisions were rarely made in case they were not fully supported by others. In conventional terms the first would have been seen as a strong person and the second as a weak one but, in practice, the strength often turned out to be a weakness for the organisation as a whole and the weakness at least gave room for others to have an input to decision-making. Neither was ideal, however, and by understanding how such individual differences can be demonstrated through language patterns you have, as a consultant, a way into exploring and enhancing individual development, group dynamics and business effectiveness.

2. *Towards/away from*

- *What they are like*

  Towards people tend to be goal- and result- oriented, whereas away from people tend to see the difficulties involved in courses of action and be motivated by avoidance.

- *How to find out who falls into each category*

  You can recognise a towards person, because they talk about what they want to achieve and what it will be like when they have reached their objective. Conversely you can recognise an away from person because they seem to find obstacles and problems when change is suggested.

- *How to relate to them*

  With towards people you will need to share their enthusiasm, while also helping them become aware of any possible obstacles in the way. With away from people you will need to acknowledge their concerns, while helping them see how results can be achieved.

- *Consultancy implications*

  A change-management programme is much more likely to work well when people are results-oriented. If the top managers are goal-oriented, but staff are not, there can be conflict, uncertainty and stress generated by any change process. This is why it is usually more helpful to tackle concerns before promoting benefits (see also 'Force-field analysis' in Chapter 7). If the top managers are more away from in their thinking you will have a harder job to convince them to move towards implementation of any course of action that could result in major changes to their own, or the organisation's, situation. Towards people are excellent at focusing on goals and staying on track, but may not see possible problems in the way. Away from people may not always enthuse about new ideas, but they can have a healthy balancing effect on over-optimism and may anticipate problems early enough to ensure they are avoided.

Example

In one organisation for which I worked there were two directors. One director was very positive and goal-oriented while the other was more away from. The two rarely saw eye to eye – or even liked each other – but their differences facilitated a healthy balance between optimism and pessimism, which kept their area of the business reasonably well on track.

---

3.   *Procedural/flexible*

- *What they are like*

   Procedural people are most comfortable when things are predictable, stable and systematic. They like order and organisation and like to know what they have to do, and how. Flexible people thrive on choice and options; they like to be able to choose their own way of doing things and like the freedom of making decisions based on responding to what is current at the time.

- *How to find out who falls into each category*

   Procedural people are often easy to spot as they have predictable ways of doing things and tend to be well organised. If you disturb something on their desk they will probably quickly move it back to its right place, and they can be uncomfortable if they are interrupted before they have completed a sequence of activity. Flexible people tend to dislike having to follow anyone else's procedure or being told how to do a task. If you give a rule book to both kinds of people, the procedural one is likely to believe that if a course of action is not covered by the rules it can't be done, whereas the flexible person is likely to think that if it isn't in the rule book they can do exactly what they like.

- *How to relate to them*

   The procedural person will need explanations of how things should be done and may well find it hard to be innovative or respond easily to changed circumstances. The flexible person will respond best to being given the freedom to choose how to do things and will enjoy being presented with options and a varied range of activities.

- *Consultancy implications*

   Procedural people are often found in large, bureaucratic organisations; they are also likely to be resistant to change if it disturbs the way they have done things in the past. Flexible people may find it hard to be pinned down to a set way of doing things and may keep coming up with new ways of doing things well past the time when a job should have been completed. Procedural people are very effective in structured situations; they are happy implementing systems, although they may not have the ability to actually devise the systems they like to follow. Flexible people are good at adapting to change, but may find it hard if their situation requires much structure and formality.

Example
I sent an invoice to one organisation, but it took months to get paid. When I queried it I was given a range of 'reasons' for the delay, one of which was that it had coincided with their year end and they were unable to pay any invoices for six weeks (!) while they carried out their internal procedures. In another organisation an invoice had been mislaid but, when I raised this with them, they offered to bypass their usual system and produce the cheque manually so I could receive it quickly. Although following procedures is often essential, which of the two organisations do you think keeps its customers happiest?

4. *Detail/overview*

- *What they are like*

  Detail people, as the word implies, thrive on 'small chunk' information. They enjoy working on tasks with identifiable, discrete elements and they often need a large amount of information to be provided before they can make a start on an activity. Overview people prefer the big picture and are happy with very general outlines of situations and events.

- *How to find out who falls into each category*

  Detail people's conversation is often lengthy and full of facts, figures and the minutiae of their experience, whereas overview people tend to skim over things, generalise and paint a broad picture.

  Detail people will take a long time to make sure that everything is correct and in its place, whereas overview people are often uninterested in small points and may overlook things that are too small for them to notice.

- *How to relate to them*

  You will get on well with detail people if you recognise their need for information and understanding, take time to listen while they work through all aspects of a situation and provide them with additional information as they go along. Overview people are likely to expect you to pick up their ideas and needs from a more skimpy outline and can get frustrated by what they perceive as information overload, or by the need for lengthy explanations and analysis.

- *Consultancy implications*

  If your client is a detail person you will need to provide full explanations of all you do and you will have to be prepared to listen for long periods while they explain points that you may grasp very quickly. If you only give a broad outline to detail people they can find it hard to understand and they can therefore be somewhat incapacitated by not having enough data on which to act. If, on the other hand, you are working with people who only want an overview, you may find they limit their effectiveness by attempting to act with only a rough idea of what needs doing – they can pick up the wrong ideas or have too little information on which to act. They can, however, very quickly grasp the significant aspects of a situation and need only a little information before taking action.

Example

I was invited to tender for work for a major public sector body. The invitation-to-tender pack contained around a dozen documents, including such things as a tender form, information booklet on the organisation, reports on recent initiatives, profiles of top staff, and so forth. Also included were requests to provide financial information, references, copies of policies on health and safety and equal opportunities, insurance policies, examples of similar assignments, thoughts on associated issues, and so on, and so on. At the same time I received an e-mail asking if I would be interested in doing an assignment for another, fairly major, organisation and, if so, would I e-mail them back with my availability and a broad outline of my expertise. Although both detail and overview are appropriate in particular situations, which of the two above mentioned approaches do you think I welcomed more, and what would your own response have been to either of these?

5. *Similarity/difference*

- *What they are like*

  Similarity people like things to be unchanging and tend to notice things they can recognise or that are consistent. Difference people like things to be varied and will notice when something stands out in some way or when a pattern is disturbed.

- *How to find out who falls into each category*

  People who seek similarity are likely to have a history of similar jobs, or stay in the same job for a long time. They often talk about similarity; for example how a place they visited was like somewhere else they know. People who seek difference may change jobs more often and get bored if things are very predictable.

- *How to relate to them*

  Acknowledging people's needs for similarity can mean showing them how a change can still maintain some aspects with which they are familiar, while needs for difference will require emphasis on the novel aspects of a situation.

- *Consultancy implications*

  In consultancy it is the similarity people who can be resistant to change, while difference people often relish it, simply for its newness and difference from what has happened in the past. Clients who prefer similarity can feel threatened by proposals for innovation, while clients who are difference-oriented may feel you are not coming up with excellent proposals if you retain much of the status quo.

Example

A colleague went on holiday recently, to a place he had been several times previously. A comment he made on his return was that "... the nice thing about it is that it doesn't change – it's just like putting on a comfortable old suit." Another colleague went on holiday and the sole criterion for selecting the location was that, although she had some concerns about the environment, she "... hadn't been anywhere like that before and would never have the opportunity again."

Noticing people's motivational patterns and responding to them will make them feel more comfortable with you, as this is an extension of the process of 'matching', which I outlined in Chapter 9 as being the foundation for rapport. Building on this rapport in order to extend people's horizons will enable you to exert influence so that growth and development can take place, but you must gain the confidence of people with whom you are working if your influencing is to be effective.

In consultancy, you can begin the process of becoming aware of client patterns very early on. Company literature often brings out corporate motivational patterns (although beware in case they simply reflect the preferences of their copywriters/designers). Telephone conversations and initial meetings give you a chance to confirm or further elicit patterns. And any contact you have with people within a client organisation is likely to reveal some of their ways of being motivated and responding to situations. The more you build this awareness into your thinking and acting, the more likely you are to be well received and the more chance you stand of having your recommendations accepted.

Self-test

Before using the information I have given you, take a few minutes to consider yourself and assess your own motivational patterns at work. In the table that follows, you will find each of the categories I have mentioned in this section; I have given four different contexts in which to consider each of the categories.

The reason for the four categories is that you may well demonstrate different patterns in different contexts, and this activity should help you assess whether that is the case. For example, people tend to be external when they go to a doctor, an accountant or a plumber – they expect that person to have more expertise in the particular area and, because of that, tend to rely on their opinions and suggestions. On the other hand, many people tend to be internal when choosing food, a place to live or an evening out – they tend to use their own judgement rather than ask others what to do. Of course there will be exceptions to each of these, but the point I am making is that people do differ in how they behave in different situations. I hope you will find the following activity useful and interesting to do.

The four contexts you will find in the 'test' that follows are:

- Employment – in this column you can consider what your patterns tend to be if you are an employed person.

- Consultancy – in this column you can consider what you think your tendencies would be as a consultant.

- How you are now – in this column you can put down what you think your present patterns are.

- How you would like to be – if you would prefer any of your patterns to be different, this is the place to indicate what those differences would be.

As an example, you may think you are not very procedural as an employee, but would need to be more so as a consultant; or you may think you have been very detail-oriented in the past but would like to become more of a broad picture person in the future. Tick the relevant boxes below for your answers.

Pattern	Employment	Consultancy	How you are now	How you would like to be
Internal				
External				
Towards				
Away from				
Procedural				
Flexible				
Detail				
Overview				
Similarity				
Difference				

Although consultancy assignments differ, to be effective you probably have to have some of each of these patterns, for the following reasons:

Internal: so you can think independently and be confident about your own opinions.

External: so you can listen to your clients' and associates' views and can be open to feedback.

Positive: so you can set and work towards objectives and help your clients do likewise.

Negative: so you can anticipate possible obstacles and take avoiding action.

Procedural: so you can be systematic and also help clients to plan and organise activities.

Flexible: so you can respond to change and offer a variety of solutions.

Detail: so you can take account of all elements of a situation and provide adequate information for others.

Overview: so you can put projects and issues in context and see the whole picture rather than only parts.

Similarity: so you can notice patterns in assignments and in client issues.

Difference: so you can work on a range of projects and spot the elements that cause variations.

However, unless you are a technical specialist working on very precise elements, or are helping clients deal with things that have gone wrong, in consultancy it will probably be most useful to have more of a bias towards internal, positive, flexible, overview and difference.

If you have been honest in your answers, you should have some ideas now about how you might come across to your colleagues and clients and whether you need to change any of your customary ways of working to fit in with specific clients or colleagues.

Observation test

Now you have done some self observation, you might like to carry out a little test of your observation skills. Take a few people – they may be work associates, friends and family or actual or potential clients – and have a go at assessing their motivational patterns from the information I have given you. Again, you can map this on the chart that follows.

Pattern	Person 1	Person 2	Person 3	Person 4	Person 5
Internal					
External					
Towards					
Away from					
Procedural					
Flexible					
Detail					
Overview					
Similarity					
Difference					

Once you have done this you will have an idea of how each of these people compares with you, how their own patterns are likely to influence their thoughts, feelings, behaviour, relationships, management style and results, and how you might best influence them in order to achieve a successful outcome. You might also have some clues as to why you get on better with some of those people than with others and why some of those people do or don't get on well with each other, or with other friends or colleagues.

So we have covered some of the major motivational patterns you will find in people. Utilising these patterns, and combining this knowledge with your rapport skills and with the influence techniques covered in the first part of this chapter should really enhance your ability to get results, both for yourself and for your clients.

Final Points

All the rapport-building and influencing techniques I have mentioned in this chapter, and the preceding one, will only work if you exercise your observation skills to begin with. In order to know what behaviour and language will be most effective for you to adopt, you will need to notice other people's behaviour and language, so you can adapt what you do in order to match and influence them.

You should therefore work on your observation skills as a precursor to these activities. Some of the ways in which you can do this are:

- Watching facial expressions and eye movements.
- Watching body movement, posture and gesture.
- Noticing breathing patterns.
- Listening to voice tonality, speed, volume and rhythm.
- Listening to people's actual words and to the language patterns formed by their words.
- Noticing whether individual people have a limited, or a wide, range of variation in their behaviour and speech.

It is often the minute changes in what people do that give you clues about their thoughts and feelings, and these clues are vital in some of the consultancy contexts I will be describing in the next two chapters. So practise noticing 'micro' changes in people – in their facial expressions, in their movement patterns, in their voice tonality and so forth (this process is called 'sensory acuity' in NLP) – and you should enhance your sensitivity, your responsiveness and your influencing skills in proportion to the effort you put in.

NLP techniques used in this chapter and the sections where you can find them

Matching, pacing and leading (positive influencing)
Modelling (role-modelling)
Time shifts (time shifts)
Ericksonian language (indirect language)

Metaphor (indirect language)
Trance state (indirect language)
Predicates (sensory language)
Meta-programmes (working with people's motivational patterns: internal/external; towards/away from; procedures/options; detail/general; similarity/difference)
Sensory acuity (final points)

Chapter 12
Client Interfaces

This chapter covers some of the specific contexts involved in consultancy, especially those where you may be 'on show', or have to influence and persuade.

In the sections that follow, please remember that the suggestions made are not necessarily appropriate in every country, or even in every organisation. Because of differing cultural norms and expectations, you do need to consider the actual environment in which you are operating and, if this differs considerably from that with which you are accustomed, you may need to get advice from people who are more familiar with the situations in which you are placed.

Interviews

There are a number of situations in consultancy when interview skills are required. You may need skills in being interviewed – for a job in a consultancy practice or for an assignment with a potential client. You may also need skills in conducting interviews – with clients, possibly colleagues and others involved in assignments you are conducting.

Job interviews

I have already mentioned job interviews in Chapter 3, so I will not go into this again here, except to say that you could also follow much of the advice given there for interviews with potential clients.

Interviews you conduct

As far as interviews you conduct yourself, the skills covered earlier on rapport development, information-gathering/questioning/

diagnostic techniques and influencing skills will be relevant, and you can also read the chapter that follows this for other ideas on effective communications, which will be helpful in interviews as well as in the other situations on which that chapter concentrates. This chapter will focus on interviews with client organisations.

Additionally, you might like to remember some of the earlier points about objective-setting; that is, the 'surface' objectives may not be a true representation of the underlying needs or wants. Similarly, when interviewing, it is important to help people delve beneath the surface to uncover the really important issues, elements, feelings, beliefs and so forth. To do this, and to recognise when the really significant issues have emerged, is a skill and it is only by combining all the elements I have been discussing in this book, and probably more besides, that you will be able to achieve this.

The NLP approaches that are particularly useful in this context include ◆Language skills (precision questioning, indirect questioning, cause-effect chains and so forth; ◆Shifts of perspective to take on the other person's 'map of the world'; ◆Chunking to put things into context; and ◆Sensory acuity – the ability to recognise from the other person's signals when you are getting to the real heart of what is important. Practising all these skills will help you enormously in interviewing, as in many other aspects of the consultancy process.

Interviews with potential clients

You may be required to undergo a formal interview process in order to win a particular assignment. If this is the case, the interview may be on a one-to-one basis, or may be a panel interview, where you are faced with a number of people from the client organisation and, possibly, other independent advisors of theirs. There are certain skills that are useful in such situations, and I would like to cover some of them in this section.

The skills I will be discussing here are:

- When to arrive.
- What to wear.
- What to bring with you.
- How to greet people.
- Where and how to sit.
- Whom to look at.
- How long to speak for.
- What questions to ask.

When to arrive

It is good practice to arrive slightly early. Not so early that you embarrass people because they feel that, as you have come earlier than expected, they should drop other things to see you early. Not late, or you may seem unprofessional.

Being a little early will give you a chance to prepare yourself, check you look presentable, organise any papers you need and think about the meeting to come. If you are with a new client, it will also give you the chance to look at any material available in the waiting area, such as annual reports, newsletters or promotional material, and get a feel for how things are done and what style the organisation adopts. You can also chat to any reception staff, which often gives you helpful information about the organisation.

What to wear

I have already covered Impression Management in Chapter 10, so this is just a reminder to do some research before going to the interview, so you can wear clothes that are appropriate for the occasion and the organisation.

In any case, do a last-minute check that your clothes are clean and tidy. It is a good idea to carry spare items such as ties or tights (whichever is appropriate for you!) so you have a substitute if needed.

What to bring with you

Make sure you have copies of any material you have sent in advance; the client may not have received everything, and it is easy to forget the details of what you have said in earlier communications unless you have a spare copy with you.

Bring some spare copies of promotional material, in case there are other people there who would find it useful; examples of work done for similar organisations are often helpful too.

Check you have a notepad and pen and put everything in one briefcase or other container if you can, so you don't give the impression of being cluttered.

How to greet people

If meeting new people, it is good to take the initiative and extend your hand first. A firm, but not crushing, handshake will transmit a feeling of confidence and if you combine it with a smile and good eye contact (not eyeballing people, but simply looking at their face) you will come across as positive and friendly. Remember that, as I have mentioned previously, in some cultures, it may be inappropriate to make physical contact with women, so handshakes might not be the correct thing to do.

If there are several people in the room, it is good to look, and smile, at each one in turn so they feel acknowledged.

Where and how to sit

You may have a seat indicated to you but, if not, think carefully about where to sit. A good place can be close to the other person or people; not directly facing them and not in the closest seat if there are several available. Sitting close by can give the impression that you are approachable, but not overly pushy nor confrontational.

You may also like to match (see Chapter 10) the posture of the other person/people by sitting back if they are, or leaning forward if they are; this may also give the impression that you are on the same wavelength as them. If there are several people, you can choose to match the one who is leading the meeting, or whom you feel is the most influential, or you may simply adopt a posture similar to the majority present.

Whom to look at

Maintaining good eye contact with everyone is helpful. As I mentioned above, this does not mean looking directly into people's eyes, but simply looking at them, rather than up at the ceiling, into the distance or down at the floor.

When one person is speaking, look at that person. When you are speaking, make sure you include as many people present as you can by looking at them in turn. Do not keep flitting back and forth so rapidly that you end up not having real eye contact with anyone at all.

How long to speak for

If you use your observation skills, this should become clear as the interview progresses. If you are uncertain, you can ask if they would like you to go on or whether you have said enough; you can also include some pauses to see whether someone else jumps in rapidly when they have the opportunity – this may indicate they have been waiting for you to finish.

On the whole, if people are looking engaged, responding with positive signals and asking questions, you are probably still maintaining their interest.

What questions to ask

It is important to ask some questions, or the client is likely to feel you have no real interest in the assignment. Good questions to ask are those that will help you evaluate whether you really want to do that piece of work and those that will show the client that you have picked up on important issues within the organisation.

As a general point, it is likely to be worth finding out what the major issues are in the situation; whether any similar projects have been carried out in the past and, if so, how successful they were;

whether all the top managers support the proposed activity; what the general staff morale is like; whether other people are being considered for the work; when decisions will be made; and what the time-scale is for starting.

If the interview is part of a selection process involving other consultancy firms, you may seek to find out who else has been invited to interview. If you can get this information in advance it can help in your own preparation, as you know whom you will be competing with and something about the client's choice of 'front-runners'. If you do have to compete with other firms, or other independent consultants, it becomes even more important to be clear about what makes you unique and particularly able to assist the client with the particular project. If you can find out anything about what others are offering, it can help you decide whether to be more flexible with your terms or more innovative in your proposals.

There is definitely an art to handling interviews well, and once you know some of the important elements, you will be able to hone your skills so you come across as professional, competent and likeable.

Let's now turn to presentations.

Presentations

You may need to make a presentation as part of your sales pitch to a potential client or you may find yourself making presentations to people within a client organisation as part of an assignment. You might also make presentations in other situations, such as discussing an assignment with potential colleagues and collaborators. Whatever the context, the skills are similar, and this section will give you some ways of making your presentations more interesting and effective. The topics I will be covering are:

- Accelerated Learning principles.
- Sensory inputs.
- Appealing to different sentiments.

- Visual aids.
- Timing.
- Interaction.
- Conditioning.

Accelerated Learning principles

I mentioned Accelerated Learning briefly in Chapter 7 on consultancy techniques. The main tenets of Accelerated Learning are that: ◆The front person has a responsibility for getting people into a state where they are receptive to learning; ◆People learn best when the environment is conducive to learning; ◆Taking account of differing learning styles ensures that people are helped in ways that are right for them; ◆Including elements that appeal to different senses will make learning more interesting and effective. I would like to consider these elements in what follows.

While you cannot actually force anyone into any state, you can certainly influence them. Once you accept that you can help your audience want to be informed, to learn, to be engaged and to feel enthusiastic, you will be more likely to take responsibility for bringing this about, rather than just sitting back and believing that if people aren't immediately responsive that is nothing to do with you and cannot be changed. So a positive frame of mind on your part will help this come about and give your audience confidence that you will interest them and give them useful things to come away with.

In order to make a presentation effective, you need to take account of people's differing needs and styles. When you think in this way, you will be able to arrange the environment, your manner and language, presentation materials and activities in such a way as to give everyone in your audience something to interest them and from which they can learn.

Accelerated Learning has a particular approach to learning styles and there are also other approaches, outside the Accelerated Learning field; before exploring the Accelerated Learning approach I would just like to outline one other approach to learning styles: the Honey and Mumford/Kolb model.

Do remember that the following frameworks will simply help you understand how people function; they should not be used to 'categorise' people irrevocably. Everyone has different ways of behaving (and learning) from time to time, and from context to context, so you should just use these ideas as a guide. If you are interested in pursuing this further, you will find details of books on the subject in the Bibliography.

Honey and Mumford/Kolb learning styles model

This approach to learning styles explores four ways of learning. The four styles are as follows:

Activists   – who like to be involved in things and explore.
Reflectors   – who like to have time to think and consider.
Theorists   – who like to understand the concepts behind things.
Pragmatists – who like to be able to apply things.

When doing a presentation to a group of people, it is probably best to assume that you have a combination of all these present. This means your presentation should include a practical element, where people can take part in discussion or activity of some kind; time to think (or papers given in advance, or to take away), so that people can consider their thoughts beforehand and assess their reactions afterwards; an explanation of how your ideas fit into a broader conceptual framework and of what underpins them; and an explanation of how your ideas can be put into practice and make a real contribution to their business.

Combining all these elements will give a broadly balanced presentation. If you are only presenting to one or two people, it is worth finding out all you can in advance about their individual learning preferences so you can gear your presentation to them personally.

Accelerated Learning styles framework

The Accelerated Learning framework has six categories that are generally relevant to business presentations; there are a further three (and more may be included in the future) but these additional ones are of less significance to most corporate presentations.

The six categories I will outline here are the following; the first three of these are also very important elements of NLP and I have referred to them briefly in Chapter 11.

Visual – people whose sense of sight is very important in perception and learning. These people need visual stimulation, so they will benefit from visual aids, good lighting, wallcharts, hand gestures to emphasis what is being said, and you as a visual aid (see below). If you speak without the use of visual aids, these people are likely to 'switch off'. People who use their visual sense a good deal often speak very quickly and make mental images of things that are said to them.

Auditory – people whose sense of hearing is important. These people take in information through listening, discussion and reading, so they will benefit from good voice tonality when you speak, the elimination of extraneous noise, the use of audiotapes and opportunities to talk things through. If your words do not communicate effectively, you will lose these people.

Kinaesthetic – people whose sense of touch and feeling is important. These people need both tactile and emotional stimulation if they are to be receptive, so consider the comfort of seating, heating levels and ventilation, as well as ensuring that what you say and do gets through to them at an emotional level. Kinaesthetic people may speak and move slowly as they can take time to generate feelings and responses.

Mathematical/logical – people who have a need for reason and systematic thinking. These people will need your presentation to be well structured, contain relevant facts and figures and be intellectually rigorous. They will probably spot inconsistencies and may get lost if you do not keep to a predictable structure. They will enjoy having backup information and spending time on analysis and debate.

Interpersonal – people who like working with others. These people enjoy group activity and thrive on teamwork and group discussion. You may find that these people are influenced by group decisions, and you may have to work hard to get them to express a personal opinion or to undertake sole responsibility for an activity.

Intrapersonal – people who like doing things on their own. These people can sometimes be hard to handle in a group presentation as they may either want to dominate or, alternatively, take a back seat because they do not feel comfortable being in the limelight. You will probably have to work hard to convince these people, but once convinced, they can be very positive and enthusiastic.

By taking account of each of these different learning styles, you will be able to make your presentations appeal to different people and enhance your chances of a successful outcome.

Sensory inputs

Just as, with the Honey and Mumford/Kolb model, it is advisable to assume you may have representatives of all the learning styles in any audience, so you would probably do well to assume you have people in your audience with need for stimulation in all the sensory channels. I have mentioned three above: visual, auditory and kinaesthetic. You can add to these olfactory (smell) and gustatory (taste). If you are able to stimulate all of the senses in your presentation you can create a dynamic and enticing environment and experience.

Here are some suggestions for building a sensory-rich environment, where people can learn effectively.

- Include visuals around the walls – charts, posters, Post-it® notes, photographs and so on. Have seats in a circle or horseshoe, so people can see each other.

- Play some music or use some pleasant-sounding aids, such as chimes or a bell, to call people to order. Make sure your voice is varied and interesting – loud enough to hear but not overpowering.

- Have some tactile objects around the room – for example, squashy stress balls. Use comfortable chairs, well spaced so people aren't cramped. Give yourself space to move around.

- Have a few sweets or nuts for people to chew; arrange refreshments if possible.

- Have a vase of scented flowers or use scented oils for particular purposes (for example, mint or rosemary for concentration, citrus for energy and lavender for relaxation).

While it will not be feasible to do this at most initial presentations to potential clients, remembering the significance of sensory elements can still inform your behaviour, and you may be able to include some elements in your presentation – perhaps managing your voice tonality well, using effective visual aids and generating positive feelings in your audience.

And when you do presentations to client staff, you can incorporate even more of these elements, such as room layout, the use of posters, photographs or charts, and providing refreshments, which will be appreciated.

Appealing to different sentiments

There are many ways in which you can communicate to an audience. One useful approach to consider is the use of differing sentiments. A framework that is often used for this is based on three Greek words: Ethos, Pathos and Logos.

The principle here is that there are three potential sentiments that can be used to gain people's attention. Of course, more are possible, but for the time being let's take the three to which I have referred above.

Ethos is to do with credibility. Developing ethos is about convincing your audience that you have the right to be there in front of them and that they will have much to gain from listening to you. Ethos is about demonstrating that you are competent, knowledgeable and professional. You can demonstrate this in a variety of ways. You may tell people your background and experience; you may give them examples of work you have done; you may show them that you can answer questions and explore issues effectively.

Ethos has to be earned; it does not come automatically. Once you have established a reputation in your field, you will not have to work at this so much, but it is worth assuming that credibility has to be constantly earned and to act accordingly. Ethos is also important at interviews with prospective clients.

Pathos is to do with emotion. Developing pathos is about appealing to your audience's feelings. Where there are emotive issues involved, it is easy to move down this path; in other cases pathos is something that may need to be generated. Do avoid over-emotionalising issues, however, otherwise people may avoid taking action because they feel it would be overwhelming, confrontational or stressful, or they may be wary of what you are saying because they feel you have hyped your subject.

Emotional Intelligence has become a bit of a buzz-word in recent years and, although there is now more recognition of the part that emotion, and emotional sensitivity, plays in business, you do need to be careful with the use of pathos until you know you can handle any responses your approach may generate.

Logos is to do with reason and rationality. Developing logos is about showing that you can sustain a logical argument, put forward the pros and cons of a case, present facts and figures and deal with hard data as well as personalities and feelings. Logos is possibly the most commonly found sentiment in business, as managers and consultants tend to be used to reasoning skills and data collection and handling.

Logos is also useful at interviews as well as presentations. While it can convey understanding and practicality, using only logos can make a presentation rather impersonal and detached.

The use of Ethos, Pathos and Logos combined can give a presentation a broad appeal, variety and interest. Learning to work with all three sentiments is worth pursuing in order to give your own presentations an edge and a breadth of appeal.

Visual aids

Having visual aids will give your presentation added interest and is a necessary element for people with a strong visual preference. There are many kinds of visual aids, and often the simplest work best.

Some of the options you might like to consider are:

• *Flip chart*

Simple to use; possible to detach sheets and stick on the wall or keep for future reference; good if members of the group are also going to make a contribution as they can come up and write too.

• *Overhead projector*

Good for prepared transparencies; easy to see from a distance; easy to pick up previous slides again if wanted.

• *PowerPoint®*

Professional-looking, although sometimes too slick in appearance; easy to build up images an element at a time; not very flexible – best used in predetermined sequence; if it goes wrong you need a backup.

• *Post-it® notes*

Useful for flexible displays of information, or for generating and sifting ideas.

- *Objects*

  Visual aids can be anything you choose to show; for example models, puppets (yes, really), photographs and anything you find in the room that can be used to demonstrate a point.

- *Yourself as a visual aid*

  Because of what I have said above about the importance of learning styles and sensory perception, people with a visual sensory preference are likely to need their visual sense to be stimulated if they are to pay attention and learn. If you wear very neutral clothes, you do not create a focal point or any visual interest in yourself; this is likely to mean that some people will 'switch off' because there is little visual interest to be obtained by watching you.

  So, think about this when presenting and aim to wear something that is visually interesting. For men, as you are most likely to be wearing a formal business suit, the interest may come from your tie. Wearing a tie with a subtle but interesting design and some colour that contrasts with your suit will help. Having some shade of red in your tie (bright red, burgundy, orange, pink, rust, etc.) will also help as this tends to make you look more energetic and healthier – select whichever of these shades looks best on you. For women, visual interest can come from jewellery, scarves, or other colour and design details on your clothes. If you are in doubt as to what works best for you, you can engage the services of an image consultant to help you choose (see Resources List).

Also remember that your movement is part of the impression you create, so avoid irritating people through the use of repetitive movements, and use your posture and gestures in ways that create an impression of enthusiasm and competence. If you can also arouse some curiosity, that will help your audience keep interested; make sure you don't overdo this, however, or you may be seen as too unconventional to be accepted. And do remember to face your audience or they may feel you lack interest or confidence and become apathetic in response.

Timing

If there is a time limit on your presentation, keep to it. People may have other commitments, and it demonstrates professionalism to manage your time effectively. If the presentation is open-ended, aim to go on for as long as is necessary to cover the issues. If the presentation is lengthy, have some breaks – either formal ones for refreshments, or short 'comfort breaks' for two or three minutes at a time. Let people know in advance what the time frame is, so they can plan and so they know when to anticipate a break. Start on time unless there is a really good reason to do otherwise; it will be fairer on those who have arrived on time and will help you keep your finish time accurate.

Interaction

Make sure you interact with your audience and encourage interaction between its members. If you stand in front of a group and declaim, you may lose their interest; being involved with the group and interacting with people will be friendlier and more supportive of their involvement. So use good eye contact, ask questions, invite and respond to questions from them. You can also help people interact with each other by inviting group discussion and by asking for comments on points made by members of the group.

Conditioning your audience through associations

This is an interesting concept. People very readily make associations between things. For example, if you once drank some milk that had curdled, you would probably check out each new bottle to ensure it was fresh. And if you knew somebody who spoke in a particular tone of voice, you would probably draw similarities between that person and any other people you met later who spoke in a similar way.

You can use this concept of association when presenting, to get your audience to respond in particular ways when you do certain things. For example, if you move around when you present, and always speak in a positive manner when you stand in one part of the room and in a more negative manner when you stand in another part of the room, the audience will begin to associate those two spots with positive and negative attributes. If you then say something when in the 'positive' spot, the people are more likely to respond well to it than if you had not previously 'conditioned' them to feel good about that spot.

A similar technique can be used if you have information to present that may not go down too well – for example a high total fee for a particular piece of work, or the fact that you are not available for a particular period when the client might have wanted you. In this case, you should avoid physically holding on to the information, for example by reading from a document you have in your hands, as this makes you part of that information and the client may develop negative feelings towards you, as well as towards the information itself. A better process is to distance yourself from the information, perhaps by putting it on a flip chart and then standing back from it and looking at it from close to the client. In this way you can both consider the potentially negative information in a more detached manner. Again, this technique can be used with interviews as well as presentations.

So there are many aspects to a good presentation; if you make sure your presentations are well planned to meet their objectives, are representative of you as a person and take account of the needs of your audience, you are well on the way to being successful.

Now let's turn to the next topic, meetings.

Meetings

There will, no doubt, be many occasions when you need to either attend, or chair, meetings. Effective meeting management will be helpful to everyone; it can speed things up, enhance morale and motivation and achieve results. Here are some ideas for making your meetings more effective.

Clarify your role
Sometimes your role is clear from the start. If, for example, you have convened the meeting, it should be apparent that you will be responsible for its conduct. Sometimes, however, you will be invited to meetings where client management will be present, as well as client staff, or possibly other people from outside. If this is the case, you should make sure you, and the meeting convenors, are clear about your role at the meeting: will you be there as an advisor, as a backup to management, as a facilitator, or as an impartial observer? If you do not clarify this early on you could find you are put in a compromising position during the meeting itself.

Arrive early
As with interviews, it is good to arrive early for meetings, especially if you are in the chair. By getting there early you can choose where to sit. You can greet people when they arrive; this is especially important if you are chairing the meeting, as you can check whether anyone seems to be in a frame of mind that will not be helpful to the meeting, and try to deal with this before the meeting starts. You can also have a pre-meeting chat to other people, which can be useful if you want to get agreement on how to approach certain items or check whether expected action has been taken.

Have a well-structured agenda

If you are in the chair you will probably be responsible for producing an agenda for the meeting. The person who produces the agenda has a good deal of control over the meeting itself and is likely to be able to determine which items are taken when, how much time is spent on each and what information is presented to people attending. Putting times to agenda items is useful, so everyone knows how long the item has been allocated and those participating can be moved on if discussion becomes too lengthy.

Keep to agreed timing

Meetings can be productive, but they can also be time-wasters. It is important to keep to the anticipated timing, both for each item and for the meeting as a whole. It is also important to start on time, so that those who have arrived in good time are rewarded for doing so; if you delay until everyone is there you may find, another time, that others arrive late because they felt their time was wasted on the last occasion when they arrived early.

Produce useful minutes

Good minutes are a reminder to those who were present, and a summary to those who were not present, of what took place. They should therefore be detailed enough to make sense, while not being over-wordy. Minutes should be circulated in good time so that people are reminded of any necessary action. A specific action sheet, which summarises the points on which action needs to be taken, and gives the name, or initials, of the person taking the action, is useful as a reminder and a subsequent check on activity.

Observe people

Noticing how people are behaving and reacting will help you manage a meeting, anticipate conflict, check for boredom or lethargy, notice if someone wants to make a point or ask a question and check reactions to your own contributions. Some specific signs to look out for are fidgeting, attempts to speak, non-participation, clock-watching, attempts to exclude others, sarcasm, paper-shuffling and misunderstanding.

Manage the process

Managing the process of a meeting is vital if you are in the chair. I have already mentioned managing time; other process-management methods include involving or excluding people as appropriate; managing disagreement if it starts to get out of hand, stopping 'sub-meetings' where people have conversations between themselves while the meeting is in progress, helping people to reflect on ideas and proposals and ensuring a balanced discussion on all topics. It can be helpful to have a contract at the start of each meeting, whereby everyone agrees to participate fully, give and accept feedback positively, say if there are things they do not understand, ask for information if they need it and keep to agreed timing and any other rules for the meeting.

So these are some aspects of meetings which it is helpful to consider. Good meeting management is a great aid to effectiveness, and sharpening your skills in this area will be a useful asset. Let's turn now to the final element in this chapter – negotiating.

Negotiations

Negotiating is something you will have to do at various stages, either formally or informally. You need to negotiate fee rates and other conditions of service with your clients; you may need to negotiate about working relationships with staff in your client's organisation; you may need to be involved in negotiations with unions or staff associations for clients, depending on the nature of your work with them; you might also be responsible for negotiating on a client's behalf, or as part of a client team, with outsiders. In all these cases some key skills will be useful. Here are some of the elements of effective negotiating.

Agreeing objectives

It helps to set an outcome that makes sense to both parties. This may sound obvious, but if you do not do this, you may find that you have different expectations that can never come together. Even if you do not have the same desired result, you can at least agree on the kind of agreement you would like to make, which will be a good starting point.

Understanding the other person's perspective and values

Being able to see things from the other person's point of view is important, as it helps you understand what they want and how they function. You can never truly be in another person's position, but anything you can do to understand their perspective will be useful. Finding out about the other person's values – what is really important to them – is part of the overall process of understanding someone else. When you know what a person values, you have useful information on what you can do to influence them and what you can offer that they will appreciate.

Focusing on interests rather than positions and issues rather than people

The more you take on a set stance, the less likely it is that you will achieve your desired result. The alternative to adopting stances is considering interests. This means you consider what is important to you, rather than having a rigid position on what you are aiming for; in this way you can be more flexible and are more likely to be successful. Similarly, if you deal with personality and personal interest, rather than the underlying issues that concern people, you will be less likely to achieve success. Try to put aside differences between you and others and concentrate on the important issues that you are trying to handle. In this way, you can retain objectivity and still have a good relationship with the other party, despite any differences of opinion.

Dealing with issues as they come up

Some people approach negotiating in a very structured way. They go in with a fixed agenda and do not depart from it. Often, however, it is more useful to take issues as they come up, so they can be tackled as 'live' realities, rather than artificially divided. Working in this way takes a good deal of skill and may be likened to doing a job interview by following what the candidate says and only reverting to a structure if they run out of steam or go off the point. If you can follow a natural process of discussion it is often more helpful and also gives you a better idea of how the other person functions.

Looking for common ground
Whatever the topic, there will probably be some factors on which you agree, or in which you have a common interest. It is useful to seek out these factors, as they can enhance the relationship and prepare the ground for later agreement on other issues.

Generating options
The more options you have, the more likely it is that you will find a point of mutual agreement. Although this may not always be the case, it is worth producing a range of options, which can then be considered for agreement. You could use brainstorming (see Chapter 7) in order to generate the options, or you could simply do it through conversation; whatever process you use is likely to help flexibility of thinking and action.

Reframing
This can be very useful in negotiating. Reframing simply means putting a different slant on things, or interpreting them in different ways. If you present something that has not been well received, you can re-present it with a different emphasis. If the other person is asking for something that appears untenable, you can show how a different view of it could lead to an alternative solution.

Reverse disagreement
This is a technique whereby, if you have to take a contrary stance, you give the reasons first. So, instead of saying "We can't start until October because we have other commitments until then", you say "We have other commitments at present and so we can't start until October", or, even better, "We have other commitments at present, so we can start in October". By giving reasons first, you make it less likely that the other person will perceive what you are saying as a rejection. There is also evidence that using the specific word 'because' when you give a reason will be particularly powerful in gaining acceptance.

'Yes set'

This is a process that is often used in sales and can also work in negotiating. Once a person has become accustomed to agreeing with you on several matters, it can predispose them to agree with you on others. So the technique relies on getting 'Yes' answers to a range of questions (and 'No' can also mean 'Yes'; for example when you say to someone, "You haven't been to Sheffield, have you?" and the response is "No, I haven't", the 'No' actually means "I agree with you that I haven't been there"). This process may sound simplistic but it often works in practice. You do need to make sure, however, that the questions you ask are going to get 'Yes' as an answer (or a 'No' which implies 'Yes' – as explained above), or the process will have unpredictable results.

Conditioning, signalling and packaging

Conditioning is a process whereby you make moves towards agreement, but without making any definite commitments. The language used for this is usually 'If -then'. So you might say, "If you were able to guarantee us X days' work, then we might be able to lower our daily rate to £x." The process is testing responses to get a feel for what the outcome might be.

Using, and recognising, 'signalling' is a useful aid here, signals being signs that a person is, or is not responding favourably to what is being discussed. The observation skills I have mentioned in other chapters will be put to good use in this context.

Packaging is important as unskilled negotiators often give some things away too early in the process and then find they have no scope for further bargaining. Packaging means putting together all the elements of your case, so you treat them as a whole and have room for bargaining. When putting forward a proposal for an assignment, you might use the elements of time-scale, cost, supporting materials, flexibility and so forth. If you have to give way on some, you might gain ground on others.

Seeking 'win-win' outcomes

Although there may be some times when both parties cannot win, on the whole a negotiation is likely to go better when both parties gain something from the interaction. If you can work jointly towards an outcome where there is mutual gain, you are likely to maintain a positive relationship and make it easier for effective negotiating to take place another time.

Dialogue

This is a very specific use of a common word and more can be found on it as a technique in Yankelovitch's book listed in the bibliography. Dialogue is a good process to use when seeking 'win-win' outcomes. Dialogue may be distinguished from debate (where people try to score points) and discussion (where people argue from fixed interests). With dialogue, both parties aim for a 'win-win' outcome, listen meaningfully and suspend self interest while the process of talking continues. Some specific elements of dialogue are: ◆Showing empathy; ◆Clarifying assumptions; ◆Avoiding being judgmental; ◆Focussing on common interests; ◆Minimising mistrust; ◆Expressing emotions accompanying strongly held values; ◆Encouraging relationships; ◆Listening well; ◆Separating dialogue from decision making; ◆Avoiding scoring points; ◆Using specific cases to raise general issues.

Labelling

Labelling is a process whereby you indicate the nature of your intervention before it takes place. For example, "I would like to ask a question", "Can I make a point" and "I have an observation" are examples of labelling behaviour.

Expressing personal feelings

Contrary to what some people think, effective negotiators often express their feelings openly – for example, "I feel we are getting bogged down in detail", "I am disappointed that we are going over the same ground again", "I am really happy with the progress we have made so far". Points like this communicate very well how someone is reacting and make the process of interaction more open and explicit.

Bargaining

Having done the preliminary work, the actual bargaining needs to take place. If your testing and packaging have been effective, bargaining may, in reality, simply be a matter of summarising what has already been explored. You may, however, have to go through a specific bargaining stage, and at this point, you will want to have information on your own position and that of the other party. If you work out the following elements either before or during the negotiation, or in an adjournment, you will be well equipped to embark on the bargaining stage with confidence.

You will need to work out three elements, for yourself and for the other party. The elements are a) ideal position, b) realistic position and c) fallback position. Your ideal position is what you would like in an ideal world, and their ideal position is what they would like, ideally. Your fallback position is the minimum you would settle for; theirs is the minimum they would settle for. Your realistic position is a range within which you could reach agreement, and their realistic position is a range within which they could reach agreement. It is only when there is overlap between what you are able to settle for and what they are able to settle for that agreement is possible.

Bargaining ranges

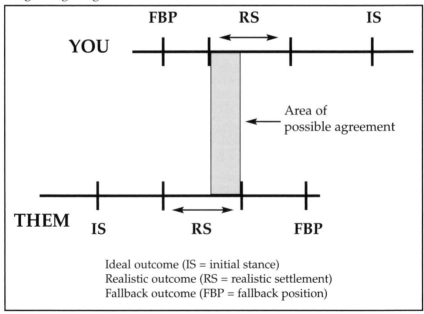

The more accurately you can estimate the other party's position on these elements, the easier it will be for you to obtain a good settlement.

Anticipating problems

Good negotiators tend to think ahead, and if they believe there could be difficulties further down the line, they will raise them as issues before they become a problem. You may think it is easier to ignore potential problems, as they may go away, but realistic handling of potential problem areas is likely to result in a better, and longer-lasting, outcome.

Finally, there may be times when an 'off-the-record' chat outside the negotiating process itself can be both friendly and productive.

Final Points

This chapter has dealt with a number of contexts that are common in consultancy work. Many of the skills I have covered overlap, so if you have developed skills in one of these areas you will be able to transfer them, fairly easily, into another. Together with the other skills covered in the book, the ones I have discussed here will be good additions to your overall effectiveness.

NLP techniques used in this chapter and the sections where you can find them

Meta-model (interviews you conduct – precision questioning)
Perceptual positions (interviews you conduct – 'map of the world')
Chunking (interviews you conduct – context)
Sensory acuity (interviews you conduct – recognising signals)
Anchoring (conditioning your audience through associations)
Reframing (reframing)

Accelerated Learning techniques used in this chapter

Environment
Learning styles

Chapter 13
Helping Others Develop

This chapter will introduce you to some of the skills involved in helping other people to achieve results.

In consultancy, sometimes you will have a very explicit role in developing other people and helping them to become more effective. At other times, you may simply help them without it being made obvious. Whatever the situation, this kind of activity is becoming more and more common in consultancy, and the following ideas will, I hope, help you become more skilled at such development activity.

Facilitating

Facilitation, fairly literally translated, means 'making things easy'. In consultancy, there are many situations where you may be called upon to facilitate. The most common of these is facilitating a meeting, but you might be asked to facilitate a discussion between two individuals or you might need to facilitate the acquisition of a subsidiary company. Whatever the situation, there are specific skills involved in facilitation that will help you in your task.

I have already covered several skills in this book that are vital to facilitation. Some of these are observation skills, rapport skills, and a range of interpersonal skills. In this chapter I will concentrate on those skills that are more specific to facilitation itself. In what follows, I will be referring to group facilitation for simplicity, although most of the points I will be covering also apply to work with individuals.

Process, not content
A good facilitator will be involved in process, not content. By this, I mean that as a facilitator, it is your job to manage *how* people achieve their results, not *what* results they achieve. So your first job

is to accept (and, if facilitation is new to the people you are working with, to explain) that your focus will be on *how* activity takes place.

Knowledge of the subject matter

Some facilitators prefer not to have any knowledge of the subject matter of the events they are facilitating. They say that without this knowledge, they are not tempted to explore their own opinions regarding the issues, and can remain outside, helping others to explore their own ideas. Other people feel that they do need a knowledge of the topic and issues if they are to help the other people involved to get the most from their interactions. Whichever view you take, the important thing to remember is that the more detached you can remain from the subject matter, the more effective you are likely to be and the less you can be criticised for taking sides or for leading people to inappropriate conclusions.

Explanation of role

It is important that you explain your role right from the outset, so that everyone knows what to expect. Because facilitation is not leading, or chairing, or directing, some people will be unfamiliar with the role and may find it unusual, so the more you can do to explain the reasons for your role and how you will actually be working, the easier it will be for others to understand and accept.

Specification of goal

It is important that both you and anyone else involved are clear about the objectives of the session. Having agreed goals will keep people focused and allow you to check, at the end, that the aims have been achieved.

Environment

Certain environments are more conducive to facilitation than others. Ideally, with group facilitation, it is helpful to have seats in a circle or horseshoe shape, so that everyone can see everyone else. It is sometimes best for you not to be situated at the front as if you were the group leader. Comfortable seating, good light, adequate heat and periodic refreshments will help people relax and be able to work effectively. You will generally need some means of recording the proceedings; this could be someone to act as note-taker, or it could be a flip chart, a screen that can be copied from, or Post-it® notes that can be collected up afterwards. It is helpful if you can avoid disturbances and ensure that people do not come and go or use mobile phones and pagers while they are present.

Time management

Managing time is one of your functions as a facilitator. Although you could delegate this to someone else in the group, you will be more in control of the process if you manage it yourself. If you are not to be looking at your watch all the time, it helps to have a clock situated in your line of vision.

'Helicoptering'

A good facilitator needs to be able to 'rise above' events and be detached. In NLP this is called being dissociated; in other circles it is called 'taking a helicopter view'. Being able to see things from differing perspectives and with an objective, rather than a subjective, manner, will enable you to observe what is going on, take an overview and imagine what the other people's experience is like. This, in turn, should help you manage the process in an effective and balanced manner.

Noticing signs

Being aware of the many subtle indications of thoughts and feelings that come through people's behaviour is a key skill to the next point – managing interactions. Using your peripheral vision is useful here, as it will enable you to notice things that are going on outside your direct visual range. Some of the things you may notice are eye movements, facial expressions, slight body movements and so forth. Receptivity to all of these will enhance your sensitivity and thereby your responsiveness to the group as a whole. A simple way of developing awareness of peripheral movement is to hold your arms in front of you, pointing your fingers straight ahead, then move your arms to the sides while still looking forwards. See if you can extend your awareness of the movement over increasing distances.

Managing interactions

There will be many things going on in the group that may need attention. For example you may need to bring in people who are being very quiet; they may have views they would like to express but feel intimidated or lack confidence in their own opinions. You may also need to control people who are being dominating, or others may feel annoyed or pushed out. You may need to deal with conflict, or potential conflict, between people; if people are being openly antagonistic, or if you are picking up signals that they do not see eye to eye, you may have to intervene in order to enable the group as a whole to continue functioning. And you may need to deal with people having discussions between themselves rather than participating in the group activity.

You will certainly need to handle questions, some of which may be directed at you, but most of which are likely to be between people in the group. Your role will be to make sure people wanting to ask a question have been noticed, to help clarify the question if the others do not understand it, to make sure the group listens to both the question and the response, to check that the questioner has been responded to in an acceptable manner and to find out if anyone else wishes to ask follow-up questions or to explore that particular topic any further.

Another thing you will need to manage is any discussion that seems to be getting out of hand. This can happen, for example, if people get excited and several speak at once, or if opinions get heated.

Keeping on track

Another task for you is to ensure that discussion stays on the relevant subject. It is often easy to stray off the track, be diverted into unnecessary detail or overgeneralisation, go round in circles or fall into chat mode rather than task-orientation mode. While there is a place for diversion and relaxation, you should be clear about when this is appropriate and deal with other instances effectively so the group stays focused on its goals.

Clarifying, reflecting and summarising

There may be times when people do not understand issues, or each other, and you have a role to play in helping achieve clarity. You may do this by explanation, or you may do it by drawing information and thoughts out of others. Whichever route you choose, the group will be able to function better when you help them understand what is being said and experienced.

Helping people understand can also be aided by the process of reflection. The word 'reflection' is often used to mean thinking about an issue and weighing up its different aspects; it can also mean the process of paraphrasing or giving people back their ideas in a slightly different form, to check exactly what they mean. Both these processes are useful in facilitation. Giving time to think, and helping check meaning, will be useful for the group as a whole and may also help particular individuals to refine their thinking within the group.

Summarising is useful at different stages. Certainly it is important at the end of a session, so everyone is agreed on what has been achieved and what action may be taken next. However, summarising can also be useful at other points, to check agreement, progress and understanding. You could also summarise people's contributions.

Putting a new slant on things
This is about helping people to think about things differently. There are several ways in which this can be done. One way is to

use what is called 'reframing'. Reframing means putting a different interpretation on something; for example loss of a job can be seen as a threat to security, or it can be seen as an opportunity for new development – 'reframing' the situation can help you deal with it in different ways.

Another way in which you can help people is through the use of metaphor and analogy. Using these processes, you can draw parallels between one issue and another. You can do this either openly and explicitly, explaining your choice of metaphor or analogy, or you can simply use the parallel examples without drawing attention to them, so that people can absorb what you are saying at a more unconscious level.

Acknowledging
It is important that people you are facilitating know that they are being acknowledged. This does not mean that you, or others, have to agree with them, but that you should let them know that their points have been heard and their feelings understood. Sometimes this can be hard to do, especially if you do not personally agree with the points being made, but it does help integration of the group and generally leads to good levels of interaction and can prevent any conflict escalating.

Checking energy levels
This means both theirs and yours. Facilitation can be hard work because you have to concentrate all the time; you may not seem to be doing much, but you are constantly engaged and active. The group may also become low on energy for various reasons, and if energy is low, they will be unable to function well. If you sense low energy levels, do something to raise them: have a break for refreshments, open a window, get the group engaged in some physical movement (you can tell them it is to raise the energy levels, and there are many examples of such activities in books on training). Whatever you choose, make sure the energy level has risen before moving on, otherwise people will be wasting their time, and yours, by being there and not being on good form.

A good facilitator is constantly alert, has eyes in the back of his or her head, remains calm and assured and involves people to the best of their personal capabilities. Facilitation skills are well worth developing.

Some processes I have personally been asked to facilitate, in a consultancy role, are:

- 'Away days' where a group (sometimes a management team, sometimes a board of directors, sometimes a departmental group) needs time away from their normal work surroundings to examine current issues, consider long-term strategy, work on teambuilding or any one of a variety of issues that face people in a business context. An external facilitator in such circumstances can help the group focus on process and bring a detached perspective to what could otherwise be a very inward-looking activity.

- Interactions between individuals who are in some form of conflict. This may be two work colleagues, it may be a manager and member of staff or it may be other forms of relationship. Here an external facilitator is usually seen as unbiased and is therefore able to assist both parties to consider and exchange views in a more detached way than if they did it on their own or were facilitated by someone else from within the organisation.

- Development sessions, where a group of people have come together to learn and enhance their performance. A good example of this is an Action Learning 'set' (see Bibliography), where people within an organisation meet to help each other explore and resolve real live work issues. An external facilitator in these circumstances can help keep the process on track without having a vested interest in the operational outcome.

Now let's turn to the next topic, coaching.

Coaching

As a consultant you may find yourself in the role of coach – perhaps not officially, but almost certainly incidentally. As you work with clients and colleagues there are likely to be numerous occasions when you will be helping someone else, or a group of people, to learn new skills, change their attitudes and collaborate, for example. To do this effectively, you will need particular skills, and I would like to cover a few of them here. In what follows, I refer to individuals, but the techniques are equally applicable to groups.

Stages of coaching

Assuming you conduct coaching as an agreed process, there are five stages that you can consider.

- *Analysis*

  At this stage you assess the current performance (present state) and the target performance (desired state) of the person to be coached. Once these are both understood, the gap between them becomes apparent and a programme of coaching can be devised to help the person move from one to the other. You may need to involve both the learner and any significant colleagues – for example the learner's manager – in this process.

- *Planning*

  At this stage you consider the programme that will be implemented, the elements of learning, the time to be allocated, the resources needed, the support required and the monitoring and evaluation necessary. You will need to check your own availability and commitment as well as that of the learner.

- *Implementation*

  At this stage you carry out the coaching, adapt where necessary to fit the learner's style and motivation and any changed circumstances or requirements, and keep in touch with any other people who have an interest in the learner's activities.

● *Evaluation*

At this stage you assess the effectiveness of the programme and the development of the learner. You can review the approach, the techniques and the factors enhancing or diminishing success.

● *Future focusing*

At this stage you consider the longer term and assess whether an ongoing programme of follow-up or additional support is required.

Whether you are following a formal coaching programme or simply offering low-key support and advice, there are a number of elements that are important to consider; some of these are as follows:

Focusing on the person being coached

To be a good coach you need self-awareness skills, so you can monitor and manage your own thoughts, feelings and behaviour. However your attention needs to be focused on the other person if you are to help them effectively. To do this you need to use your visual observation skills in order to notice what the person is doing; you also need to use your listening skills to hear what they person is saying (or not saying!).

Some of the things you can watch for are facial expressions, eye focus, body movement patterns, apparent energy highs or lows, responses to your own observations, distraction, information and activity overload.

Some of the things you can listen for are positive or negative statements, variations in tone of voice, signs of understanding or confusion.

It helps to take in observations as information rather than to evaluate them instantly. This means noticing things (for example a facial expression that seems to indicate confusion) and then checking what is actually going on, as you may find your original perception was incorrect.

It also helps to imagine what things are like for the other person – both their work activity and their experience of the coaching situation. You can do this by taking on his or her perspective; in that way you can gain useful information about the person's needs and also have some insights into how your coaching style and processes come across.

Understanding the person
You might debate whether it is ever possible to understand another person, but in coaching, it is important to have at least some basic ideas about the person with whom you are working. Some of the things you can seek to understand are.

- Values: what is important to the person.
- Motivation: how the person becomes stimulated to take action.
- Learning styles: how the person learns best.
- Goals: what the person wants to achieve.

The better you can understand the person, the easier it is to gear your coaching to them as an individual and towards their specific needs.

Listening, questioning and giving information
Key skills in coaching are those of giving and getting information. Listening and questioning are especially important, as it is through the process of assessing the learner's thoughts, feelings and behaviour that you will understand that person's outlook, motivation and understanding. The more you use non-directive methods of questioning, that is following up what the learner is saying or doing rather than imposing your own style, the more you will help the person explore their own situation and ideas. However, there may well be times when you need a more direct

approach in order to expand the learner's thinking and direct him or her towards specific outcomes and processes.

Giving feedback

As you observe things you can feed them back as observations. You can turn them into positive or negative comments, but you can also feed them back simply as information; there will be times when each of these approaches can be more effective.

When giving feedback it is helpful to remember:

- To separate the behaviour from the person, so that you are commenting on what the person *does* rather than *what sort of person* does that kind of thing.

- To balance negative feedback with positive if possible, so the overall impression is not simply of adverse criticism. Make any criticism constructive so that the learner can use it in a practical way.

- To base feedback on facts rather than opinions. Of course there will be times when you do need to express an opinion on what has been done, but it is generally more helpful to focus on the facts themselves. For example, "I noticed you fidgeted when I mentioned how much time was left before your report has to be submitted" rather than "I thought you looked uncomfortable when I mentioned how much time was left before your report has to be submitted". The former tells the person what their behaviour is, so they have an opportunity to modify it, rather than simply stating your own thoughts on what they are doing.

- To make feedback specific, so the person understands exactly what you are referring to.

- To provide feedback on elements that can be changed. A person can generally change their behaviour; they can also change their thoughts, feelings and beliefs. However some things are rather less likely to be changed, or are impossible to change. I was once asked to advise a senior executive on appearance. One of this person's characteristics was his bushy eyebrows, which others had felt were making him come across as unkempt and quirky. However these eyebrows were an intrinsic part of the person, and although he could have had them tidied up, he would not have felt this was compatible with his self-image. This feedback would be unlikely to be accepted.

Being open, trustworthy, supportive and empowering
The more you can create an atmosphere in which you can work amicably, the easier your task becomes. Some elements of this are:

- Being open: so that you express your thoughts and feelings and give information freely.

- Being trustworthy: so that people know that confidentiality will be respected and it is all right to make mistakes.

- Being supportive: so that the person knows you will be there for them as an individual, even if you do not agree with everything they do.

- Being motivating: so that you provide positive encouragement and also help the person overcome any negative beliefs they may have about their own levels of ability, or about other people's opinions of them.

- Being empowering: so you enable the person to own and take responsibility for their goals, behaviour, thoughts, feelings and results.

Having an understanding of the person's role and requirements
The better your understanding of what the person has to achieve, the easier it will be to coach him or her. And the more you can apply a structure to what the person has to perform, the easier it will be to help the person become aware of how the elements of their performance relate to each other and contribute to their overall success.

Being a role model

As well as coaching by explicit guidance, it is also useful at times to coach by example. If you can demonstrate, either openly or simply by being observed, effective ways of functioning, you are likely to help the person you are coaching to enhance their skills.

Increasingly, there is a trend towards distance coaching, for example coaching via telephone or e-mail. There are specialist organisations set up to develop and provide such coaching expertise, and this trend looks set to expand further in years to come.

Some things I have coached people in, as a consultant, have been how to:

- Manage a team.
- Remain calm and assertive.
- Manage image.
- Deal with performance-management issues.
- Facilitate.
- Listen and gather information.
- Deal with emotional responses.
- Relate to people of different types.
- Interview.
- Run meetings.

Finally, in this chapter – mentoring.

Mentoring

Mentoring is becoming more prevalent in many business areas and consultancy is no exception. As a consultant you may be called upon to act, formally, as a mentor; more often you will find yourself undertaking this role in a less overt manner. Knowing some of the key skills of mentoring will be a help to you in each of these situations.

The word 'mentor' originates from ancient Greece. According to legend, Mentor, an old and wise friend of Odysseus, was asked by Ulysses to look after his son, Telemachus, while Ulysses was away.

Mentor also had another form – that of the goddess Athena. And Athena was renowned for her wisdom and was a particular protector of craftsmen. So mentoring became associated with guidance, protection and the overseeing of a young person by an older one. Apprenticeships for craftsmen were an early industrial development, and mentoring schemes are now commonplace in British industry and elsewhere.

Today mentoring describes the process whereby a person helps another to understand, learn and develop. Although in its original usage it was a one-way process, mentoring can have benefits to both parties – if you act as a mentor to someone else you are likely to enhance your own development too. Julie Hay (*Transformational Mentoring* – see Bibliography) refers to Developmental Alliances as 'Relationships between equals in which one or more of those involved is enabled to increase awareness, identify alternatives and initiate action to develop themselves'. This is a much broader definition of the concept than that traditionally used.

Mentoring tends to be a longer-term activity than coaching and can extend over many months or years. If you act as a mentor to someone, you will need to take the role seriously and consider whether you can give long-term commitment if that is what is required.

There are many ways in which mentoring can take place and these are some of the elements often found in the mentoring process:

- Acting as a sounding board.
- Giving support.
- Giving guidance.
- Sharing knowledge, information and wisdom.
- Helping evaluate outcomes or results.
- Confirming decision-making processes.
- Giving feedback.
- Role-modelling.
- Helping explore learning processes.
- Providing motivation.
- Helping to handle the process of change.

As a mentor, it is important to recognise the extent to which you can help the learner; there may well be some aspects that are beyond your own capabilities. It is helpful then to be able to refer the person on to another source of help, or to develop your own skills in order to help the person further.

It is also important to recognise that in mentoring, as in counselling and therapy, it is only too easy to let a professional relationship drift into a personal one. It is important to keep these distinctions in mind, as professional and personal relationships can become blurred and give rise to either personal or ethical problems.

As a consultant, you can often find yourself in a mentoring relationship. It is quite common for this to happen when working with people who are in the top management team of an organisation. Chief executives often feel isolated and unable to share their thoughts and ideas with others within their organisation, and senior managers sometimes need support that they feel they cannot get from their colleagues. It is important that your role in such situations is well defined, as a number of ethical issues may be raised that could possibly cause complications.

If you do act as a mentor, either to a colleague or to someone within a client organisation, there will be skills you need in order to be successful. Many of these will be the same as those I have mentioned under coaching. The mentoring relationship, however, is usually a less directive one than coaching and, because of this, your skills as a mentor will tend to centre on empowerment, reflection and being a role model for your learner.

I have had many examples in consultancy of acting as a mentor to clients; in fact it seems to be a recurring element of what I do. I think if you establish a good relationship and do produce results that are valued, this encourages a climate where you are likely to move from straight consultancy into more of a mentoring mode.

Some people I have taken on this role with include:

- Chief executives.
- Senior managers.

- Functional staff.
- Other consultants working within the same organisation.
- My own support staff.

And, although I have never been on the receiving end of a formal mentoring process, there are many people I would mention from whom I have learned in various ways and would recommend as mentors to others if I were asked.

Final Points

In this chapter I have covered the techniques of facilitating, coaching and mentoring. There are many business contexts where these techniques can be used; some of the most common are:

- Skills development.
- Attitude change.
- Career development.
- Change management.
- Teambuilding.
- Motivation.
- Creativity.
- Confidence enhancement.

Each of these contexts can make different demands of the facilitator, coach or mentor, but all of them will require the range of skills and approaches I have mentioned here.

Finally, before we leave this chapter, you might like to consider whether you personally need to be facilitated, coached or mentored. As a new consultant you will have many things to learn, different roles to adopt, different relationship issues and so forth. You may well find it beneficial to seek out people who could help you in this process.

Some people who could be suitable in this context are more experienced consultants, trusted friends and professional coaches. You could also consider reciprocal arrangements (as in co-counselling) whereby you get together with a colleague to offer each other facilitation, coaching or mentoring when needed.

Once you become experienced in these activities you can help others in your client organisations to develop the skills, so you are not simply guiding them, but helping them on a lifetime of learning.

NLP techniques used in this chapter and the section where you can find them

Dissociation (helicoptering)
Reframing (putting a new slant on things)
Role-modelling (being a role model)

Chapter 14
Business Writing

This chapter will introduce you to some of the skills involved in producing written material for a range of purposes involved with consultancy.

I always think of writing as one of those strange skills, like cooking, singing and decorating. Most people do all of these at some time, yet they will often say that they 'Can't write, cook, sing or decorate a room'. What they believe is that they haven't been trained to, or do not possess an innate ability to, do that activity. And writing is rather like that; everyone can write a few words, a shopping list, a letter, a note to a colleague, but they may lack the confidence to put words together in a specific format for a particular purpose. So this chapter is designed to help you feel more competent at writing business documents fluently and effectively, so they communicate your meaning accurately and influentially to your chosen recipients.

Let's start with a reminiscence. A job I held early in my career was in local government. At that time and, in some ways, to the present day, there were a range of levels of 'importance' within the staffing of the council. Really important people could have their names typed on their letters and they could sign for themselves. Rather less important people could have their names on, but could not actually sign the letters. Those even 'lower' could send letters out, but could neither have their name on, nor could they sign.

One of the people with whom I shared an office fell into the middle category; he was entitled to have his name on his letters, but had to send them through to our head of department to sign. One day he dictated a very brief letter; it simply said, "Please send me a brochure on …" He sent it through for signature. Shortly afterwards it was returned. His words had been crossed out, the message on the top of the page read, "Re-type" and his simple request had been changed to: "I shall be obliged if you would send me a brochure on …"

This example often gives rise to amusement, or bemusement and disbelief, when I recount it, but it is true. At the time, and in that environment, this was considered 'good' business writing. So what is good practice nowadays, and how can you achieve it? Let's consider the various types of business document you may be involved with in consultancy, and find out how you can produce effective and interesting documents easily and enjoyably.

Types of business document

I have included here most of the common documents and also a few that, although not solely business-oriented, are likely to be useful aids or products in consultancy work. The documents have been split into three broad categories, although some of these do overlap in parts.

- Business documents.
- Publicity material.
- Client documents.

Let's take each of the categories in turn and see how they can be tackled.

Business documents

Letters

Business letters should generally be short, concise and to the point. If you can keep your letter to one side of A4 it is usually best. For anything longer, a continuation sheet is often preferable to using both sides of the paper (although less helpful to maintenance of the rain forests). If you continue on the back of a sheet, it is surprising how many people do not turn it over and so miss what is on the second page.

Having headed paper is essential if you wish to convey a professional image, and laying out your letter so it looks balanced on the page makes it pleasanter to read. Using reasonably wide margins will also help the reader and will prevent your letter looking cramped and wordy.

Make sure you date each letter, and if you are replying to another communication, include any reference you have been given. Give a subject heading that clearly expresses the broad content of the letter. Check you have the correct name, title and address of your recipient and help the person to understand a little about you by putting your personal title (Mr, Mrs, Ms, Dr and so on) as well as your job title if you use one.

It is often better to show that you are taking the reader into account, or assuming a relationship, rather than simply promoting your own interests. To do this you can use language such as "You may be interested in ...", or "It would be helpful if we could discuss ...", rather than "I am sending copies of ...". There is some evidence that the more you use the words 'You' and 'We', the more the reader is inclined to respond well to you.

It is also friendlier-sounding to use active rather than passive words. For example, "We have set up a working party" (active) rather than "A working party has been set up" (passive).

Use separate paragraphs for each new topic and make sentences reasonably short so they can easily be understood. Also ensure you make clear what your purpose is in writing the letter, and if you expect any action from the recipient, make sure this is clearly spelled out.

Memos

Memos are used for internal purposes, for one member of an organisation to communicate with another. They should be short and straightforward and, preferably, contain one topic only.

If your memo is not already on a pre-printed form, ensure it contains your name and contact details as well as the name, title and department of the person to whom it is being sent.

Faxes

A fax should have a cover sheet so the recipient knows what it is and where it has come from. To this end, the cover sheet should include your name, date, contact details, number of pages and topic. Each sheet should then be numbered; although most fax machines print a page number on each sheet as it comes through, this facility will not let the recipient know when a whole page of the original is missing.

Remember that, if the recipient does not have a plain-paper fax, your communication will come through on flimsy, curled-up paper, will not look as professional as a letter and will fade with time. So unless your message is extremely urgent, avoid faxes for communications that need to make a strong image statement.

E-mails

The current tendency is for e-mails to have fewer criteria regarding standards of presentation than other forms of written communication, so they often contain typing mistakes and poor grammar. Even though this is common, it does still look unprofessional, so it is worth making your messages as well-constructed as you can.

Lengthy e-mails can be harder to read than typed or printed documents sent through the post, so make sure the typefaces you use are clear and large enough to be read easily.

Publicity material

Brochures

A brochure is not essential for a consultant, but many clients will ask if you can send them something about yourself and your practice. If you do have a brochure, it simplifies the process and looks professional. Nowadays, it is very feasible to produce your brochure by desktop publishing, so you do not have to have a printed one, which is expensive and can rapidly become outdated. If you do produce your own brochure, however, do make sure it is well designed; you may wish to have a professional designer do this for you, even if you then run the brochures off on your own computer rather than having them printed in bulk by a print firm.

There are a range of ways in which brochures can be produced. One option is to have a looseleaf version, with a folder, so you can insert appropriate sheets each time and update them easily.

Another option is to have a single A4 sheet, folded to give an A5 leaflet (or several of these, each with information on different aspects of your work to use as appropriate). Or you can have multiples of pages, A4 or A5, stapled or stitched together, or a foldout version that opens to show a number of pages, but closes up to a smaller size. You could also have more individual forms of publicity material, but the more unconventional it is, the higher the risk of alienating more traditional client organisations (and of attracting more adventurous ones).

The choice of paper/card, size, typeface, layout, colour and graphics will reflect your own personality and image, so do think carefully before deciding what you will have. There are many designers who can help with this, and if you do decide to have your brochure printed, your printer will probably have access to in-house designers who can do the design job for you.

The content of your brochure should be relevant to your business and convey the impression you choose. The language you use will be a major contributory factor, so although there are no hard and fast rules about what to say, using formal or informal language will create different impressions. What you do write will be more effective if you consider the different readers you may have. In Chapter 11 I have outlined some ways in which you can communicate effectively with different people, and using these techniques in your brochure will make it more accessible and interesting to its recipients.

If your brochure is the only thing you send, it should have contact details, an outline of what products and services you offer and some biographical information on you and the business. Other things you can include are: ◆Your mission statement and philosophy; ◆In which geographical regions you are prepared to work; ◆Examples of past clients (and short examples or case studies of work conducted for them); ◆Any working relationships you have with other consultants.

Remember to update your brochure regularly and check whether additional items need to be included or old ones removed.

Newsletters

You could find it helpful to have a newsletter of your own and you could find yourself helping a client to produce a newsletter for internal readership or for their own customers. The same principles will apply to both, although there can be differences in approach and style, depending on the size and composition of your client base.

A newsletter should be current, informative, contain short items, be targeted to the readership, be on time if it appears on a regular basis, be recognisable and achieve its purpose. The purpose of a newsletter can vary; for example, it might be: ◆To inform, ◆To motivate, or ◆To sell.

If you produce a newsletter of your own, its main purpose will probably be to keep in touch with your clients and to influence existing and potential clients to use your services. It will therefore need to provide something of value so that it is read and taken account of. One of the things I do in my own newsletter is to include a technique or example that can be used to help the client's business; mention any further training I have done recently, so it is clear what additional skills I have; promote any particular new products or services; and perhaps mention a current assignment or two.

This kind of newsletter can be more informal and 'chatty' than most business documents, as it is designed to be interesting and eye-catching. Using colour and graphics can help, and photographs can also be a good addition.

If you are thinking of helping a client produce their own newsletter, you may well need some professional advice. There are various books available on the subject, some of which I have listed in the Bibliography, and there are some professional bodies that function within this field – I have given details of some of these in the Resources List.

C.V.s

Having an up-to-date c.v. is useful, as it can give helpful information to possible clients, associates and agents.

Your c.v. should be brief (one or two sides of A4) and give an outline of your qualifications, work experience, strengths and achievements. Quantify achievements where possible, so your actual results can be demonstrated.

When applying for a job, only send a c.v. if it is expressly requested; if you are asked to complete an application or tender form, do not send a c.v. instead, or refer to your c.v. instead of completing the appropriate parts of the form. A c.v. is a useful instrument, but only when it is used appropriately.

Books and articles

Writing books and articles is a good way to make yourself known, enhance your business image and generate new work. If you find writing easy, then this is worth doing; if you find it harder you will have to decide whether it is worth developing the skill in order to gain the benefits it can bring.

Articles can be written for professional magazines, the local or national media and, increasingly, Internet publications. Although you may get paid for articles, it is probably best not to expect this and to treat their production as a marketing exercise rather than a fee-earning one.

It is usually best to contact editors and see what they would like rather than to write articles 'on spec', although you may be successful with unsolicited items if you have something to offer that is very new, topical, or particularly relevant to the publication's readership.

With books, again it is best to find out what publishers would like. If you write without knowing whether there is a market for your offering you may find you have put in a good deal of time and then have difficulty in placing your manuscript.

Anecdote

Somebody once said that there was no point in reading a new book because he had already read every word in it elsewhere, although not necessarily in the same order!

Client Documents

Capability statements

A capability statement is a document which tells a potential client what you are capable of doing. As such, it needs to be focussed on the particular matter in hand and comprehensive enough to give a good feel for what you can do, while being relatively concise. A capability statement does not say what you will do for the client, but explains what your strengths and expertise are so the client can judge whether you are the person for the job.

Proposals

A proposal is the document that you send to a client to set out how you would respond to that client's needs. There are many formats for proposals, but some common features are the following:

- *Summary of need*

  This is simply rephrasing, or repeating, the client's expressed requirements, so it is obvious what the proposal addresses. Using the client's actual words is often likely to come across better than using your own words to para-phrase what they have said themselves.

- *Description of you and your organisation*

  This is to introduce yourself and your business, describe any aspects of each that are relevant to the assignment, and high-light particular strengths and relevant experience.

- *Statement of approach and style*

  This is to indicate how you work and what the client is likely to experience when working with you. Examples of elements you can include here are: ◆Speed, ◆Flexibility, ◆Informality, ◆Practicality, ◆Collaboration, ◆Supportiveness, ◆Openness, ◆Confidentiality.

- *Action to be taken*

  This is the main element of your proposal and contains your ideas for what should be done to meet the client's needs. In this part you should include whatever information summarises your thoughts, in as much detail as the client needs in order to understand what you propose and to decide whether to commission you. Some of the things you can put into this section are: ◆What stages there will be to your activity; ◆What processes you will use; ◆Whom you will need to meet with, and when; ◆When you might submit interim or final reports.

- *Benefits*

  This is to provide a summary of the benefits the client will receive if the work is carried out.

- *Requirements*

  This is to let the client know what your expectations of them will be. Some of the things you might mention are: ◆Support from top management, ◆Access to information, ◆Administrative support or office space if appropriate.

- *Fees and terms of payment*

  This is to indicate your fee structure and your terms of payment. You should also state your requirements for expenses and whether you are registered for VAT (or any other tax levied in your own country). See Chapters 3 and 5 for more on charging and billing systems.

  Terms of payment should indicate whether you bill on a time basis (say at the end of each month) or to a fee level (say when work completed exceeds a certain value). You can also say you expect payment within a time period, for example 30 days from invoicing, and also add on interest if you are not paid by then. Most clients will have their own payment procedures however, and you may find it difficult in some cases to get payment in the times you specify. This can be one point to discuss before starting the assignment.

It may also be worth indicating whether your fees will only remain in force for a period of time; if the client delays a decision for some time your fee rates might have increased, yet you could find yourself committed to a lower rate if your proposal has contained fees that are valid indefinitely. You could also include an item on your procedure for charging if the client cancels the assignment at short notice or part way through.

- *Timing*

If you have not already included this in your main section on action to be taken, you should indicate here what your availability is, when you could start, how long you estimate the work will take and so on. Some of the time elements may already have been specified by the client, but it is useful to have it in the proposal as a reminder.

- *General terms*

This section is to give the client information on how you operate. For example: ◆Whether you will be doing the work or whether a substitute or an associate might replace you; ◆What will happen if you are ill or incapacitated; ◆What the position is regarding ownership of intellectual property. (This latter point is an interesting one, because many consultants produce material that is either presented to clients, or used by them, and there can be difficulties with copyright and ownership unless these issues are clarified in advance.)

- *Guarantees and disclaimers*

Some consultants put clauses in their proposals saying they do not guarantee results; others offer their services on the basis that if specified results are not forthcoming they will reduce or waive their fees. Although relating to a training course and not a consultancy project, one organisation I know recently offered a 110% return of fees if the customer was not satisfied that the course met expectations. Either course of action – a disclaimer or a guarantee – will have consequences in client attitude and perception and in financial security, so neither is to be undertaken lightly.

- *Conduct and ethics*

  You may wish to mention this topic and outline any particular principles you follow; you may also want to say whether you adhere to the codes of conduct of any professional bodies. Your client may include some requirements regarding confidentiality, use of materials, etc. in their contract with you, but it gives a professional feel to your proposal if you include elements such as this where appropriate.

Tenders

Some organisations will ask you to tender for work; this is often the case with public-sector organisations where there has to be evidence of public money being spent wisely, or with very large-scale assignments where competitive tendering is commonplace. The letters ITT refer to this process and mean an invitation to tender. Tendering can be a lengthy and time-consuming process, so you will need to think carefully before embarking on it.

If you pursue a tender process, you will probably need to write for an information pack, read material that may be substantial, possibly telephone to discuss some of the details before responding, complete an often lengthy and detailed form, provide references, send details of your accounts for anything up to the past three years, and give details of work done for similar organisations or on similar projects. As a small point, it is worth sending tenders by recorded mail as they usually have very specific dates for return and it helps to have evidence of postage in case of non-delivery. If successful at the first stage, you will probably be invited to an interview and asked to give a presentation of your ideas; you may be given a topic for your presentation for which you will need to do preparatory work and produce visual aids or handouts. If the presentation is successful you may be invited back for one or more further interview/discussion sessions before getting the work.

The process of attending presentations is referred to as 'beauty parades' in the consultancy profession and the whole process can be very demanding on time and resources. You are unlikely to be paid expenses for attending selection interviews, so you can also incur substantial costs for producing materials, travelling and accommodation. And if you are tendering for public-sector work, it may not be very well paid, so you could find it is not cost-effective to embark on this process at all.

Example

I generally do not get involved in tendering, but earlier this year I did tender for some work, together with a colleague. We were shortlisted and invited to do a presentation. When we arrived, the interview panel was led by the chief executive of the organisation who, from the outset, seemed detached and almost out to find fault. When we responded to questions by saying that the organisation would need to adopt certain attitudes or courses of action if they were to be successful in implementing the project they had in mind, we felt we had challenged their mind set and they would not be very open to change. We were not offered the work, which was not a surprise to us. In my experience, when you get an immediate impression that you and the client can get on well and there is some common understanding of approach and interest, then things are likely to continue working well. Where there is not this immediate rapport you can, as I suggest in Chapter 10, create it, but I would personally prefer to work with people I already have some affinity with. I think this is something you can generally assess very quickly, probably from the first telephone call or the first few seconds of an interview.

And...

Just as I completed the above example I received a telephone call from an organisation that had contacted me the week before and invited me to an interview as part of their selection process for an assignment. They had a very tight schedule and needed to see two or three people very urgently. The phone call was to let me know they had chosen another consultant on this occasion, but would like me to work with them in the future. The feedback was good, especially as it was unsolicited and positive. You might well find it useful to ask for feedback on any occasions when you are unsuccessful in a tender or other selection process. It will help your future effectiveness and build on the relationship you have with your potential clients.

Reports

A major element of consultancy work is reporting back on findings and giving recommendations. Some consultancy projects may not require a formal report, but can be handled effectively through meetings, discussions and oral presentations. It is, however, more common to produce reports, and you will need to develop skills in this area, especially if you work on large-scale projects or have to communicate with people in dispersed locations.

Some kinds of report you may need to produce are

- *Progress report*

  A progress report can be useful when people need to know, on a regular basis, how things are getting on. Progress reports can show which aspects have been dealt with, what costs have been incurred to date and how people are responding to interventions. Some clients will need progress reports so they can provide information on your assignment to parent companies or to other stakeholders. The period for such reports will need to be relevant to the particular client, but monthly reports are often a good way of handling updates. Progress reports should be reasonably concise and it is often helpful to detail work outstanding as well as work completed.

- *Interim report*

  An interim report is generally produced either when an assignment is lengthy and there needs to be some consideration or evaluation of its progress, or when issues have been identified that require speedy action or changes in direction of the assignment itself. An interim report should be brief if possible and does not need to include all aspects of the assignment, simply those that need to be considered at this stage.

- *Draft report*

  A draft report may be produced where there are organisational issues that need sensitive handling. If a final report is likely to contain controversial recommendations, sensitive material about individuals or major cost implications, it is generally preferable to discuss them with the client before they are documented or published. Another reason for producing a draft report is if there are different interest groups within the organisation, for example a senior management team and a board of directors or trustees, and you want to ensure that the final report is one that the managers feel comfortable in presenting to the board. It is important, therefore, that your relationship with whoever commissions your work is such that you can discuss this kind of issue and that you are not asked to act in an unethical way by distorting your recommendations to fit with internal politics.

- *Final report*

  This is presented at the conclusion of the particular assignment. The report may be sent as a written document or it may be given at a supporting presentation, where you can talk through the elements of the report and answer questions on the report and the work that resulted in its production.

Reports can, of course, vary in their presentation, but a good approach is to include the following:

- A short summary at the start, so that anyone who needs to understand its main points can access them quickly, without having to read the entire document.
- Your methodology in conducting the assignment and writing the report.
- Any assumptions you have made in the report.
- Credits of any reference sources and any people whose assistance helped in your work.
- A brief statement of rationale for the assignment being conducted and the report written.
- The body of information you wish to present, including issues, facts and figures.
- Conclusions.
- Recommendations, with financial, staffing, time, political and any other implications made clear. If you have options for recommendations, it helps to indicate which one you think should be adopted.

- The benefits to the client of adopting the recommendations you have made.
- A suggested action plan for implementation, including activities, roles and responsibilities, time-scales and ways of measuring achievement.
- Any appended information that is useful but more appropriate to have in an appendix than in the body of the report.

The style and format of your report will need to take into account:

- *The subject matter*

  There are particular conventions within certain areas that may influence how you produce your report. For example, some topics may need statistical analysis, financial tables and technical data, while others may need philosophical debate or political awareness. No one approach will be suitable for all topics.

- *The culture of the organisation*

  The organisation itself will have conventional ways of doing things, and your report will be better received if it takes account of these internal conventions. Of course you can present something that inspires simply because it differs from convention, but in the main, you are likely to gain a better response when you consider the organisational elements with which you have been dealing.

- *The politics of the organisation*

  While remaining within the limits of ethical behaviour, it is important to take account of internal politics and check that a) you are writing for the appropriate audience to act on the report, b) you take account of any divergence of opinion and are sensitive to this in producing your report, c) what you are recommending can actually be put into practice, given the internal relationships and opinions that exist.

- *The individuals to whom it will be presented*

  This means you will need to take into account aspects such as personal learning and motivational styles so that the language you use in the report, and the way it is designed, enables each person to get the most from it and to be receptive to its recommendations. I have covered various ways of communicating with people in other chapters, and it is worth taking these elements into account, both when producing your report and when presenting it in person.

Presentation materials

If you are called to an interview or presentation as part of a selection process, or if you have to give a presentation as part of an assignment itself, there are some supporting materials you may need to produce; these include visual aids and handouts.

You may choose to use a PowerPoint® presentation, which you can take on disk and run from a laptop computer. This will look professional, but does have some limitations. It is easier to use PowerPoint® graphics in a sequence, so if you wish to vary your presentation it can be difficult. If there is a problem with your disk or computer you may not be able to use it at all. It can also look so slick that it becomes impersonal and packaged and takes away from your individuality as a consultant.

An alternative is to use overhead projector transparencies and carry a portable overhead projector, or ask for the use of one for the presentation (ask in advance so you can be sure that one will be supplied). This process is more flexible, but does mean you need to select the relevant slides and shuffle them in and out of covers. This can, however, give you time to think and time to develop your relationship with the people to whom you are presenting. You can also select which slides to use as you are presenting and whether to leave some out or include some additional ones if appropriate. You can also have some blank transparencies to create additional slides.

If using either of these two approaches, remember not to put too much information on any one 'page', and to add some colour and graphics for interest. If presenting figures, remember that not everyone is comfortable with statistical information and try to make your material as user-friendly as possible. Graphs and charts rather than cold figures can help with this.

You could also use a whiteboard, but this will mean erasing each item as you go along and will mean you are standing at a wall, possibly quite detached from your audience. You could also use a flip chart, which is very much more immediate and responsive to the ongoing discussion. This will not look as formal as the other processes and may well be more appropriate if your potential client is in a less sophisticated sector or working to a low budget.

You may also wish to produce handouts to support your presentation. These should be concise and sum up the main points of interest. Unless they contain points that you wish people to look at while you discuss them, give the handouts after you have spoken, otherwise people will be reading them rather than listening to you. If you do give handouts at a selection presentation it will give those present a further reminder of you, and you should put your organisation and contact details on them for reference and copyright safeguarding.

It can be helpful to have with you some small items such as a couple of marker pens, some Blu-Tack® or Sellotape®, in case of need.

Handbooks

You may find that, as part of an assignment, you need to produce a handbook for your client. This may be an operating handbook or a handbook containing collected information relevant to the organisation. Handbooks should usually be written in clear, direct and relatively formal language; passive language is usually conventional for this purpose, although if the organisation is very informal, a chatty handbook can be a possibility. A good handbook will have a contents page, a clear and logical structure, clear page and section numbering and, preferably, a date of issue at the start, or on each page if it is looseleaf.

Policies and procedures

You may need to help your client to produce policies and procedures relevant to the areas in which you are working. Again, such documents are usually written in a fairly formal manner and do need to be well structured and systematic. If writing procedures, do check that they are understandable and relevant; a procedure that may be suitable for you could be inappropriate for your client, so a good deal of discussion needs to take place to ensure that what you produce is actually workable in the client organisation.

Final Points

1.   Elements of business writing

The principles that run through all the above examples of business writing are as follows:

- Consider the purpose for which you are producing a document.

- Communicate simply, clearly and in a well-structured manner.

- Make sure your communications are geared to your particular audience.

2.   Principles of communication

I have talked a good deal about various elements of communications and, in the long run, effective communication depends on both sender and receiver being aligned in their understanding. This can be a tremendously difficult task, and it may help you to know about aspects of communication that are enshrined in linguistic theory.

Two elements can be taken into account; they are as follows:

● *Our perception of reality*

Assuming there is a reality 'out there', we perceive and experience it through our senses. Our senses (sight, hearing, touch, taste, smell) can be considered as 'transformers', that is, they transform reality into perception and experience. And our perception is filtered through our senses so that if, for example, we have poor hearing, there may be certain tones we do not hear, or if we have a degree of colour-blindness, there will be certain shades of colour we do not see. So our perception is partial and subjective and, consequently, so is our experience.

● *Our communication of perception and experience*

Once we have a perception or experience, we can begin to communicate it, but our communication depends on our language (and, of course, our non-verbal language too). So, if our language skills are limited, we will not be able to describe our perception or experience. Imagine the difficulty in describing the many shades of green you see in any landscape. So our communication is also partial and subjective.

Effective communication, therefore, is a miracle, and anything you can do to enhance it, and to make explicit your meaning to those with whom you are communicating, the better.

3. *Clarity and comprehension*

In order to make your writing accessible you can consider the 'FOG index'. The FOG index is an estimate of how simple or complex a piece of writing is. There are different ways of calculating the FOG index; as the original one is quite complex, the one I prefer to use is as follows:

Select the document to be assessed. Take a sample of three or four typical sentences from the document. For each sentence, count a) the number of words it contains and b) the number of words in that sentence with three syllables or more. For each sentence multiply a) by b). Then take an average of the resulting figures from each of the sentences.

Example
In this example two documents are being compared:

- *Document one*

Sentence one has 8 words and one of these has 3 syllables:
    total score 8 x 1 = 8

Sentence two has 9 words and one of these has 3 syllables:
    total score 9 x 1 = 9

Sentence three has 8 words and two of these have 3 syllables or more: *total score* 8 x 2 = 16

Total score for the three sentences is 8 + 9 + 16 = 33
Average is 33 divided by 3 = 11
So the FOG index for that document is 11

- *Document two*

Sentence one has 16 words with 6 of these having three syllables or more: *total score* 16 x 6 = 96

Sentence two has 18 words with 5 of these having three syllables or more: *total score* 18 x 5 = 90
Sentence three has 14 words with 6 of these having three syllables or more: *total score* 14 x 6 = 84

Total score for the three sentences is 96 + 90 + 84 – 270
Average is 270 divided by 3 = 90
So the FOG index for that document is 90

The higher the FOG index the more complex the writing, so document two is clearly more difficult to read than document one. There is no ideal figure for the FOG index because a paper in a learned journal, or a paper with lengthy technical terms may have a higher FOG index but still be appropriate for its readership. However, in general, unless your report has to be written in complex language, simpler writing will be more accessible to, and more appreciated by, most readers.

4. *Writing on the Internet*

There are some specific points worth remembering here. (The source for much of what follows is Lesley Allman, writing in *Communicators in Business* magazine.)

Studies by 'web guru' Jakob Nielsen revealed that reading from computer screens is 25% slower than reading from paper – and doesn't feel as comfortable. So he recommends that people write 50% less text when the writing is to be read on screen. Simple language and bullet points work better than complex writing.

It is worth thinking of a commonly used acronym: KISS (Keep it Simple, Stupid or Keep It Short and Simple). This has recently been given an update to fit in with electronic communications: Keep it Short and Scannable. Scannable is important because, according to Morkes and Nielsen, only 16% of web users read word for word, with 79% scanning pages instead, picking out key words, sentences and paragraphs. Because of this, highlighting, subheadings, lists and section breaks make the process easier.

In addition, Nielsen and Morkes show that, of the intranet sites they studied, those written in objective language rather than promotional, scored 27% better for ease of use, because with the promotional language people spent time wondering if what they were reading was true, rather than absorbing the information itself.

Other elements worth remembering are giving dates and sources for information, which add credibility. The letters used to summarise all the points mentioned here are SS&C (Succinct, Scannable and Credible). Morkes and Nielsen refer to the important factors as: concise, scannable and objective. On test web pages attention paid to each of these criteria improved usability by as much as 58%. When all three were combined the improvement rate was 124%, and when information was split into more pages with more hyperlinks to secondary information, the rewritten pages scored 159% higher than the originals.

So, good writing on the Internet is equally important as other formats and should not be disregarded because the medium seems an informal one.

5. *Written versus spoken language*

Remember that there is a difference between the spoken and the written word, so ensure that your presentations are spoken (don't read from a prepared script or they will sound stilted and formal) and your written documents are well structured grammatically (don't write from transcripts of spoken language or they can be difficult to understand in written form).

6. *Divergence and disability*

When producing written material (and when conducting other consultancy activities, such as making a presentation, running a meeting or doing a survey) it is important to ensure that all potential recipients of what you are doing are enabled to benefit from it.

As far as written documents go, it is important to ensure that they are accessible to:

- *People with poor eyesight*

  If your documents have to be read by people whose eyesight is poor, remember to use clear, large typefaces, plenty of white space and good formatting. It can be very frustrating to attempt to read a poor-quality fax, an e-mail in microscopic print or a report with tables of undecipherable figures.

- *People whose native language is not your own*

  If your documents are likely to be seen by people who are not fluent with the language in which they are written, you need to pay attention to the use of words and phrases that are specific to a particular language or culture, either adding or removing words from the text as appropriate. If producing items for large organisations with multi-cultural workforces you may even need to have certain documents translated for general consumption.

- *People without inside knowledge of the field or organisation*

  Sometimes documents go to people who are unfamiliar with the terms, concepts or individuals referred to. Because of this it is worth avoiding such things as: ◆Jargon; ◆The use of people's initials, unless everyone will know to whom they refer; ◆Reference to processes that may be unfamiliar to readers. Accessibility is the objective, so check your documents for words that may not mean much to some people.

7. Legal issues

When you write something that is published (and letters, faxes, e-mails and similar documents are all a form of publication) you need to consider whether any issues are raised which could have consequences in law. For example:

- Make sure you do not libel people.
- Make sure you do not disclose confidential or personal material without prior agreement.
- Make sure you do not infringe copyright.

Much is currently being written about publication on the Internet, and there are some interesting cases of each of the above issues in respect of e-mails and discussion-group postings. In an article in *People Management* in June 2000, Ellen Temperton said, "E-mail is often seen as a transient form of communication, akin to the spoken word. Yet the document can be printed, kept and subsequently produced in court. Unguarded language in messages can be the basis for constructive dismissal, defamation and discrimination claims. It can also create binding contracts where none were intended, breach third-party intellectual property rights and disclose confidential information." So it is well worth checking what you write for sensitivity and truthfulness before you go into print.

8. Ensuring quality

Finally, whatever your document, check it is the highest quality you can achieve. Pay attention to both content and process;

content is what is in the document and process is how you produce it. Make sure it is well structured and flows easily. An excellent way of checking on accessibility is to give your written documents to someone else to read aloud to you. You may be surprised how they come across and you may get some understanding of how to improve them. And, while on quality, remember computer spelling and grammar checks, but also do it yourself; even the best software often overlooks errors.

Finale

Consultancy can be a fascinating and rewarding field in which to work. Whether this is true for you depends on your temperament, your ability to recognise and create opportunities and your enthusiasm for helping people and organisations to develop and thrive.

There is no single profile for successful consultants, although there are some traits and behaviours that are common to many. Neither is there any single set of consultancy 'rules' that will guide you through the complexity of assignments. There are, however, many resources, of which this book is simply one, and it is well worth taking advantage of the accumulated information and wisdom that is available before taking your own path along the route to consultancy success.

The areas covered in this book are simply a personal view of what is involved in consultancy. Of course there are other opinions, and other areas, that could be included. As a consultant, however, you will need to be able to sort the useful from the irrelevant, come to your own conclusions and build your own model of what consultancy is and what it can do.

One area I have not covered in depth is that of client education. As a consultant, your major reason for existing is to help your clients to grow their businesses and enhance their personal effectiveness. To this end, it is important that you do all you can to help them to help you to help them – yes, you have read this correctly! So how can you set about this?

I have already given some ideas in other chapters about ways in which you can help others develop, so here is a reminder, and perhaps an expansion, of what will help your clients maximise their use of you.

- **Role-modelling** – by acting in ways they can learn from, you enable clients to watch, listen and learn from what you do. If you are authentic ('being yourself') and congruent (being 'internally consistent') and do things like listening, clarifying purposes, providing adequate information, remaining calm, focusing on the important issues and so forth, they should be able to pick up these points, incorporate them into what they do personally and use them to relate to you in ways that will help the overall progress of the assignment.

- **Being explicit** – when you say what you think, how you feel, what you will provide, what you need and what you expect – including support from whoever commissions you to undertake the project – it helps people to understand and to respond. By being upfront about things, you build an open and trusting relationship and help your clients to be open about what they want from you.

- **Sharing responsibility** – although you are being paid for your inputs, unless you are taken on solely as an additional resource, in which case the term 'consultant' is probably a misnomer, a collaborative relationship with your client will benefit both of you. By treating your client as a partner, rather than an employer, you can jointly consider the issues, implications, activities and outcomes involved in assignments and have collaborative ownership of the total process. In this way you are likely to have a more successful result and the client is likely to gain more understanding of the implications of consultancy roles and processes and have more commitment to implementation of recommended action.

- **Encouraging generative learning** – by simply doing a job you may solve a problem or achieve a one-off result. By teaching your clients how to consider and deal with issues you give them much more valuable business – and life – skills. This approach to learning is called 'generative' because it is a continuing process of development and one where lessons are learnt about how to conceptualise, how to see connections and how to continually enhance one's skills.

Theoretically, you could do yourself out of a job if you champion all the above approaches, because clients would be capable of running their affairs without outside help. However, the world being what it is, there are more than enough people and organisations around who can benefit from a fresh eye and ear, so doing your best to develop learning organisations will benefit both your clients and you. I wish you success in the process.

And if you are ever a buyer of consultancy services, I hope you will remember what it is like at the deep end, the cutting edge, the firing line, or however you would describe the consultant's lot, and offer a friendly and sympathetic response to whomever you select.

Resources List

Organisations that Promote the Interests and Benefits of Consultancy

With the growth of consultancy has come development of a range of professional bodies, some are membership organisations and some are trade associations; I have listed some of them here. There are also numerous organisations that act on behalf of consultants, as agents, franchisees and the like, helping find work and provide professional contacts. The professional membership bodies serve a range of functions, including:

- *Accreditation*

    This is generally to do with showing that particular members have specific levels of knowledge and skill. Once a member has achieved certain standards they are admitted to particular grades of membership and allowed to use letters of designation after their names. This is a good indication to anyone using their services that they have achieved appropriate standards of performance.

    Professional bodies may also accredit external organisations providing services for their members; for example training bodies may be accredited, or suppliers of resources used by those practising in the profession.

- *Regulation*

    Professional bodies also aim to regulate the practice of their body of knowledge and skill. Regulation may be carried out through requirements to be a member, to undertake regular training, to comply with codes of ethics and conduct and so forth. Regulation often works through inducement, such as recognition, but it may also work through sanction, such as the provision for disciplinary action should required practices not be complied with. As well as regulating individual consultants, there is also regulation of practices, through

337

Certified Practice schemes, and there is regulation of training through accreditation of training providers.

- *Membership services*

  The range of services offered to members varies from organisation to organisation. Commonly provided services
  include information and advice; legal help; insurance;
  library services; jobs registers; training; networking opportunities; conferences, events and exhibitions; publications;
  advertising opportunities and referrals; room hire, catering
  and accommodation; discounts on products and services of
  external suppliers.

- *PR, marketing, membership development and fund-raising*

  Most professional bodies have provision for developing
  their presence, attracting funds and increasing membership.
  These functions are vital to survival and growth, so that
  members' interests can be served, and may involve media
  liaison, sponsorship, membership drives, sales of products
  and services and so forth.

- *Job search, temporary work and consultancy assignments*

  Some bodies offer job-search services to members. These can
  include registers of job opportunities, counselling and mentoring, and agency services for employment or consultancy.
  Where there is a register of approved people, inclusion on
  the register tends to indicate a particular level of ability and
  a recognition of competence by the professional body.
  Continued inclusion on such registers may depend on regular references from users and offer the possibility of using
  the professional body's logo and endorsement on business
  stationery.

- *Information and advice*

  Many professional organisations have library and information services, helplines available to members and/or the
  public, Websites and discussion groups. Some bodies will

have paid or voluntary advisers on topics such as legal, career and development issues.

- *Professional development and training*

  Another feature of professional bodies is their emphasis on ongoing development. CPD (Continuing Professional Development) is a term commonly used to denote a requirement to demonstrate ongoing activity through training, reading, work shadowing and other learning processes. Another way in which bodies assist their members to develop is through counselling and mentoring, activities that are growing in popularity.

- *Publications and events*

  Producing magazines, newsletters and research reports and running meetings, training events and conferences are other ways in which professional bodies develop their presence and add value to their membership.

- *Social contact and networking*

  The opportunity to meet others in similar fields, and to meet potential clients or customers, is a growing field of activity. Special interest groups and learning networks are now commonplace, where members with particular interest in specific aspects of their field can meet, learn, exchange ideas and generate business opportunities.

- *Representation and lobbying*

  Finally, representing their members, and lobbying on behalf of them, are issues that are of major importance in certain professional bodies. There is often the opportunity to convey opinions to government bodies, and there is also the chance to influence decision-makers when members' interests are at stake.

Contact details for consultancy organisations

International

International Council of Management Consulting Institutes (ICMCI)
Global association that certifies professional management consultants with the CMC appellation.
Currently operating in Argentina, Australia, Austria, Bangladesh, Bulgaria, Canada, Cyprus, Denmark, Finland, France, Germany, Greece, Hungary, India, Indonesia, Ireland, Italy, Japan, Malaysia, Norway, Netherlands, New Zealand, Nigeria, Poland, Singapore, South Africa, Spain, Sweden, Switzerland, United Kingdom, United States of America.
850 Long View Road, Burlingame, California, 94010 - 6974.
www.icmci.com
ICMCI also organises a world conference.
See www.mc-worlcon.com

UK

Institute of Management Consultancy (IMC)
Professional body for the management consultancy industry.
5th Floor, 32/33 Hatton Garden, London EC1N 8DL.
Tel: 020 7242 2140; Fax: 020 7831 4597
www.imc.co.uk

The Management Consultancies Association (MCA)
Trade body for consultancy, with members coming from the major employing organisations. Open to firms with at least 15 full-time consulting staff and in practice for at least five years.
11 West Halkin Street, London SW1X 8JL.
Tel: 020 7235 3897; Fax: 020 7235 0825; e-mail: mca@mca.org.uk
www.mca.org.uk

The Richmond Group
A 'virtual' consortium of independent management consultants, all of whom are CMCs and Members or Fellows of the IMC. The group provides meetings, conferences and networking

opportunities to members and a consultancy resource and assurance of quality to clients of its members.
17 D'Abernon Drive, Stoke D'Abernon, Cobham, Surrey, KT11 3JE.
Tel: 01932 865 146
www.richmond-group.co.uk

BCB

A private-sector trade association of consulting firms and individuals, working internationally. BCB runs the 'British Consultants of the Year Awards' in association with *The Times* newspaper.
1 Westminster Palace Gardens, Artillery Row, London SW1P 1RJ.
Tel: 020 7222 3651; Fax: 020 7222 3664; e-mail: mail@bcb.co.uk
www. bcbforum.demon.co.uk

USA

Institute of Management Consultants
2025 M Street N. W. Suite 800, Washington, DC 20036-3309
Tel: +1 202 367 1134 or +1 800 221 2557; Fax: 202 367 2134;
E-mail: office@imcusa.org
www.imcusa.org

Association of Management Consulting Firms (AMCF)
A global membership association and trade body for consultancy firms that raises awareness of consultancy matters, promotes professional standards and lobbies on behalf of the industry.

USA Headquarters: 380 Lexington Avenue, Suite 1700, New York, NY 10168.
Tel: +1 212 551 7887; Fax: + 1 212 551 7934; e-mail: info@amcf.org
www.amcf.org

AMCF Europe: Avenue Marcel Thiry 204, B-1200 Brussels, Belgium.
Tel: 32 2 774 9528; Fax: 32 2 774 9690; e-mail: eyam.amcf@ey.be

Association of Professional Consultants (APC)
A Californian consortium of independent consultants.
www.consultapc.org

National Consultant Referrals Inc.
A free consultant referral service for small businesses.
Consultant's Mall. A site for finding consultancy services
Consulting Central. A resource for consultants, prospective consultants and consultancy buyers
Brain Bid. A matching service for contract work; project requirements, consultant profiles and confidential bids all produced on-line.
Consulting Tools. A discussion group for service providers to share information and discuss problems relating to the consultancy industry.
All the above can be accessed via the APC site above.

Information Central for Management Consulting Worldwide
MCNI website at:
www.mcni.com
Click on the associations below for links to their Websites
Association of Internal Management Consultants
Academy of Management Managerial Consultation Division
Association of Management Consulting Firms

Profit, Inc.™
A network of experienced consulting professionals, and affiliated companies, working with SMEs (small and medium-sized organisations).
e-mail: consultants@profit-inc.com
www.profit-inc.com

EUROPE

European Federation of Management Consultancy Organisations (FEACO)
3/4/5 Avenue des Arts, B1210 Brussels, Belgium.
Tel: 32 2 250 0650; Fax: 32 2 250 0651; e-mail: feaco@feaco.org
www.feaco.org

Association of Management Consulting Firms (AMCF) (see also AMCF USA)
Avenue Marcel Thiry 204, B-1200 Brussels, Belgium.

Tel: 32 2 774 9528; Fax: 32 2 774 9690; e-mail: eyam.amcf@ey.be
www.amcf.org

AMCF also has associations with Brazil, Canada and Japan.

Becoming qualified and recognised as a consultant

Recognition is often a matter of reputation. Once you have carried out successful consultancy projects, you are likely to find you are recommended and sought after through word of mouth. The more you do successfully, the more people are likely to recommend you and praise your work. Recognition can also come through accreditation by a recognised consultancy body or completion of an accredited training programme. The fact that you have gained a professional qualification is one way for potential clients to assess your competence.

Internationally, there is now a recognised qualification – CMC, which stands for Certified Management Consultant. It is the only career qualification for practising consultants; it is portable and recognised in 30 countries worldwide. The qualification is open to members of professional bodies that are affiliated to the International Council of Management Consulting Institutes (ICMCI); currently there are 25 such bodies. Only members of the ICMCI can award the CMC qualification. To gain the qualification, evidence of professional capability has to be provided, in accordance with the ICMCI Uniform Body of Knowledge.

In the UK, the assessment process for CMC is competence-based and involves provision of evidence of competence, experience, education and training; it is essential to have practical experience as a consultant before applying. In the UK there is no specific time period for experience, but it is unlikely that if you have less than three years' experience you will satisfy the requirement. Also, in the UK, there is a facility for nationally recognised Credit Accumulation and Transfer, allowing competencies to be recognised between different accrediting bodies, minimising the need for duplication of validating evidence.

Some ways in which you can demonstrate competence are:

- An assignment study, where you write up a consultancy assignment, showing your activities and your learning from those activities. The assignment study should cover four elements: management consultancy; management; professional specialism; and socio/technical/economic/political (that is external issues) awareness.

- A professional record, which consists of a c.v., summaries of assignments, evidence of ongoing training and development, evidence of qualifications, evidence of contractual arrangement with clients, evidence of compliance with codes of professional conduct and ethics and evidence of and reflection on your learning from assignments and/or academic study.

- References from clients, in which they comment on your work, the issues you handled and your professional, technical and consultancy skills.

- An assessment interview, where you can make a presentation and answer questions on your assignment study and your professional record.

Some of the aspects of consultancy on which you may be assessed are marketing, sales, client relationships, ethics, analytical and diagnostic processes, negotiating, contractual arrangements, proposals and presentations, implementation, information sourcing, change management and conflict resolution, evaluation and process management. Full guidelines on application for the CMC qualification are available from the relevant body in your own country, and details of international management consultancy bodies are given in the preceding section.

Training Providers

EUROPE – Top International Business Schools 1997/8

Cambridge University Cambridge
CESMA ESC Lyon, France
City University London
Cranfield School of Management Cranfield, Bedfordshire
Durham University Durham
Edinburgh University Edinburgh
EA Paris, Madrid, Oxford
ENPC Paris
ESADE Barcelona
Henley Management School London
ICADE Madrid
IESE Barcelona
IMD Lausanne, Switzerland
Imperial London
INSEAD Fontainebleu, France
Instituto de Empresa Madrid
ISA at HEC Paris
Koblenz Koblenz, Germany
KU Lurven Leuven, Belgium
Lancaster Lancaster
London Business School London
Manchester Business School Manchester
MBA Sci Po. Paris
Nijenrode Breukelen, Netherlands
Nottingham Business School Nottingham
Rotterdam School of Management Rotterdam
SDA Bocconi Milan
Solvay Business School Brussels
Strathclyde Graduate School of Business Glasgow
Warwick University Coventry

USA – Top International Business Schools 1997/8

Arthur D Little School of Management Boston
Babson Graduate School of Business Massachussetts

Bentley Graduate School of Business Massachussetts
Carnegia Mellon School of Industrial Administration Pittsburgh
Columbia University New York
Cornell University New York
Dartmouth College Hanover, New Hampshire
DePaul University Chicago
Duke University – FUQUA Durham, North Carolina
Emory University – GOIZUETA Atlanta
Georgetown University Washington DC
Harvard Business School Boston
Indiana University Indiana
Michigan University Michigan
MIT-Sloan Boston
New York University – Stern New York
Northwestern University – Kellogg Chicago
Purdue University Indiana
Stanford University San Francisco
Thunderbird – AGSIM Arizona
University of California at Berkeley San Francisco
University of California at Irvine Los Angeles
University of California at Los Angeles Los Angeles
University of Chicago Chicago
University of Pennsylvania Wharton, Philadelphia
University of South Carolina Colombia
University of Rochester Rochester, New York
University of Virginia Darden, Virginia
University of Washington – OLIN St. Louis
University of Wisconsin Madison, Wisconsin

Source of European and USA business school data:
Inside Careers – Cambridge Market Intelligence Ltd/The Institute
of Management Consultancy (UK).

Providers of diplomas, certificates or MSc degrees in
management consultancy

UK

Ashridge Management Centre Berkhamsted, Hertfordshire
Civil Service College Sunningdale, Berkshire

Nottingham Business School Nottingham
University of Salford Salford
University of Strathclyde Glasgow
Sheffield Business School Sheffield
South Bank University London

Some of the independent training organisations that provide practical consultancy skills

Consultancy Skills Training
32 York Road, Cheam, Surrey SM2 6HH, UK.
Tel: 020 8642 9568; e-mail: cst@cst-ltd.co.uk
www.cst-ltd.co.uk

Maresfield Curnow
The Bishop's Avenue, London N2 0AP, UK.
Fax: 020 7431 6084; e-mail: barry_curnow@compuserve.com

Training organisation specialising in the application of NLP to consultancy

Management Magic
Pentre House, Leighton, Welshpool, Powys SY21 8HL, UK.
Tel: 01938 553 430; Fax: 01938 555 355;
e-mail: management.magic@border.org.uk
www.border.org.uk

Consultancy Publications

UK

Effective Consulting
Pentre Publications, Pentre House, Leighton, Welshpool, Powys SY21 8HL, UK.
Tel: 01938 553 430; Fax: 01938 555 355;
e-mail: editor@effectiveconsulting.org.uk
www.effectiveconsulting.org.uk

Professional Consultancy (The bi-annual Journal of the IMC)
5th Floor, 32/33 Hatton Garden, London EC1N 8DL.
Tel: 020 7242 2140; Fax: 020 7831 4597
www.imc.co.uk

Management Consultancy (Magazine)
VNU Business Publications, 32-34 Broadwick Street, London W1A 2HG.
Tel: 020 7316 9000; Fax: 020 7316 9250;
e-mail (editor): mark_brenner@vnu.co.uk
www.managementconsultancy.co.uk

Management Consultants News (IT-focused; free publication)
Prime Marketing Publications Ltd., Witton House, Lower Road, Chorleywood, Herts WD3 5LB.
Tel: 01923 285323; Fax: 01923 285818; e-mail: icn@pmp.co.uk
www.pmp.co.uk

Inside Careers 2000
A guide to a career in consultancy.
Cambridge Market Intelligence Limited, The Quadrangle,
49 Atalanta Street, London SW6 6TR.
Tel: 020 7565 7900; Fax: 020 7565 7938
Associate Publisher: The Institute of Management Consultancy (UK) – see above.

Management Consultancy Decisions International
Sterling Publications Limited, Brunel House, 57 North Wharf Road, London W2 1XR.
Tel: 020 7915 9660; Fax: 020 7724 2089
e-mail: Info@SterlingPublications.com
www.sterlingpublications.com

USA

C2M (Consulting to Management)
858 Longview Road, Burlingame, CA 94010-6974.
Tel: +1 650 342 1954; Fax: +1 650 344 5005;
e-mail: c2m@c2m.com
www.c2m.com

Consultants News
Management Consultant International
Consulting Magazine
What's Working in Consulting (a magazine for independents)
All available on subscription from Kennedy Information,
Tel: 800-531-0007 (Only available in USA)
www.kennedyinfo.com
www.consultingcentral.com
Also available from Kennedy Information: a report entitled 'Management Consultancy 2010, The Global Outlook for an Industry in Transition'.

EUROPE

FEACO Survey on the consultancy market
Available from feaco@feaco.org

Consultancy recruitment firms

UK

Beament Leslie Thomas Recruitment Consultancy Limited
Quality House, 5-9 Quality Court, Chancery Lane, London WC2A 1HP.
Tel: 020 7495 3404; Fax: 020 7405 3310; e-mail: team@blt.co.uk

USA

Association of Executive Search Consultants (AESC)
'Representing leading executive search firms worldwide.'
500 Fifth Avenue, Suite 930, New York, NY 10110.
Tel: +1 212 398 9556; Fax: +1 212 398 9560; e-mail: aesc@aesc.org
www.aesc.org

UK Websites specialising in e-recruitment

www.totaljobs.com
www.jobsift.com
www.monster.co.uk
www.opp.co.uk
www.personic.com
www.proteus.web.com
www.rec.uk.com
www.search-direct.com
www.source.com
www.stepstone.co.uk
www.topjobs.net

Other Useful Internet Sites

The National Professional Services Register
www.npsr.co.uk

The Recruitment and Employment Confederation
www.rec.uk.com

Agencies/Intermediaries

People Agenda Management Consulting
12 Canon Harnett Court, Warren Farm, Stratford Road, Wolverton
Mill, Milton Keynes MK12 5NF, UK.
Tel: 01908 227 111; Fax: 01908 226 100;
e-mail: people.agenda@virgin.net
www.Chamberlain-Walker.co.uk

Russam GMS (Interim Management)
48 High Street North, Dunstable, Beds. LU6 1LA, UK.
Tel: 01582 666 970; Fax: 01582 471 757;
e-mail: hq@russam-gms.co.uk
www.russam-gms.co.uk

Other Useful Bodies

The Association for Neuro-Linguistic Programming (ANLP)
PO Box 10, Porthmadog LL48 6ZB, UK.

The Federation of Image Consultants (TFIC)
Mallory House, 27 Verulam Road, St Albans, Herts, AL3 4DG
Tel: 07010 701 018; e-mail: info@tfic.org.uk

Speakers' Associations

UK
The Professional Speakers Association of Europe
PO Box 247, London W4 5EX
Tel: 020 8742 7788; Fax: 020 7842 2396;
e-mail: psa@netcom.uk.co.uk
www.professionalspeakers.org

USA
National Speakers Association
1500 South Priest Drive, Tempe, AZ 85281.
Tel: (480) 968-2552; Fax: (480) 968-0911;
e-mail: marsha@nsaspeaker.org
www.nsaspeaker.org

Industry Information

Top consulting firms in order of fee income

UK (1998)

PricewaterhouseCoop...
Cap Gemini
KPMG
Andersen Consulting
P A Consulting Group

Ernst & Young
Deloitte Consulting
McKinsey
SEMA
Gemini Consulting
Logica
ICL Group
CSC
Arthur Andersen
Arthur D Little
Towers Perrin
OSI
IBM Management Consultancy
A T Kearney/EDS
Druid

Since these figures were produced, some of the above organisations have merged.

Source: *Management Consultancy* 10th annual survey of the top consulting firms

The survey has many more firms listed, as well as breakdowns by sector.

USA (1999)

Andersen Consulting
PricewaterhouseCoop...
Deloitte Consulting
Ernst & Young
CSC
KPMG Consulting
Cap Gemini
McKinsey & Company
Mercer Consulting Group
Arthur Andersen
Booz, Allen & Hamilton
Towers Perrin
A.T. Kearney

AMS
Sema Group
Hewitt Associates
The Boston Consulting Group
debis Systemhaus
Logica
Keane, Inc.
Source: *Consultants News* ©1990, Kennedy Information LLC,
Fitzwilliam, NH
Tel: 800-531 0007 (Not available outside US)
www.kennedyinfo.com
www.consultingcentral.com

The listing of firms has the top 50 and also lists the number of consultants employed, both in the USA and globally. The top firm has
well over 50,000 consultants worldwide.

Bibliography

The following list gives some books which you will find useful in developing your skills further. I have listed them under particular chapters, as they contain material which relates to the subject matter of those chapters, but some of the books have applications to other chapters and also to topics not covered in this book.

Chapter 3
Starting a career in consultancy

Inside Careers – Management Consultants (2000). Cambridge Market Intelligence Ltd. in association with the Institute of Management Consultancy. (UK)

Fee and Pricing Trends in Management Consulting (1999). Kennedy Information Research Group. (USA)

Networking for Success (2000). Carol Harris. Oaktree Press.

Active Job Seeking (Audiotape) (1995). Carol Harris. Management Magic.

Chapter 4
Defining and establishing your business

Awesome Purpose (1999). Nigel MacLennon. Gower.

Tactics (1985). Edward de Bono. William Collins.

Management Processes and Functions (1990). Michael Armstrong. Institute of Personnel Management.

Chapter 5
Finance, marketing and selling

The 24 Hour Business Plan (1990). Ron Johnson. Hutchinson Business Books.

Chaos Marketing (1995). Torsten H. Nilsonn. McGraw Hill Book Company.

Shaping Customer Focus (1999). Philip Atkinson and Ian Millar. Transformations (UK) Ltd.

Kompass Registers (Produced annually). Volume 1: *Kompass Products and Services Register*. Volume 2: *Company Information*. Volume 3: *Parents and Subsidiaries*, Volume 4: *Industrial Trade Names*. Reed Business Information. UK.

UK Census returns (information for marketing purposes) available from Census Customer Services, Office of National Statistics, Segensworth Road, Tichfield, Fareham, Hampshire PO15 5RR. Tel: 01329 813586.

Chapter 6
Project management, monitoring results, developing skills, culture, divergence, ethics

Project Management: The People Challenge (1997). Roland Bee and Frances Bee. Institute of Personnel and Development.

Project Management: Planning and Control (1995). Rory Burke. John Wiley and Sons.

Effective Learning: Training Extras (1995). Alan Mumford. Institute of Personnel and Development.

Lazy Learning (1994). Diana Beaver. Element Books.

Creating Culture Change: Strategies for Success (1990). Philip Atkinson. Rushmere Wynne.

Business Etiquette (1994). David Robinson. Kogan Page.

The Dance of Life (1982). Edward Hall. Doubleday. (The nature of time.)

An Executive Guide to Employing Consultants (2000). Richard E. Zackrison and Arthur M. Freedman. Gower.

Chapter 7
Consultancy concepts, skills and techniques

The Mind Map Book (1993). Tony Buzan. BCA in arrangement with BBC Books.

The Psychology of Personal Constructs. Volume 1: *Theory and Personality* (1991). George Kelly. Routledge.

Rapid Problem Solving with Post-it® Notes (1997). David Straker. Gower.

How to Be a Better Decision Maker (1996). Alan Barker. Kogan Page.

How to Be a Better Problem Solver (1996). Michael Stevens. Kogan Page.

NLP: New Perspectives (1999). Carol Harris. Element Books.

Introducing NLP (1990). Joseph O'Connor and John Seymour. HarperCollins.

Super Teaching (1995). Eric Jensen. Turning Point Publishing.

7 Kinds of Smart (1999). Thomas Armstrong. Plume Books.

The Art of Systems Thinking (1977). Joseph O'Connor and Ian McDermott. Thorsons.

Tools for Dreamers (1991). Robert Dilts et al. Meta Publications.

Intellectual Capital (1997). Leif Edvinsson and Michael S. Malone. Piatkus.

The Art of the Long View (1991). Peter Schwartz. Bantam.

Scenario Planning (1998). Gill Ringland. John Wiley Ltd.

Chapter 8
Confidence, motivation, emotional control, positive thinking

Finding Flow (1998). Mihalyi Csikczentmihalyi. Basic Books.

Total Confidence (1994). Phillipa Davies. Piatkus

Creative Imagery (1989). William Fezler. Simon and Schuster.

Super Self (audiotape) (1995). Carol Harris. Management Magic.

Time Line Therapy and the Basis of Personality (1988). Tad James and Wyatt Woodsmall. Meta Publications.

The Voice Book (1988). Michael McCallion. Faber and Faber.

Personal Effectiveness (1993). Alexander Murdock and Carol Scutt. Butterworth-Heinemann.

Unlimited Power (1988). Anthony Robbins. Simon and Schuster.

The Breath Book (1999). Stella Weller. Thorsons.

Chapter 9
Memory enhancement, time management, stress avoidance

The Complete Time Management System (1989). Christian Godefroy. Piatkus.

The 80:20 Principle (1998). Richard Koch. Nicholas Brealey Publishing.

The Twenty Minute Break (1991). Ernest Rossi. Jeremy P. Tarcher.

The PhotoReading Whole Mind System (1993). Paul Scheele. Learning Strategies Corporation.

Speed Reading in Business (1989). Joyce Turley. Crisp Publications.

The Speed Reading Book (1971). Tony Buzan. BBC Books.

Memory Skills in Business (1988). Madelyn Burley-Allen. Crisp Publications.

Master Your Memory (1998). Tony Buzan. BBC Books.

Accelerated Learning (1985). Colin Rose. Accelerated Learning Systems.

Chapter 10
Impression management and rapport creation

Your Total Image (1990). Phillipa Davies. Piatkus.

101 Ways to Make a Professional Impact (1996). Eleri Sampson. Kogan Page.

The Image Factor (1994). Eleri Sampson. Kogan Page.

Creating A Good Impression (audiotape) (1994). Carol Harris. Management Magic.

Training Extras series (*Assertiveness, Listening Skills, Asking Questions, Constructive Feedback, Negotiotiating and Influencing, Reports and Proposals*, etc). Various authors and dates. Institute of Personnel and Development.

Emotional Intelligence (1996). Daniel Goleman. Bloomsbury.

Chapter 11
Influencing

Words That Change Minds (1997). Shelle Rose Charvet. Kendall Hunt.

People Pattern Power (1998). Marilyne Woodsmall and Wyatt Woodsmall. International Research Institute for Human Typological Studies

Figuring Out People (1998). L. Michael Hall and Bob G. Bodenhamer. Crown House Publishing.

The Structure of Magic Volumes 1 and 2 (1975/6). Richard Bandler and John Grinder. Science and Behaviour Books.

Body Code: The Meaning in Movement (1979). Warren Lamb. Princeton Book Company (Action Profiling).

Metaphors in Mind: Transformation through Symbolic Modelling (2000). James Lawley and Penny Tompkins. The Developing Company Press.

Handbook of Internal Communications (1997). Eileen Scholes, ed. Gower Publishing.

Chapter 12
Interviews, presentations, meetings, negotiations

Getting to Yes (1981). Roger Fisher and William Ury. Hutchinson Business Books.

Getting Past No (1991). William Ury. Business Books.

The Magic of Dialogue (1999). Daniel Yankelovitch. Nicholas Brealey Publishing.

Thick Face, Black Heart (1995). Chin-Ning Chu. Nicholas Brealey Publishing. (The Asian approach to influencing.)

Negotiating Tactics (1997). Peter Thompson et al. Wyvern Crest Publications.

The Asian Mind Game (1991). Chin-Ning Chu. Macmillan.

Influencing with Integrity (1997). Genie Laborde. Crown House Publishing.

Chapter 13
Facilitation, coaching, mentoring

A Practical Guide to Facilitation Skills (1993). Tony Spinks and Phil Clements. Kogan Page.

Coaching and Mentoring (1995). Nigel MacLennan. Gower.

The Complete Facilitator's Handbook (1999). John Heron. Kogan Page.

Facilitating Change (1997). Barry Fletcher. Gower.

The Manager as Coach and Mentor (1995). Eric Parsloe. Training Extras. Institute of Personnel and Development.

Transformational Mentoring (1995). Julie Hay. McGraw-Hill.

Learning Alliances (1998). David Clutterbuck. Institute of Personnel and Development.

Action Learning in Practice (1997). Mike Pedler. Gower.

Action Learning at Work (1997). Alan Mumford. Gower.

Performance Coaching: The Handbook for Managers, H.R. Professionals and Coaches. (2003). Angus McLeod. Crown House Publishing.

Chapter 14
Business writing

101 Ways to Better Business Writing (1996). Timothy R. V. Foster. Kogan Page.

You Have a Point There (1953). Eric Partridge. Hamish Hamilton Ltd. (Punctuation)

The Complete Facilitator's Handbook (1999). John Heron. Kogan Page.

Writing Works (1995). Krystyna Weinstein. Institute of Personnel and Development.

Create Impressive Documents (1996). Steve Hards. Briarwood 1000.

Active Job Seeking (c.v. information; audiotape) (1995). Carol Harris. Management Magic.

Books on consultancy

Flawless Consulting (1981). Peter Block. Jossey-Bass Pfeiffer.

The Flawless Consulting Fieldbook (2001). Peter Block. Jossey-Bass Pfeiffer.

The Seven C's of Consulting (2000). Mick Cope. Financial Times/ Prentice Hall.

Management Consulting (1996). Milan Kubr, ed. ILO.

High Income Consulting (1993). Tom Lambert. Nicholas Brealey Publishing.

The Top Consultant (1994). Calvert Markham. Kogan Page.

How to Be Your Own Management Consultant (2000). Calvert Markham, ed.; contributions by Richmond Group members. Kogan Page.

Consulting for Dummies (1997). Bob Nelson and Peter Economy. IDG Books.

Million Dollar Consulting (1998). Alan Weiss. McGraw-Hill.

Index

7 Steps to Emotional Intelligence
Patrick E. Merlevede MSc
with Denis Bridoux and Rudy Vandamme

Goleman taught us the importance of Emotional Intelligence. Since the publication of his EI 'exposition', a whole array of Emotional Intelligence books has appeared, with each title purporting to put those theories of EI into practice. This book goes deeper. Revealing the structure beneath Emotional Intelligence, *7 Steps* utilises its unique framework to combine EI and *Neuro-Linguistic Programming (NLP)* – the study of excellence that examines how behaviour is neurologically formulated. *7 Steps* confidently integrates the insights of EI and NLP to promote a greater understanding of how emotions work – and *how they can be worked upon.*

Paperback, 418 pages, ISBN: 1899836500

Presenting Magically
Transforming Your Stage Presence With NLP
David Shephard BSc, DES &
Tad James MS, PhD

Have you ever been enthralled by a masterful presenter or trainer? Have you longed to effortlessly entertain and motivate your audience just as they seemed to do? At one time it was considered that such captivating performances were possible only if you were one of the fortunate, 'natural-born' presenters. Now, with the application of advanced human communication technologies such as NLP (Neuro-Linguistic Programming) and Accelerated Learning, *everyone* can learn to present magically.

Whether you are a newcomer or a seasoned professional, ***Presenting Magically*** will provide you with masterful tips and techniques that will transform your presenting skills. Introducing the secrets of many of the world's top presenters, this is the most comprehensive book available on the application of NLP to presentation.

Hardback, 256 pages, ISBN: 1899836527

Change Management Excellence
Putting NLP to Work
Martin Roberts PhD

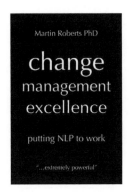

Working with many top British and American companies over the last thirty years, Martin Roberts has developed an enviable reputation for solving problems seen by others as insoluble. He attributes this to his ability to adapt and apply to business problems techniques derived from the field of psychology. These include: NLP, Behavioural Modification, Gestalt therapy and Transactional Analysis.

This book is about how to achieve excellent Change Management using a variety of techniques. Many of the methodologies presented here have never previously been published, and the book contains many new concepts and applications for consultants, would-be consultants and everyone involved in change within a business setting. It also provides an intriguing insight into why many fashionable 'cook-book' approaches to change run into problems – and how to avoid repeating them.

Paperback, 304 pages (est), ISBN: 1904424678

Understanding NLP
Principles & Practice - Second Edition
Peter Young

Understanding NLP opens a doorway into a more imaginative and coherent way of understanding and using NLP. This completely revised edition unites the many strands of NLP using an elegant paradigm which Peter Young calls the Six Perceptual Positions model. The book provides numerous examples of the paradigm in practice.

Many NLP concepts are tracked back to their origins, and some of the metaphors used to explain NLP are reinterpreted. New material includes: the NLP Presuppositions, Polarity thinking, Logical Levels, an expanded view of Outcome Setting, and a clarification of Perceptual Positions. There are new chapters on the Art of Asking Questions, and Working with Parts and Roles.

This practical guide for the NLP practitioner, coach or therapist, has numerous suggestions about good practice and offers many practical tips on actually doing NLP and utilising the Six Perceptual Positions model. As a result, readers will develop a better understanding of different kinds of clients, and be able to make more effective interventions for creating change.

Paperback, 320 pages, ISBN: 1904424104

www.crownhouse.co.uk

Communication Excellence
Using NLP to Supercharge Your Business Skills
Ian R. McLaren

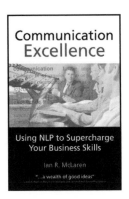

How good are your communication skills? Do you always convey the correct message, or do you sometimes feel that you are not fully understood? What this book provides is a ten-lesson course that will transform you into a consistently excellent communicator. Drawing on psychology, linguistics and Neuro-Linguistic Programming, it teaches you how best to interact with colleagues, bosses, officials, family and friends, and become adept at new and effective communication techniques. Providing essential training in key NLP-based methods, **Communication Excellence** presents powerful exercises in: rapport-building; anchoring; changing beliefs; calibrating; matching, pacing and leading. These techniques will increase your ability to: manage; market; sell; influence; inspire; innovate. Communicating its own insights in a crystal-clear manner, **Communication Excellence** is an invaluable tool for all those in business who need to communicate effectively. *Essential advice for everyone wishing to convey the correct message!*

Paperback, 240 pages, ISBN: 189983639X

www.crownhouse.co.uk

Me, Myself, My Team
How To Become An Effective Team Player Using NLP
Angus McLeod PhD

In **Me, Myself, My Team**, Angus McLeod looks at the team within each of us, and at each of us as part of a team. Providing a wealth of ideas to help the reader find new perceptions and new courses of action, **Me, Myself, My Team** asks the questions:

- **WHO is leading?**
- **WHERE are we pro-active?**
- **WHO is following?**
- **WHERE are we reluctant?**
- **HOW does the commentary inside our head get in the way of effective communication with others?**

By answering these questions with acute observations, **Me, Myself, My Team** sets the success criteria for high performing teams, and calculates effective solutions that will make a difference in both communication and motivation. Having its foundation in the belief that *openness and flexibility are the primary keys to personal effectiveness*, it promotes the need for *real* empowerment of the self – and not the so-called 'empowerment' bestowed by senior managers. Upbeat, friendly and full of practical ideas, this is an exceptional management book that demonstrates how we really can achieve the greatest success by being a team player.

Paperback, 144 pages, ISBN: 1899836381

www.crownhouse.co.uk

USA, Canada & Mexico orders to:
Crown House Publishing Company LLC
4 Berkeley Street, 1st Floor, Norwalk, CT 06850, USA
Tel: +1 203 852 9504, Fax: +1 203 852 9619
E-mail: info@CHPUS.com
www.CHPUS.com

UK, Europe & Rest of World orders to:
The Anglo American Book Company Ltd.
Crown Buildings, Bancyfelin, Carmarthen, Wales SA33 5ND
Tel: +44 (0)1267 211880/211886, Fax: +44 (0)1267 211882
E-mail: books@anglo-american.co.uk
www.anglo-american.co.uk

Australasia orders to:
Footprint Books Pty Ltd.
Unit 4/92A Mona Vale Road, Mona Vale NSW 2103, Australia
Tel: +61 (0) 2 9997 3973, Fax: +61 (0) 2 9997 3185
E-mail: info@footprint.com.au
www.footprint.com.au

Singapore orders to:
Publishers Marketing Services Pte Ltd.
10-C Jalan Ampas #07-01
Ho Seng Lee Flatted Warehouse, Singapore 329513
Tel: +65 6256 5166, Fax: +65 6253 0008
E-mail: info@pms.com.sg
www.pms.com.sg

Malaysia orders to:
Publishers Marketing Services Pte Ltd
Unit 509, Block E, Phileo Damansara 1, Jalan 16/11
46350 Petaling Jaya, Selangor, Malaysia
Tel : +03 7955 3588, Fax : +03 7955 3017
E-mail: pmsmal@streamyx.com
www.pms.com.sg

South Africa orders to:
Everybody's Books CC
PO Box 201321, Durban North, 4016, RSA
Tel: +27 (0) 31 569 2229, Fax: +27 (0) 31 569 2234
E-mail: warren@ebbooks.co.za